More Praise for *Corporate Integrity*

"Managing beyond compliance demonstrates vision and leadership, key indicators in measuring the elusive 'quality of management,' which investors strive to define and invest in. Companies that demonstrate leading-edge thinking and climb the integrity ladder are those that will provide superior returns to shareholders over the long-term. This book provides some practical tools to help companies get where they need to be in the 21st century."

Michael Jantzi, Jantzi Research Inc.

"Even as corporations today rile at the thought of further compliance, the unavoidable reality looms...they absolutely require a millennium sherpa to guide them through the rapidly shifting obstacle course of global change to ensure their footing. Donna Kennedy-Glans is one of those rare creatures, with the vision, expertise and knowledge to guide corporations upwards, through these moving targets to make their place as tomorrow's corporate leaders."

Ellis Kirkland, Chairman and CEO, Kirkland Group of Companies

"Amazing! Donna Kennedy-Glans has the facts and figures to prove that integrity doesn't just make good ethical sense; it makes good business sense. This book could revolutionize the way that corporations and those whose lives are impacted by them do business together."

Cynthia Bourgeault, Episcopal priest, writer and retreat leader, and author of The Wisdom Way of Knowing: Reclaiming an Ancient Tradition to Awaken the Heart

"Donna Kennedy-Glans provides a practical guide for organizations who view corporate integrity as a business opportunity. Utilizing the concepts and tools presented in *Corporate Integrity*, organizations can increase business results while establishing a reputation for the highest levels of accountability."

Mark Samuel, Author of The Accountability Revolution *and* The Power of Personal Accountability

"This valuable book deals with a subject that must become a road map for corporations in this century. The values of corporate integrity, moral responsibility and transparency are critical to corporations as they can be manipulated by nontransparent governments, particularly in developing countries. As much as these principles are a must for private and public corporations, they are also essential for many governments in the world."

H.E. Dr. Abdul-Kareem Al-Eryani, Former Prime Minister, Republic of Yemen

"I have seen Donna in action and she is a bulldog about making sure companies think beyond compliance. She doesn't let companies get away with saying that they are doing everything right because they are following the rules. Likewise she wants NGOs to be more accountable to companies."

DeAnna Woolston, Western Colorado Congress

"This book touches on a very important issue for both corporations and governments.... To achieve integrity across a society is the responsibility of all governments, corporations, and individuals. I congratulate you for an excellent work."

H.E. Dr. Abdulla Nasher, Republic of Yemen Ambassador to Canada

"The management tools provided in this book outline a proactive approach to regulatory compliance that all but guarantees improved public perception, greater risk reduction, improved regulatory compliance and greater profitability."

Steve Potter, Director, Bureau of Resource Management and Development, Division of Mineral Resources, New York State Department

"As someone who works with companies daily to support greater understanding of their impact on, and ability to manage their effects on, human rights, I recommend this book highly and will refer to it often!"

Krista Hendry, Director, Human Rights & Business Roundtable, The Fund for Peace, Washington D.C.

Corporate
Integrity

Corporate Integrity

A TOOLKIT FOR MANAGING BEYOND COMPLIANCE

**DONNA KENNEDY-GLANS
& BOB SCHULZ**

JOHN WILEY & SONS CANADA, LTD.

National Library of Canada Cataloguing in Publication Data

Kennedy-Glans, Donna
      Corporate integrity : a toolkit for managing beyond compliance / Donna Kennedy-Glans.

Includes index.
ISBN 13 978-0-470-83569-9
ISBN-10 0-470-83569-9

      1. Business ethics. 2. Corporate governance. I. Title.

HD57.7.K466 2005   658.4   C2005-900321-9

Production Credits:
Cover design: Mike Chan
Interior text design: Natalia Burobina

John Wiley & Sons Canada Ltd
6045 Freemont Blvd.
Mississauga, Ontario
L5R 4J3

Printed in Canada

10 9 8 7 6 5 4 3 2 1

To our parents

Eleanor and Wallace Kennedy
and
Ann and the late Bob Schulz

for inspiring integrity

Ten percent of the royalties paid to authors from the sale of this book
are dedicated to
BRIDGES SOCIAL DEVELOPMENT
(www.canadabridges.com),
a humanitarian organization focused on supporting women in development

Contents

Preface
A Moral Compass

The failure of ethics in business is front line news these days. In response, regulatory agencies are drafting more integrity rules and most corporate managers I know are scrambling to comply. Managers are looking to strict compliance with rules and regulations, internal and external audits, and insurance to reduce the impacts of integrity risks to their corporate bottom-line. Through work in-the-trenches with companies, it is my experience that compliance is not enough to navigate integrity dilemmas. The big rewards are in moving beyond compliance. Before you hire another auditor to comply with ever increasing rules and regulations, why not think about managing integrity beyond compliance. This book will give you the strategic integrity management tools that not only reduce your bottom-line risk, but also contribute to your top-line revenues.

The business tools in this book have been tested through what I call *"ground-truthing"* processes, and are shared with you through application to real-life scenarios. Business drivers for integrity in organizations are identified first, and then the focus switches to helping you with the *how* of operationalizing business integrity practices. This book will guide you through the practical realities of becoming a **Moral Compass** within your organization. *Corporate Integrity* is not about making you *feel good* about corporate ethics; it is about helping you *do something* about managing integrity so your organization can achieve greater success.

Like you, I have been learning about the complexity of integrity dilemmas since childhood: To be effective, we need to bring our whole person to the task of being a **Moral Compass**. As a young girl growing up in a multi-ethnic farming community in southwestern Ontario, I learned early to recognize the invisible threads that bound individuals together within a community. Our family farm was embedded in the heart of the tobacco belt of Canada. Migrant workers flowed into our community in the spring when the tobacco seedlings were planted, and left again at the first frost in the autumn. At times, our community struggled to absorb these migrant workers—from Quebec, eastern Canada, Eastern Europe, Africa, the Caribbean, and Mexico. These migrants challenged the social status quo, impacted our sense of security, and influenced neighborhood youth. But, we were economically dependent on the contribution of these seasonal workers. Like it or not, our lives were interwoven. Those tobacco farmers who recognized the value of respectful relationships with these migrant workers yielded financial and nonfinancial rewards—their workers were motivated and reliable, and their family life was not threatened.

I also experienced first-hand the complex intersection of corporate investment and society when my parents' farm was expropriated by Ontario Hydro. I witnessed my parents' helplessness and experienced my own. Others in the community thought that my parents should be thrilled with the financial stability that a corporate buy-out provided, but, these people didn't understand. Ontario Hydro had the legal right to force my parents to relocate from a family farm. Although the company's negotiators were well intended, they did not seem to truly comprehend the enormity of the personal impacts that came with their check and a forced relocation.

Even as a teenager, I understood the power of written media, through writing editorials for a local newspaper and running the high school newspaper. My father, my personal integrity hero, took me aside and spoke to me of the work I was doing: *"Leadership is being extended to you. There is an accountability that comes with that leadership. You must learn to think beyond 'me' to 'us'."* A blunt message of responsibility that was to become my mantra.

My journalism career took a bit of a detour though, and I became a lawyer. Law was attractive; it gave me a framework to examine business integrity and social justice, and offered me insight into the strengths and the limitations of legislative and judicial authority on integrity dilemmas. By some twist of fate, I was hired to work in the international projects in the oil patch, and ultimately in executive roles. From the start, I was thrown into projects in the developing world—Indonesia, Pakistan, Algeria, Colombia, and Papua New Guinea, to name but a few—and I loved it.

Hands-on experience with energy projects in these countries gave me the unique opportunity to explore the interconnectivity of the corporate investor, the host government, and the local citizens. Partners in these commercial projects needed each other. Vietnam had oil reserves, but lacked the funds and technical expertise to develop the reserves; Western companies had the dollars and the know-how. Notwithstanding this co-dependency, both the local and foreign partners preferred to build brick walls around investment projects to constrain interaction between foreigners and locals. Just as I had experienced in my childhood, the local community wanted to shield its citizens from outside influences. My history had taught me that this strategy would not work; I knew it had to be about "*us.*"

Participating at *the corporate table* in both head-office boardrooms and at operational field sites forced me to act as a *bridge* between management principles and operational reality. Understanding opportunities and challenges from both a management and an operational perspective enhanced my ability to identify solutions to perceived dilemmas. This bridging role also fostered the ground-truthing of assumptions and logistics. Head-offices have incredible intellectual capital. But, as I learned, if head-office strategies were not applied to projects in a real and meaningful way, the disconnect between the management vision and operational reality compromised everyone's objectives and credibility. Lawyers in head-office could edict lofty directives about sexual discrimination, but if the personnel in a field office in Egypt did not know how to apply these standards within Islamic communities, the likelihood of corporate management policies being implemented was predictably slim. Ground-truthing was not just relevant for companies. When international environmental agencies made claims about environmental degradation by corporate investors in the Amazon, I challenged these organizations to ground-truth their claims through direct observation.

Over time, I earned a reputation as someone who asked the tough questions. When my corporate colleagues were uncomfortable talking about the reality of bribery in Ecuador, or were squeamish discussing conflicts of interest in Saskatchewan, I would find a way to get the issue on the table. From personal experience, I know that the barriers to speaking up on specific internal integrity dilemmas can be formidable. Creating an accepted process for managing integrity dilemmas, in any organization, can diffuse some of this personal risk.

Some people claim that they can compartmentalize their work life, their spiritual life, and their personal life. These same people claim that in a project, they can put government in a box, impacted citizens in a box, and corporate investors in a box. Compartmentalization is a very tempting theory, but I feel our seemingly watertight compartments have long been flooded. When you work as an employee with a company, or work along a corporate supply chain, you are connected to that company and to its impacts on society. When you make decisions about integrity, inside a boardroom or at your family dinner table, your decisions are influenced by your values as a whole person. In the farming community where I spent my childhood, tobacco growers are now converting their farms to grow ginseng and other crops, or selling out. As part of the tobacco supply chain, farmers feel the negative social stigma; they deal with their own inner conflict about their role in an industry that causes cancer. Public furor over the perceived lack of integrity within tobacco manufacturing companies has a direct impact on the lives of tobacco growers, their families, and the local community. There is no rational way for us to put big tobacco companies, cancer victims, and tobacco growers into individual boxes.

There is another theory that is thrown out routinely in discussions about corporate integrity. People frequently assert that *"doing the right thing"* can be defined in black and white terms: *"You will know the right thing to do."* Others take a very Pollyanna view of the world, declaring: *"If only companies would behave more responsibly, environmental degradation would end."* Seeing the world in black and white is quite alluring—it condones blaming individuals and organizations for enormous wrongs. This is a simplistic view that rarely helps individuals or organizations to define or manage the complex integrity dilemmas that we struggle with in the twenty-first century. There were many bitter lessons that reinforced these learnings, and the business imperative to manage integrity beyond compliance. Let me share a few of these learning experiences from Indonesia, Colombia, and Nigeria.

I cut my corporate teeth in Indonesia. I initially pereived Indonesia as a place of boundless lush jungle, but this perception was abruptly jarred after my first visit to a seismic camp in Kalimantan. We flew over clear-cut islands—not just clear-cut forests, but small islands shorn of trees. With enormous gasps, we stared down in shock at the scarred land. Then the finger-pointing began:

"The Indonesian Government is allowing this to happen. They are getting the profits."
"No, it is a foreign company that is doing the clear-cutting and making the money."
"I heard that the locals are taking bribes and letting local companies in to clear-cut."

By inadvertently seeing the issue of clear-cutting in black and white terms, my colleagues struggled to identify a *"culprit"* to blame. It is more likely that there was no single organization or individual responsible for this outcome. It is also likely that the clear-cutting occurred incrementally. It is not likely that someone recommended: *"let's go clear cut whole islands"*. When we look at integrity dilemmas in black and white terms, we fail to recognize the complexity of the issues, or to recognize the imperative for multi-party alignment in the solutions. *The good, like the bad, doesn't happen with one visionary sword carrier, it comes when a whole group of engaged individuals and organizations begin to agree to do something differently.*

In the late 1980s and early 1990s, many companies invested in Colombia because the country was largely stable. Over the course of the 1990s, security and governance in Colombia were incrementally undermined by drug lords and guerrillas. Like most investors, the head-office management team that I worked with observed the growing erosion of stability in Colombia with unease. The tipping point came when a convoy of trucks carrying oil field equipment for our project was torched by guerrillas, from end to end. Thankfully, no one was injured, but the enormity of our problem crystallized in the space of about two hours. As champion of an *above-ground risking* process in the company, I was sent to Colombia to lead an investigation into what happened, and to assess options. I knew that an exit from the country was a preferred option. However, withdrawing from Colombia would have had enormous negative impacts for the Colombian Government, and for company personnel and contractors. Through very tense dialogue, we were lucky to identify an option that was palatable for everyone—we asked the Colombian Government for permission to transfer our drilling commitments from a guerrilla-infested region of the country to safer ground. We had reacted, and it worked—jobs were preserved and the company maintained its credibility and its commercial opportunity. This response was only possible because the company had a strategy in place for managing integrity dilemmas.

Sometimes, our most powerful learnings are drawn from our greatest integrity challenges. In the mid 1990s, I was a Vice President with an international oil company. A corporate decision to invest in Nigeria necessitated that the company re-evaluate its boundaries, and re-assess its accountabilities. I'll forever be grateful to my corporate colleagues for their courage in allowing those conversations. At the time of the company's commitment to drill for oil in Nigeria, Canada's Foreign Affairs Minister was leading the charge to have Nigeria thrown out of the Commonwealth. Transparency International ranked Nigeria at the bottom of the corruption index. I vividly remember the day that a colleague walked into my office to inform me of the corporate decision to do business in Nigeria. I gasped. Weren't we aware that Nigeria was a pariah state; that corruption was pervasive; that Abacha was an evil dictator; that Shell's experiences were horrific; that local communities were bearing the full weight of investment (oil spills, contaminated water, gas flares) yet received little or no allocation of the benefits of development. Didn't we realize that the recent death of Ken Siro-Wiwa was a defining moment in relationships between investors and host communities (and that his brother was residing in Canada)? The litany of questions was unstoppable. I was incredulous.

But, the decision was made. How then to live with this decision, and not compromise the corporation, our personnel, and our stakeholders in the process? It could easily have turned into a public relations nightmare. Through persistent and credible dialogue, we kept repeating the mantra that we wanted to be part of the solution in Nigeria, not part of the problem.

Slowly, we built trust. I traveled to Nigeria, many times, to meet with citizens, local advocacy organizations, other investors, and local governments. I met with the local representative of Transparency International in his offices above a chicken coop in a remote district of Lagos. We asked questions. We listened. We heard their stories, perceptions, goals, and fears. We saw their mandate to change Nigeria—Vision 2020—and became familiar with the steps in their journey. We then reflected on what we could do. How could we really be part of the solution in Nigeria? I endorsed two strategies: the company should be a bold advocate for gas flaring reduction or elimination, and the company should deal with corruption head on through alliances with others.

With these mandates, we marched forward, organizing a gas flaring conference in Abuja and many steps later bringing an international group together in Kananaskis, Canada to talk about how to reduce gas flaring in Nigeria. At that conference, we first heard the news that Sani Abacha had died in the arms of two prostitutes. Under the new leadership of President Obasanjo, companies with a recognized ability to manage integrity issues, including gas flaring and corruption, have been highgraded as investors.

Some people have asked me along this journey: *"Why did you become a moral compass for corporations? Why didn't you align with an advocacy organization or a government to promote integrity in companies instead?"* The questions are fair. In fact, over the last few years, much of my work has been focused on bridging relationships between corporations and governments; corporations and advocacy organizations; and corporations and host communities. Keeping my focus on corporate integrity is very deliberate. Since the early 1990s, corporations have funded and managed a majority of the world's development projects. Corporations' ability to influence citizens and communities is now greater than that of governments. When you are in a position to impact others, you have a choice: you can either demonstrate responsive leadership, or you can fail to be a leader. *Governments, advocacy organizations, and other corporate stakeholders should not be expected to stand by idly when corporate leaders fail to assume leadership on integrity.*

In 2000, I was diagnosed with a tropical virus contracted in Vietnam, and spent 8 months recovering. As my body slowly rejuvenated, I discovered I was no longer content to work with companies to punch through the ceiling on corporate integrity; I also wanted to raise the corporate integrity floor. Alliances with other individuals sharing similar objectives were critical. To gain a better understanding of how companies could be motivated to contribute to human development within host communities, either independently or in partnership with humanitarian organizations, I participated in several missions to Vietnam and Yemen. Ultimately, I founded Bridges Social Development as a not-for-profit vehicle to foster these alliances (www.canadabridges.com). I came to realize that the tools and practices that I had been applying in for-profit corporations were equally relevant to non-profit organizations. You will discover that the simple, practical tools in this book can be used to help any organization, community, business, or family live in integrity.

Until recently, proponents of *corporate social responsibility* have been somewhat skeptically received by leaders in the public, private, and voluntary sectors. Through my work with companies, and key corporate stakeholders, it was becoming glaringly obvious that many external stakeholders were dismissing corporate responsibility as *"fluffy"* public relations rhetoric. Even within corporations, there was a great deal of confusion, even disillusionment, as compliance with rules became equated with corporate integrity.

I believed that it was time for a book on business integrity management practices that would help those willing to overcome their apathy. I consulted with Bob Schulz—a teacher of management practices for three decades. Bob's students have thanked him by honoring him with countless teaching awards. He has recognized, and nourished, the deep hunger in young people to rationalize the need to find a kinder way to treat the world while earning a good living. Bob believed that the corporate community was ready for this message. I invited him to become my coauthor.

As we worked through this book, the question we kept asking ourselves was: *"When organizations manage everything else so well, why do they fail to strategically manage integrity?"* All too often, company managers attempt to put integrity in a box, usually an unwieldy box labeled *"ethics"*.

Here are the business tools you need to take corporate integrity out of its box and become a Moral Compass capable of directing your own organization to integrity and greater upside potential.

Donna

Integrity Bridges (www.integritybridges.com)

Acknowledgments

In the midst of the unraveling of the Enron empire, a friend challenged me to write a book to share business integrity learnings and best practices. *"People don't know how to measure or manage integrity, and they need someone who has been in the trenches of companies to guide them."* Kaycee Krysty, a sage financial adviser based in Seattle, Washington, takes much credit for launching the vision of this book.

During the writing of this book, my husband, Laurie, and sons Graydon, Mitchell, and Liam offered unconditional support. This family is my rock. Laurie's understanding of my driving curiosity to explore relationships between corporations and communities, and to champion corporate integrity in head offices and on the ground, is the only foundation upon which this work can be done. My sons' gentle teasing about my integrity quest—*Do you know how challenging it is to have a "mother of integrity"*—is playful and supportive. In earlier years, when teachers would inquire of my sons about my travels to the third world, they would delight in informing their classmates that their mother was *"working on corruption."* Without my family's unwavering support, this book could never have been written.

We would also like to thank our editors at John Wiley & Sons for their trust, and for their partnership, in the co-creation of this book. When I called Elizabeth McCurdy of Wiley in 2003 to inquire about Wiley's interest in a corporate integrity book, she was collaborative and engaging. Karen Milner, Business Editor at Wiley, was patient and supportive, providing an inspiring mix of professionalism and personal engagement. When I suggested to Karen that we meet at Wiley's offices during one of my visits to Ontario, Karen chose instead to travel to southwestern Ontario to meet me at my parents' farm. Karen and I rambled through local tobacco and ginseng fields, picked raspberries, and joined my family for a farm-style lunch; she chose to observe first-hand what motivated this passion for integrity.

The journey from visioning, to writing, to publishing was an unfamiliar path for us. Wisdom from those with experience in translating business experience into practical guidance was critical. Bruce Cohen, a well-established business author with Wiley, shared that wisdom in an unstinting and transparent way. Bruce's coaching was invaluable, and gratefully received.

Bob's administrative assistant, Joan Taylor, became our right arm in designing Integrity Grids and other graphics needed to share our business tools with readers. Joan's cheery and composed disposition, and her commitment to this shared effort, was a calming influence in the face of ambitious deadlines and grinding edits. Lynn Sales provided timely software guidance whenever requested.

My sister, Diane, offered resolute support and wise counsel. Friends, including Janis, Rick, Jay, Molly, Kathleen, Susan, and Leslie, provided steadfast assurances of the need for this book, and its messages.

The approach taken in the book was guided by our interaction with leaders from all sectors—governments, not-for-profits, corporate, and citizens. Without their soul-baring questions, we could never have written a book that offered insight into the real world of corporate integrity, or the hope of practical strategies and solutions.

The personal and public commitments to integrity by the late Ralph Scurfield, and always-humble Dick Haskayne, namesake of the Haskayne School of Business at the University of Calgary and a long time public advocate of corporate integrity, offered strong institutional grounding for this work. As well, the support of Vice-Dean Carol Stewart, Area-Chair Vern Jones, and Dean Michael Grandin of the Haskayne School of Business availed Bob the time and resources necessary to focus on the book.

Although I am certain that he did not appreciate his impact at the time, an epiphany moment for me occurred in a lunch with Vic Zaleschuk, a former CEO with Nexen Inc. and member of several corporate Boards of Directors. Vic is a savvy business leader, with his eyes firmly on the bottom line: his impassioned oratory emphasizing the critical need for corporations to value integrity and passion provided timely affirmation of the need for this book.

Introduction

What is Corporate Integrity?

Corporate integrity is the alignment between a corporation's explicit intention to define its values and its role in society, and its manifestation of this organizational intention in the commitments and actions of corporate personnel.

Why does Corporate Integrity Matter?

At the dawn of the twenty-first century, the credibility of business as a whole has been discredited by the actions of a few corporations motivated by greed. While it can be argued that the overwhelming majority of companies demonstrate integrity, the onus of establishing integrity has now shifted to corporate management teams. As a consequence, a corporation's ability to define and embed integrity in the hearts and minds of all corporate personnel, beyond head-office policies, has become critical to corporate credibility and profitability.

Evolving Expectations and Integrity Dilemmas

Corporate integrity is the subject of much dialogue. The collective understanding of what constitutes corporate integrity is evolving. Some people prefer to think of integrity in terms of right and wrong, or black and white. But a corporation's ability to clearly define *the right thing to do* in an increasingly interconnected and complex world is challenging; integrity dilemmas are on the rise for corporate managers.

All this dialogue about corporate integrity has generated some frameworks for consensus-building. Representatives from the public, private, and voluntary sectors generally concur that bribery and corruption, human rights abuses, and dual standards for environmental standards have negative impacts. As well, these groups generally agree on the merits of transparency, pluralism, allocation of benefits to local communities, and governance. Questions still remain about the appropriate and feasible role of corporations in minimizing these negative impacts and promoting positive impacts.

Motivating Corporate Integrity Behaviours

As integrity expectations for corporations continue to be expanded and clarified, the question then becomes one of how to motivate corresponding corporate behaviours. Some question the will and sincerity of corporations to commit to enhanced integrity standards on a voluntary basis, and endorse strict regulation of corporate behaviors and weighty penalties for noncompliance. Others believe that corporate innovation can be stifled by over-regulation, and insist instead that corporate leaders will adopt voluntary integrity practices to secure competitive advantage in the marketplace. The debate as to whether corporate behaviour is best motivated by carrots or sticks, or a combination of carrots and sticks, is likely to continue.

Managing Beyond Compliance

What is critical to evaluate at the present time is corporate preoccupation with compliance; corporate managers in most organizations are increasingly focused on ensuring compliance with rules and regulations. **Compliance is a minimum standard of corporate performance and is often insufficient response to a corporation's integrity values.** Managing to compliance only allows corporations to be responsive to existing expectations of stakeholders.

Beyond compliance thinking is an imperative for corporate management teams intent on strategic and proactive management of integrity. Managing integrity beyond compliance allows corporate management teams to anticipate the trajectory of evolving integrity expectations and practices. Managing to compliance may keep a company out of legal courts, but managing beyond compliance will foster a corporate "win" in the court of public opinion and in the marketplace.

Purpose of This Book

This book is intended to guide corporations and their key stakeholders in the strategic leadership and establishment of business integrity values beyond compliance.

Our goal is to share our experiences and lessons gleaned from years of coaching and advising organizations operating in environments where corporate integrity is routinely threatened. Such dilemmas include relationship challenges with host governments and local communities, assaults on corporate reputation by the media and advocacy groups, corruption, political risks, and security threats.

Corporate Integrity: Tools and Applications

The tools provided in this book have been applied to real business situations and are intended to assist corporate leaders and key corporate stakeholders in their pursuit of practices to embed business integrity. Overall, this is a practical how-to book that tailors, aligns, and consolidates business tools that enable companies to effectively and efficiently operationalize business integrity values.

Terminology

The words "corporate" and "corporation" are used in a general context. Thus, large and small organizations, whether incorporated or not, are considered under the term "corporations." Also, there is no distinction made between private sector corporations and public sector corporations.

PART 1

New Frontiers in Managing Corporate Integrity

New Frontiers in Managing Corporate Integrity

What Does Integrity Mean?

Let's start with an understanding of what *integrity* means. When speaking of integrity, some people think in terms of right and wrong, or black and white. Some people think of others as being either honest or dishonest. Some people think of corporations as either having business integrity or lacking business integrity. However, it is frequently difficult to say whether a corporate action or inaction is 100 percent right or 100 percent wrong. "Doing the right thing" often means different things to different people.

Almost every definition of integrity includes reference to characteristics of *probity* and *honesty*, but it is worth noting that while honesty and probity are embodied in integrity, integrity goes beyond honesty to incorporate a wholeness that defines corporate character. Integrity is defined with reference to the state of being *whole*, *complete*, or *undivided*.

Some situations are very clear. Specifically, it is illegal for corporations in most economies to pay money under the table to agents who bribe government officials in order to secure advantage in a contract award.

However, the consequences of illegal actions in different investment environments around the world are not always black and white. Instead, many situations have interwoven strands of complexity. Is a corporation acting with integrity if it invests in a host country where the government in power acts with prejudice against minorities within its population? How does this analysis change with the manner and degree of repression by the host government against such minority groups? It is not a simple task to assess whether corporate actions demonstrate integrity or not.

A single act by a single employee can be seen as a lack of integrity for a person or corporation. One inconsistent action of dishonesty or improbity can compromise a corporation's reputation for integrity. Conversely, widespread and long-term consistency by all corporate employees is required to embed integrity.

Integrity is not a fixed end state. Legal and ethical "goal posts" are moved in response to stakeholder expectations. For example, shareholders have recently become suspicious of accounting manipulations and fortuitous cashing of options and bonuses, and have become more vocal in their skepticism. In response, the allocation of open-ended stock options to directors and managers is declining in favor of performance-based shares distributed only when an individual leaves the company.

Where Are We? How Did We Get Here? Where Are We Going?

Where are we? How did we get to this state of confusion, even anguish, about the integrity of companies? Why is public pressure for increased corporate responsiveness to business integrity values gaining momentum? And where are we headed?

Where Are We?

Within the last decade, business has sped well past the expectation that corporations are responsible only for making a profit for shareholders and to look after employees fairly. Business and society are now in a grayer zone, with few official judges or rules. It is little wonder that corporate stakeholders are confused about who is the "good guy" and who is the "bad guy."

Unlike financial reporting systems, corporations have few defined processes or standards to measure, assess, verify, or report on business integrity. Verification of corporate alignment between integrity commitments and practices may be prescribed by law or required by corporate procedures, but these assessments are generally conducted after negative events. Control systems for managing business integrity are evolving—

corporations are experimenting with balanced scorecards, triple bottom-line reporting that addresses financial and nonfinancial attributes, and even verification systems. Accountability processes are in an evolutionary state.

How Did We Get Here?

How did we arrive at this new frontier of business integrity expectations for companies?

- Economic liberalization and political reform in the world has seen exponential growth since the fall of the Berlin Wall in 1989. Social reform has been a natural corollary to these economic and political developments.

- Globalization has changed the way corporations communicate and has made corporate actions more transparent.

- As well, corporations have become the engine for development growth. In the late twentieth century, the private sector surpassed the public sector as the source of capital for economic growth in developing countries.

These evolutionary catalysts have produced expanded corporate influence and expanded corporate accountabilities.

Recent integrity breaches by high-profile and trusted corporate leaders have jolted society into the collective realization of these contextual changes. Now corporations are forced to ask key questions:

- What are the roles of government and multilateral organizations in regulating corporate integrity?

- To whom are corporations accountable?

- Who decides?

- Who measures?

- Who rewards or punishes corporate behavior?

Where Are We Going?

Corporate leaders face unprecedented pressure to respond to stakeholders. Stakeholders expect credible assurances from corporate management about business integrity and accountability. Corporations' stock price and market capitalization depend on their *credibility* in delivery of these assurances. For example, the share price for Royal Dutch/Shell Group fell sharply in January 2004 in response to the company's admission of a 20 percent overstatement of proven reserves. Assuming moderate oil prices of U.S. $25 a barrel, this overstatement of oil reserves alone represents more than U.S. $67.5 billion in potential future revenues. As the company articulated plans to accurately redefine reserves and replaced top managers, Shell's stock price gradually recovered, but not in full alignment with the industry sector.

Sometimes corporate credibility is compromised due to external forces. In the face of the tampered Tylenol bottles, Johnson & Johnson withdrew all Tylenol bottles from pharmaceutical shelves at a cost in excess of U.S. $100 million. In order to restore public confidence, Johnson & Johnson championed the conversion to tamper-proof containers.

Managing to Compliance

Corporate managers are all too familiar with the accounting, governance, and ethical failures of leading companies. The fallout from Enron and WorldCom, and then Parmalat, has triggered public demands for both increased regulation of corporations and assurances of corporate compliance with these regulations.

Corporations are forced to commit substantial resources to keep abreast of emerging and evolving governance requirements, and to ensure compliance. Implementation of the detailed compliance and process verifications prescribed by the Sarbanes-Oxley Act has doubled audit fees and time commitments for executives and directors in many U.S.-based corporations and their supply chains.

With this increased focus on compliance, corporate management may develop a false sense of security and inadvertently neglect key issues such as business development, corporate strategy, competitive advantage, and organizational culture. Corporate managers trapped in the treadmill of compliance can easily lose sight of the objectives of the rules that they are complying with on a day-to-day basis.

In the face of pressure to comply, managers will focus on observing third-party rules on a reactive basis rather than proactively managing business integrity. When the rules and regulations governing corporate behaviors originate from multiple governmental and nongovernmental sources, corporations struggle to ensure that they meet all the regulations. Opportunities for strategic assessment and proactive management of integrity outcomes can be compromised because corporations are overly focused on strict compliance with rules and regulations.

Managing Business Integrity Beyond Compliance

Compliance with laws and regulations is a necessary corporate motivator, but complete compliance with rules by all employees of a company will not guarantee business integrity. A business culture of integrity is needed to address the complexity of modern corporate issues. A culture of corporate integrity will naturally foster individual employee compliance.

Some corporate leaders recognize that compliance is a minimum standard of corporate performance that may fail to respond to their key stakeholders' legitimate expectations. For example, an automotive manufacturing plant may proactively and voluntarily adopt global health, safety, and environmental standards that extend beyond compliance with less onerous local regulations. Although the manufacturer is not legally required to adopt global standards, the company can voluntarily and proactively respond to the expectations of their employees, suppliers, and consumers.

Proactively anticipating stakeholder expectations is often less expensive in the long run when compared to short-term compliance with regulations. Retrofitting manufacturing plants to comply with emergent environmental and occupational health and safety standards is generally more expensive than incorporating these standards in the initial plant design. Corporate leaders do not need to spend more money to manage business integrity. But corporate leaders do need to be wise in their budget allocations to ensure that corporate behaviors manifest integrity.

Compliance with regulations requires efficient and effective *administration* by corporate personnel. Insightful corporate leadership requires *management* beyond compliance—a thoughtful understanding of the complexity of the decision-making processes and behaviors necessary to establish integrity within an organization.

What Motivates Compliance and Beyond Compliance Management?

Why do corporate managers choose to administer to compliance, or to manage beyond compliance? What is the business case for business integrity strategies based on compliance, or that go beyond compliance? These are critical questions.

First, let's look at what motivates *compliance* management. Why would corporate leaders choose to manage to compliance? Corporate managers who choose to manage to compliance are generally motivated by top-down leadership models, fear of legal liability and penalties, corporate reputation management strategies, rigid adherence to corporate codes of conduct, dependence on financial risk strategies, and a general sense that compliance with regulations is "the right thing to do."

Corporate managers who do not even manage to compliance are generally motivated by greed or ignorance. Greed can be encouraged or ignorance perpetuated if corporate values are not clarified or reinforced in corporate conduct codes or internal communications. Greed may also be condoned if the corporate culture reinforces or rewards integrity breaches and the consequences of noncompliance (for example, fines and penalties, financial and reputation impacts) are either not deterrents or are not well understood. Analysts' expectations for short-term share performance can also implicitly encourage noncompliance behaviors for the sake of reporting quarterly profit.

Some corporations avoid making voluntary business integrity commitments beyond legal compliance because a voluntary commitment to business integrity may create greater accountabilities for the corporation. This could mean that managers may be accountable if they fail to meet the beyond compliance standards that they set for themselves. We witnessed similar reactions two decades ago when business was encouraged to adopt voluntary environmental practices as part of responsible care programs.

Fears of legal liability associated with integrity commitments beyond compliance were perpetuated by allegations launched against Nike Inc. in the United States based on its public relations statements on integrity. In response to claims that it had mistreated workers in Vietnamese manufacturing plants producing its athletic gear, Nike countered with a public relations campaign. Nike defended the benefits of its Asian factories to host countries and sought to portray the company as being in the "vanguard of responsible corporations" seeking to maintain adequate labor standards in overseas facilities. Nike Inc. was sued in 2003 for these public statements on the basis that their corporate actions did not appear to be aligned with their corporate public relations statements.

Subsequently, Nike agreed to settle the lawsuit and paid U.S. $1.5 million to the Fair Labour Association, an independent coalition that seeks to improve factory conditions and monitoring. The outcome of this litigation has been disquieting for companies and is identified by some corporations as a barrier to communication of integrity commitments beyond compliance.

The Business Case for Beyond Compliance Management of Corporate Integrity

What is the business case for business integrity beyond compliance?

Individual corporations have unique reasons to strategically manage business integrity outcomes beyond compliance. This book is intended to help corporate managers and key corporate stakeholders to better understand corporate motivation, and to ensure that the corporate intention to manage business integrity matches the corporate integrity commitments and practices.

The business case for business integrity may include some or all of the following rationales:

- *Proactive management versus reactive administration:* Corporate management teams focused on day-to-day compliance with the myriad of rules and regulations and guidelines established by governmental and nongovernmental organizations are on a treadmill. In their quest to keep abreast of these rules, managers become reactive rather than proactive. Managers frequently lose sight of the need for strategic management of business integrity. Companies in a reactive mode have less opportunity to strategically align their multiplicity of responses to third-party rules and regulations. Opportunities for strategic assessment and management of integrity outcomes can thus be compromised.

- *Corporate Culture:* Rules-based approaches to integrity management will be more likely to characterize integrity dilemmas as black or white. In organizations facing more complex integrity dilemmas, a process-oriented integrity approach that allows for open dialogue on integrity dilemmas may foster more creative and responsive business integrity strategies.

- *Managing the "Weakest Link":* A corporation's integrity is only as strong as its weakest link. It is not sufficient for *most* employees in an organization to function at or beyond the corporation's overall integrity expectations. The weakest link within a corporation can be a lightning rod for unwanted media and stakeholder attention that will detrimentally affect the reputation and effectiveness of the entire organization. Thus, a proactive business integrity strategy strengthens the weakest corporate integrity links and reduces the risk of fallout for the rest of the organization.

- *Attraction and retention of personnel:* Corporations that strategically manage business integrity naturally foster a corporate culture that encourages creativity and risk taking. Compliance thinking can tend to stifle enthusiasm for innovation and high-performing teams. Corporations with a culture of integrity are able to attract and retain personnel (both employees and contractors) with integrity values aligned to the corporation's values, and detract personnel with integrity values at odds with the organization's values.

- *Reputation management:* Key stakeholders can become corporate critics in the absence of a strategic business integrity strategy. Corporations that manage business integrity beyond compliance are well positioned to anticipate stakeholder expectations, and to establish and reinforce corporate credibility with internal and external stakeholders, and existing and future stakeholders. Integrity commitments and practices will enhance stakeholders' perceptions of corporate financial and operational performance, and will minimize the risk of negative attention.

- *Competitive advantage:* Competitive advantage is enhanced for companies who are able to establish reliability as a "partner of choice" with governmental, voluntary, and private sector partners. This competitive advantage can enhance corporate access to commercial opportunities. As well, corporate managers should expect that their competitors will try to exploit any business integrity gaps. Benchmarking of corporate performance against peer groups includes evaluations of corporate management of business integrity.

- *Business integrity is critical to public and governmental relations messages:* Credible business integrity intentions and actions are foundational elements of effective public and governmental relations messaging; without business integrity, all other corporate messages become meaningless for most audiences and stakeholders.

- *Establish consistency of credibility with local communities:* Citizens and local organizations assess corporate integrity at individual employee and organizational levels. Organizational credibility within local communities is directly linked to the credibility of individual employees and contractors.

- *Enhance corporate ability to balance shorter and longer-term priorities:* Corporations frequently have to juggle the competing expectations of short-term financial markers and longer-term investment and sustainability horizons. Establishing a clear commitment to business integrity helps corporate managers in understanding, quantifying, and explaining to stakeholders why short-term profitability goals may need to be adjusted to accommodate longer-term integrity priorities. One example is the value of honoring commitments to employees or host communities.

- *"You do not value what you cannot quantify":* As the adage suggests, if corporations do not have clear commitments to business integrity or systems in place to monitor alignment between commitments and corporate practices, it is difficult to measure business integrity impacts. Compliance mandates focus on corporate observance of rules and regulations, and not necessarily on the achievement of business integrity outcomes.

- *Link to project and enterprise risk management:* A common motivation for strategic business integrity management is risk management. Corporations that identify the business integrity expectations of key internal and external stakeholders have a better understanding of their risks and opportunities within individual projects and overall at an enterprise level. Business integrity responses can be designed to support management of these project and enterprise risks.

- *Link to corporate governance:* Better governance of corporations is enabled through effective working relationships between boards of directors and management teams. Directors' priorities are to foster high performance and competitive advantage. Maximizing corporate performance through these effective working relationships is generally not the stuff of legislation.

- *Correlation to operational and financial integrity:* Business integrity strategy is not simply a fuzzy "nice to have." Third-party assessments of financial and operational performance of a corporation are not entirely objective. When analysts gauge corporate *performance*, the reliability of financial and operational performance indicators is subjectively influenced by perceptions of corporate integrity. Poor corporate performance on business integrity measures will undermine overall corporate accountability frameworks, including financial and operational accountability and credibility.

- *Risk of litigation and penalties:* The risk of fines and jail time for business integrity breaches motivate corporate management teams to embed business integrity management practices on a strategic basis. Legislation intended to promote integrity behaviors now has more "teeth," and regulators and judges responsible for enforcing the rules are showing little leniency. Public humiliation of corporate offenders has become a judicial objective; Martha Stewart is one high-profile example. Corporations able to demonstrate a corporate culture of integrity are more likely to be afforded some leeway for human error.

- *Recognition by social funds and socially focused stakeholders:* Increasingly, social funds and other corporate stakeholders are assessing corporate effectiveness on the basis of a company's relative performance on nonfinancial indicators, for example:

  - corporate responsiveness to environmental impacts,
  - sustainability of practices,
  - relationships with host communities,
  - contribution to societal impacts of development, and
  - non-discrimination practices.

  Having these commitments clarified and communicated, and having systems in place to assess and report on outcomes, enhances a corporation's credibility with these stakeholders.

- *Assists corporations in defining their sphere of influence:* Intentionally or through actual practices, corporate management teams define their organizational sphere of influence. Does the corporation intend to influence behaviors only within its own organization, or does the corporation intend to influence behaviors beyond its organization's boundaries? For example, corporations may wish to ensure that their business integrity commitments are adhered to not only by their own employees, but by all contractors, subcontractors, suppliers, and partners. In some cases, corporations may choose to include host governments and others within their sphere of influence. Clarifying business integrity strategy assists corporate managers' understanding of their organization's intended sphere of influence.

- *Response to consumer expectations:* Companies involved in supplying products directly to consumers will appreciate the need for this key stakeholder group to clearly understand the corporation's integrity commitments and actions. Wal-Mart, one of the largest suppliers of merchandise to consumers, is very aware of consumer expectations. As the level of consumer awareness and advocacy grows, other corporations along the supply chain increasingly benefit from establishing and reinforcing their own integrity values and practices to assuage consumer expectations.

- *Clarify the corporate role in development and society:* Business teams that have integrity strategies in place are better positioned to thoughtfully consider the role that their organization intends to play in development and society. Governments and multilateral organizations may pressure a corporation to assume a larger role in development or in society. For example, the World Bank may encourage a corporation to support local governments with transparency initiatives or infrastructure development. Corporate management teams are better able to define their corporate role in such an initiative if there is an overall organizational integrity strategy in place.

- *Enables strategic giving:* A corporation's ability to approach engagement with communities beyond compliance enables the voluntary creation of strategic relationships with communities. This can include strategic relationships, investment, and other types of participation with host communities.

- *Want to be leaders:* Some corporations intentionally choose to be industry leaders in ethics or corporate social responsibility. These companies acknowledge that sometimes legislation is catching up to evolving best practices. Leaders in these companies seek to experiment with pilot projects to test new thinking rather than following others.

- *Top-down leadership mandate:* Some leaders will choose to be integrity leaders beyond compliance. These leaders may not have integrity values that are necessarily aligned with the objectives of regulations and laws, and instead choose to commit to integrity markers that go beyond the regulatory or contractual frameworks of their operations.

- *Reputation as innovator:* Recognition of corporate entrepreneurialism and innovation is increasingly important. A company's ability to be creative in its response to integrity dilemmas will identify that corporate management team as innovative in all aspects of its operations.

Proactive Management or Reactive Tactics?

Corporations traditionally define their key stakeholder groups to include shareholders, employees, suppliers/partners, customers, and society. Corporate management must decide whether to use a *reactive* or *proactive* approach to the business integrity expectations of these stakeholders.

Stakeholder expectations for business integrity are evolving. For example, shareholders are increasingly voicing concerns about compensation paid to senior executives; employees are demanding increased transparency in hiring practices; retail outlets are requiring environmental certifications along the supply chain; and customers are inquiring about wages paid to coffee growers and the use of child labor in manufacturing.

Corporations are increasingly being asked to anticipate the impacts of their projects on society. Activists are appealing to companies to participate in community discussions about project impacts *before* the ground is broken on a new development. In addition, previously silent majorities—individual citizens and grassroots organizations—are now speaking out through the media.

Corporations can choose to *react* to business integrity gaps and resulting dilemmas, or to be *proactive*. There are financial reasons to be proactive. On the basis of net present value break-even analysis, proactively anticipating gaps is often less expensive than reactively fixing problems. Management strategies are beginning to recognize that it is more economical for corporations to budget proactively and to anticipate risks, rather than reactively paying lawyers and public relations firms to repair reputations and minimize liabilities.

The Downside to Reactive Responses

Reactive management practices are frequently exposed in bribery and corruption charges. When individuals in companies are fined and sent to jail for condoning kickbacks to officials in host governments, a company may react by imposing strict corporate rules and replacing corporate leaders. When Statoil faced corruption charges in relation to its operations in Iran, the directors of the Norway-based company immediately reacted by replacing senior executives.

Reactive management practices can produce severe consequences to individual managers. Corporate leaders can go to jail. For example, a former president of Elf Aquitaine served a thirty-month jail term for his role in lucrative commissions paid to leaders of African countries. In some jurisdictions, criminal negligence charges can be levied against individual managers who fail to protect the safety of employees. In response to the death of twenty-six men in the Nova Scotia Westray Mine in 1992, Canadian criminal law was beefed up by Bill C-45 in 2004 to allow criminal charges to be made against corporate supervisors, managers, or directors who fail to take reasonable steps to prevent injury to workers.

Personal liability for integrity breaches does not disappear easily—personal responsibility may not have a statute of limitations. Recall, for example, the 1984 Bhopal toxic methyl isocyanate gas leak at a pesticide plant run by Union Carbide, one of the worst industrial accidents in history. Twenty years after the disaster, Warren Anderson, the company's then-chairman, is still being pursued for criminal charges by Indian officials. Mr. Anderson is now in his early eighties, living a low-profile retirement in the United States, and is being held to account for an industrial accident that occurred in 1984.

Dow Chemical acquired Union Carbide Corporation in 2001. Dow's acquisition renewed interest in the Bhopal liability question. Although Dow denies any inherited liability for this corporate legacy, others are drawing links between Union Carbide's reputation and Dow's future opportunities. Political appeals to Dow are being launched by U.S. congressmen demanding that Dow address the Bhopal environmental and health impacts created twenty years ago.

Corporate liability may not disappear easily. Even though Talisman Energy Inc. sold its Sudanese oil interests to an Indian company in 2003, activist groups representing Sudanese human rights issues continue with litigation against Talisman under the U.S. Alien Torts Claims Act.

Further, environmental liabilities are challenging to assign or sell to a purchaser of assets or shares. These liabilities can be permanently attached to the historical chain of title on a retroactive basis. Liability claimants may elect to assign culpability to "deep pockets" of solvent corporations along the title chain.

The Upside to Proactive Strategies

An example of proactive management is Anglo American mining company's decision to take a more interventionist approach with host governments on human rights. The world's second largest mining group made its position known to governments that it would not stand by if the human rights of a local community were being abused in the vicinity of its operations. While the underlying corporate motivation may not be known, this proactive strategy by Anglo American is expected to forestall a wide range of possible actions by activists.

Business integrity is often aligned with "good business." Employers who decided to provide AIDS drugs to their personnel in operating environments where HIV/AIDS is epidemic are able to effectively align integrity commitments and workplace productivity. These corporations are able to demonstrate their integrity commitments to employees and society and at the same time reduce the risk of operational downtime as a result of serious illness and death. Drug manufacturing companies who decide to enhance access to HIV/AIDS drugs in Africa are also able to link integrity and good business. By saving lives and enhancing quality of life, drug companies improve their future markets and enhance their present reputations.

Managing New Frontiers in Corporate Integrity

The "finish line" in business integrity has moved and will continue to move in response to dynamic stakeholder expectations.

History demonstrates that business leaders are not only held accountable to the standards of the day, but are frequently held accountable on a retroactive basis to evolving standards. For example, a seemingly acceptable corporate decision in 1975 to use asbestos for building materials may be condemned by corporate stakeholders a decade later on the basis of new knowledge and higher standards.

Evolving stakeholder expectations create new challenges for corporations and their management teams. These new frontiers also create opportunities for corporations as competitors may lag behind in recognizing future trends or fail to manage risks. For example, companies that anticipated the demand for flexible work schedules (including telework opportunities for parents with young children) attract a wider pool of skilled employees than companies that chose to maintain historically inflexible work policies. Companies that anticipate future trends and expectations are positioned for competitive advantage. Car manufacturers that anticipate consumer reaction to emissions reduction mandates will evaluate their sport-utility vehicle markets and proactively install emission reduction technology. Companies along the food supply chain are more likely to maintain market share, and be competitive, if they stay alert to consumer demands for reduced trans fats and foods that have not been genetically modified. Restaurant owners serving farmed salmon on their menus must now consider their patrons' demands for wild salmon. Kraft Foods, the manufacturer of OREO cookies, has announced plans to reduce trans fats in OREOs and to stop marketing in schools.

To be effective and competitive, corporate leaders must anticipate current and projected business issues and risks on a proactive basis. To navigate these complex frontiers, corporate leaders require new tools:

- *Frontier 1:* Understanding perspectives related to integrity and corporations

- *Frontier 2:* Clarifying the roles and responsibilities of corporations

- *Frontier 3:* Aligning corporate integrity values, talk, and walk

- *Frontier 4:* Explaining differences between corporations regarding integrity and values, commitment, and action

- *Frontier 5:* Evaluating a corporation's accountability for business integrity and measuring integrity differences between corporations

A cultural shift from reactive to proactive management requires intentionality and leadership endorsement. Integrity management has become the norm at many leading companies, including Hershey Foods, Lockheed Martin, Waste Management, Texas Instruments, and The Home Depot. Many of these companies have made integrity a strategic objective, and not just a public relations tactic.

This book is written for the purpose of supporting corporations and their key internal and external stakeholders to better *understand* the nature of these new frontiers, to *measure* gaps between actual/current practices and the desired/future state required to lead in these new management frontiers, and to *navigate* these new frontiers with effectiveness and efficiency.

Business Tools to Navigate the New Management Frontiers

In the last few years, there have been thousands of articles written and speeches delivered to reinforce a business integrity imperative. Governments, academics, industry associations, advocacy groups, and multilateral organizations are beginning to merge their efforts to reinforce the need for business integrity. What corporate management teams now need to implement these integrity strategies beyond more talk are clear practices that enable and embed corporate actions. The tools provided in Part 1 of this book will support corporate management in the implementation of business integrity practices.

Part 2 focuses these management tools on three case scenarios. Chapter 10 focuses application of the business tools on one key issue—how corporations define and implement business integrity values in their relationships with communities.

Part 3 discusses emerging trends in business integrity. This chapter also examines what motivates and achieves enhanced corporate integrity—carrots or sticks, or a combination of carrots and sticks? Various options to stimulate corporate integrity are examined.

Frontier 1:
Understanding Perspectives Related to Integrity and Corporations

Highly visible business integrity meltdowns—Bre-X Mineral's gold scandal, Xerox's restatment of revenues, and Shell's overstatement of petroleum reserves—place all corporations on the defensive.

Advocates favoring more legally prescribed roles for corporations appear to be winning public relations campaigns, portraying images of trusting and vulnerable shareholders suffering losses that impinge on their retirement pensions and quality of life. Corporations are increasingly uncomfortable with critics' power to impugn their reputation. Business leaders feel vulnerable and defensive in this unfolding "corporate trust challenge."

This chapter digs below the surface of these diverse perspectives and then explores the breadth of perceptions on the state of business integrity within corporations by dealing with the following questions:

- Are the Enron, WorldCom, Parmalat, Bre-X, Xerox, and Shell situations anomalous or just the tip of the iceberg?

- Do corporations truly care about business integrity or is integrity merely a public relations exercise?

- How can corporate stakeholders measure and monitor integrity?

Business Integrity: An Inside Look

If questioned, it is entirely predictable that the vast majority of chief executive officers and employees of reputable corporations would genuinely express an intention to act with business integrity. What corporate leader would disavow the value of integrity?

Some key questions to ask of corporate leaders include the following:

External stakeholders: What does acting with integrity mean in practice for this corporation?

Internal stakeholders: What is our corporate commitment to business integrity? Is there alignment between our corporate talk on integrity and our corporate walk?

When a corporation has a code of conduct and/or a mission statement claiming integrity as a corporate value, the managers may believe that mere compliance with laws is sufficient. However, external stakeholders often expect that corporate integrity will mean more than just compliance with laws. For example, a corporation may assume that informing local communities of a development decision after the fact is sufficient if preliminary consultation is not required by law.

Conversely, affected citizens will expect that a corporation acting with integrity will provide early consultation in order to incorporate local expectations into decision making regardless of regulatory requirements. As a result, corporations are frequently caught off guard by the strength and vehemence of local opposition. For example, the fast-tracked construction of a meat-packing plant and abattoir adjacent to a residential area will activate placard-waving grassroots objectors if local communities are not consulted. The outrage can even spread beyond local communities to attract the attention of media and activist groups.

Chapter 6 examines the key components of a business integrity accountability framework for a company—corporate reporting on integrity commitments and actions, independent measurement and verification of alignment between corporate intention and corporate actions, and corporate management's response to deficiencies. Without an accountability framework, it is very difficult for stakeholders to effectively measure this alignment. Without an ability to effectively judge corporate business integrity, public opinion and media reporting by corporate critics predictably sway stakeholders.

Business Integrity Guidelines Are Not a Recent Phenomenon

The concept of assessing or defining business integrity is not new. In 1943, the Rotarians adopted the 4-Way Test, which became one of the world's most widely disseminated hierarchies for business ethics.

Of the things we (Rotarians) think, say, or do:

1. Is it the *truth*?

2. Is it *fair* to all concerned?

3. Will it build *goodwill* and *better friendships*?

4. Will it be *beneficial* to all concerned?

Many corporations have codes of conduct widely disseminated within the company. Even with these guidelines in place, integrity meltdowns have occurred. Clearly, there is a lack of alignment between corporate intentions to act with integrity and actual corporate practices. There is benefit in clarifying the complexity of business integrity expectations and actions.

The Integrity Ladder

To assist internal and external stakeholders in assessing corporate responsiveness to business integrity, a measuring tool has been created to establish a hierarchy of behaviors.

The Integrity Ladder encourages employees, shareholders, and other corporate stakeholders to examine corporate motivation.

RUNG	QUESTIONS TO ASK TO REVEAL MOTIVATION (COMMITMENT)	PRIMARY MOTIVATION	EXAMPLE	CONTINGENCY PLAN (ACTION)
10	Will my children and grandchildren appreciate my decisions to help others?	Concern for future generations	George Soros's personal commitment to transparency Bill Gates's personal commitment to fight HIV/AIDS	Individuals create trusts and foundations to support philanthropy Altruism
9	Are there ways to leverage my corporate budget to achieve a positive social impact that has long-term sustainability?	Both social return on corporate investment and financial return on corporate investment are intentionally of substantial importance	Corporate alliances with other stakeholders to respond to host communities health care needs	Consider impact of investment beyond the operating timetable Capacity building in host jurisdiction
8	Are there ways to leverage my corporate budget to achieve a positive social impact?	Social return on corporate investment is a desired and intended by-product of financial investment	Corporate responses to host communities' health care needs	Consider commercial and social benefit of community investment, respect for environment, and relations with host government
7	How do we leverage our corporate budget to ensure that we do no harm?	Avoid causing harm to others	Corporate decision to ensure operating budget includes environmental and social impact assessment and response	Consider universal health, safety, and environmental practices if cost effective

	Question	Compliance motivation	Example	Strategy
6	How do we comply with both the letter and spirit of applicable laws and company policy?	Compliance motivation supplemented with proactive risk management	Investments are subject to proactive decision-making process	Create multidisciplinary teams to properly evaluate and manage risks
5	What do we need to do to comply with the letter of the law and company policy?	Compliance with rules	Strict compliance with host government's environmental practices, even if inferior to international standards	Hire many lawyers to draft and interpret rules
4	Will this action or inaction detract from my public reputation or private relationships?	Reputation protection; reactive risk management	Apply different practices to less visible investments	Hire a public relations firm to engage with stakeholders
3	How do I comply with the minimum legal requirements and stay in business?	Minimum compliance	Allegations against Nike and its supply chain in Asia	Challenge legal interpretations/jurisdiction Accept double standards No sense of social accountabilities
2	How can I avoid being caught with "dirty hands"?	Personal safety/self-preservation	Allegations against Elf Aquitaine in Africa	Outsource the "dirty work" Minimize the paper trail
1	Will I go to jail?	Personal safety/self-preservation	Enron management	Plea bargain Turn in someone else
0	How do I cover up?	Personal safety/self-preservation	Richard Nixon in Watergate scandal	Hire high-priced lawyer Obfuscate

| SUMMARY OF RUNGS AND MOTIVATION ||
RUNGS	MOTIVATION
8, 9, 10	Help others
7	Avoid negative impacts to others
5, 6	Avoid negative impacts to corporation
0, 1, 2, 3, 4	Avoid negative impacts to me

A corporation stuck on rungs 0 through 3 in the Integrity Ladder is likely to have negligible expressed commitment to business integrity. A corporation that is concerned with impacts on relationships (rung 4) may be motivated to make integrity commitments as a means of preserving its reputation with others. Corporations focused on legal compliance, rules, and the need for economic order (rungs 5 and 6) will be motivated to make integrity commitments necessary to maintain an efficient operating environment—the primary motivation is compliance and risk management.

Corporations who consider the impact of their investments and operations on others—including local communities, the environment, and the host country—operate on rungs 7 through 9 of the Integrity Ladder. Gradations between rungs 7 through 9 of the Integrity Ladder reflect the extent of corporate commitment to these accountabilities. Some corporations recognize these social accountabilities as nice-to-haves, but only if their operating budgets are not affected. Other corporations are willing to expend additional capital and administrative expenses to support these objectives. Some corporations are concerned with responses to social accountabilities only during their intended period of investment, while other corporations pursue sustainability over the long term.

Rung 10, the pinnacle of the moral development index, is a corporate leader in his or her individual capacity as a philanthropist who asks the question: Will my children and grandchildren appreciate my decisions to help others? Some critics may question actions to accumulate wealth or criticize motivations to disperse personal wealth. However, individuals such as George Soros, Ted Turner, Bill Gates, and many others use their personal wealth to invest in health care, education, and infrastructure that will benefit future generations.

Applying the Integrity Ladder

Applying the Integrity Ladder tool to two mini-case studies will illustrate how this assessment tool can be used by management teams. Once the rungs of the Integrity Ladder are understood, then the internal and external stakeholders can discuss what the desired rung on the Integrity Ladder should be for a corporation.

Scenario X: Compliant Corporation Ltd.

Compliant Corporation Ltd. operates in a manner that complies fully with legal requirements. The corporation's CEO is legally trained and vigilant in ensuring that the corporation is aware of all laws that apply to its operations, including tax and commercial laws, and anti-corruption legislation in host countries where Compliant Corporation operates. The corporation occasionally considers the impact of its operations on local communities where it operates, but not in a systematic or transparent way. The corporation's mission, vision, and values statements include enthusiastic commitments to integrity. Corporate personnel who do not respect the law know that their jobs are at risk.

Corporate leadership values business integrity as a necessary prerequisite for an open economy. For economic reasons, senior management discourages investment in countries where a level playing field may be compromised by corrupt host government officials.

The corporation's integrity statements are somewhat generic in language, but the corporation's employees generally understand the CEO's expectations. Compliance with these expectations is generally observed in practice.

COMPLIANT CORPORATION LTD. ON INTEGRITY LADDER			
RUNG	PRIMARY MOTIVATION	INTEGRITY COMMITMENT	INTEGRITY ACTION
10			
9			
8			
7			
6			
5	Compliance with law and corporation policy	Compliance orientation in corporation policy	Compliance with policy
4			
3			
2			
1			
0			

Corporate commitments and actions on integrity are aligned at rung 5 for Compliant Corporation.

Scenario Y: Strategic Corporation Inc.

Strategic Corporation Inc. operates in many investment environments. Through experience, the managers have learned that effective dialogue and engagement with host communities where the corporation operates is critical to the corporation's sustainable investment and effective operations. The CEO of this corporation has recently mandated a reevaluation of the corporation's vision, mission, and values statements. Expanded commitments have been made with regard to business integrity, host communities, and the environment. These value statements also reference respect for human rights in jurisdictions where the corporation operates.

The CEO has mandated implementation of these refreshed corporate commitments and training is planned to support personnel in implementation. Key stakeholders have been informed of these undertakings.

At a head-office level, personnel understand the CEO's intentions and there is alignment between the corporate commitments and practices. The corporation is increasingly engaged in dialogue with external stakeholders on key issues. In addition, the managers want to be "part of the solution," including participating in industry discussions on emerging issues. However, at an operating level, the personnel directly responsible for managing projects do not understand what has changed and operational practices have not changed.

STRATEGIC CORPORATION INC. ON INTEGRITY LADDER			
RUNG	PRIMARY MOTIVATION	INTEGRITY COMMITMENT	INTEGRITY ACTION
10			
9			
8			
7	Elements of avoidance of harm to others	Company policy	
6	Proactive risk management	Company policy	
5	Compliance with law and company policy		Operating group is weakest link
4			
3			
2			
1			
0			

Corporate commitment and action on business integrity are not aligned for Strategic Corporation. While the corporation's professed commitment is positioned at rung 6 and shows elements of rung 7, actual practices in the operating groups demonstrate corporate integrity walk at rung 5. Therefore, senior management time should be focused on raising the corporate actions for the operating groups from rung 5 to rung 6 to achieve greater organizational alignment. After this alignment is completed, then senior management can consider moving all of the departments from rung 6 to rung 7.

The Critical Link Between Corporate Integrity and Accountability

Effective assessment of business integrity is dependent on corporate accountability processes and practices. If a corporation fails to account for its actions, corporate stakeholders are constrained in their ability to assess integrity. In an environment charged with distrust, any opaqueness in a corporation's reporting and assessing of performance will attract suspicion. Clearly, the onus is on corporations to be transparent in reporting corporate actions.

Another aspect of accountability that warrants examination is corporate response to breaches in integrity:

- Are employees held to account for actions (or inactions) that cause the corporation to fail to meet its integrity commitments?

- What is the incentive for corporate personnel to act with integrity?

- How are breaches in integrity reported? Does the corporation have a hot line or help line to allow for confidential reporting or whistleblowing?

Little Protection Behind the Corporate Veil

Within some corporations, employee complacency has been jarred. Disconnects between corporate values and actual practices are becoming increasingly uncomfortable. Employees are recognizing the downside risks resulting from vagueness in individual and collective understandings of business integrity.

Employees historically believed that there was protection behind the corporate veil. While the corporation itself may be fined for certain inappropriate actions, individuals would generally not be held accountable for corporate actions. Certainly, an employee may be imprisoned or fined as an individual for actions that were illegal. However, employees and directors often assumed they were protected from personal prosecution for actions that were sanctioned by the corporation.

However, corporate managers, and even their overly conciliatory accountants, are now charged with (and jailed for) breaches of integrity that were seemingly tolerated within corporate governance structures. Employees are now asking themselves: What questions do I need to ask in order to not be complicit in corporate misbehavior, and do I really understand the meaning of business integrity?

There Is a Need to Talk about Corporate Motivation

In order not to distort reality, it must be emphasized that not all corporations are evil. The vast majority of corporate behavior demonstrates integrity. However, there is an emerging imperative for corporate management teams to define business integrity *with integrity*, and to declare and demonstrate unwavering commitment to business integrity.

Charting corporate commitment to integrity on the Integrity Ladder will engender dialogue about business integrity. This dialogue may not be easy. This dialogue will necessarily expose the cracks between corporate policy and intention regarding business integrity and a corporation's actual practice. As well, differences between individual and corporate value definitions may make it challenging for employees to compartmentalize their work and personal lives.

Navigating in Frontier 1 requires focused management attention. Corporate managers' ability to demonstrate delivery on their integrity commitments depends on internal governance strategies, structures, and systems. Unlike technological upgrades, these governance structures cannot be fabricated off-site and installed in organizations. These strategies and systems are embedded within intangible sets of relationships, expectations, and accountabilities that are created and supported by individuals within corporations. The strength and durability of corporate governance strategies and accountability infrastructure are predicated on corporate culture.

If corporations are not proactive in responding to the stakeholder appeal for evidence of integrity, this leadership vacuum likely will be filled by regulations, laws, and other third party–imposed mandates. As Chapter 11 discusses in more detail, the United States Securities and Exchange Commission, as well as regulatory agencies in many other countries, have full support from political leaders to issue reams of regulations needed to rein in seemingly freewheeling corporate accounting practices.

These corporate integrity gaps are not only being filled by traditional lawmakers. Public distrust of corporations is also providing an opening for nongovernmental and advocacy organizations. Chapter 11 provides more detail, but one example here will be useful to explain. With the support of dozens of credible nongovernmental organizations, George Soros recently launched an appeal dubbed "publish what you pay." The campaign is targeted at extractive companies, and demands that corporations invested internationally disclose all payments made to host governments. Until recently, corporations would largely have ignored such an appeal, but, in the present climate of suspicion, corporations ignore this stakeholder appeal for voluntary action at their peril.

Frontier 2:
Clarifying the Roles and Responsibilities of Corporations

This chapter focuses on issues arising from evolving expectations about the role of corporations in society and development. It is impossible for a corporation to describe its business integrity commitments to key stakeholders in corporate vision and mission statements without first clarifying its intended and feasible role in society and development.

Corporations have traditionally defined their key stakeholder groups to include shareholders, employees, suppliers/partners, and customers. More recently, corporations have been asked to anticipate the impacts of their projects on society. In order to respond to these evolving expectations, corporations are encouraged to clarify and redefine their responsibilities and roles. Corporations must also consider how they translate these responsibilities and roles into commitments and actions in corporate visions, missions, philosophies, or cultures.

Corporations cannot be all things to all people. However, corporations do need to understand what role their key stakeholders assume a corporation is playing in society and development. To the extent that there are discrepancies between stakeholder expectations of the corporation and the roles and responsibilities actually assumed by the corporation in its vision and mission, these discrepancies need to be resolved.

As well, corporate management may also be placed in the position of reconciling divergent stakeholder expectations of corporations. For example, some shareholders will argue that a corporation is primarily accountable to its shareholders to maximize profits—this stakeholder position may not be easily reconcilable with a community stakeholder whose land value is eroded by the potential environmental impacts of a new development project.

In order to navigate the risks and opportunities presented in Frontier 2, key corporate stakeholders are encouraged to ask questions to enhance understanding of a particular corporation's roles and responsibilities, and better define corporate boundaries. This step is a necessary prerequisite to clarification and refinement of corporate commitments to integrity. The latter portion of this chapter focuses specifically on expectations of community stakeholders.

> *External corporate stakeholders ask:* What is the proper role and responsibility for corporations? How does this corporation meet these expectations?

> *Internal corporate stakeholders ask:* What do my managers expect of my corporation? Does my corporation have the motivation and capacity to effectively respond to these expectations?

Conflicting Perspectives on Corporate Roles

Many corporations have a formal business plan that includes:

> *Vision:* JKL will be the (relative ranking of number one, top five, or top quartile) in the (XX industry) within (YY years).

> *Mission:* JKL will provide (XXX goods and/or services) to the (YYY specific customer markets) in the (ZZZ geographic region).

> *Philosophy/Culture:* JKL uses a balanced scorecard to recognize the different stakeholder groups of shareholders, customers, employees, and society.

Even within the same vision, mission and value statements, and guidelines, internal and external corporate stakeholders can have very different perspectives on the corporation's roles and responsibilities. For example, some corporate stakeholders look to corporations for longer-term performance—local communities where projects are situated are a good example of a stakeholder group that expects long-term corporate engagement. Communities expect that investors will consider the environmental and socioeconomic impacts of a development on a host community—boom and bust cycles should be anticipated in certain industry sectors, and impacts to local quality of life predicted.

Public companies listed on stock exchanges frequently face challenges in reconciling these longer-term roles with stakeholders' expectations in measuring short-term performance. Public corporations must comply with the procedures and disclosures required by stock exchanges. Disclosure can create conflicts with financial analysts who are driven by quarterly forecasts of sales and earnings per share. Corporations that do not meet the estimates disappoint analysts, which can result in an immediate and substantial stock price decline.

Even business school disciplines contribute to the confusion about corporate roles. Each discipline within a business school has a different perspective on the corporate roles to be emphasized:

BUSINESS DISCIPLINE	EMPHASIS	TYPICAL STATEMENT
Finance	Shareholders	Corporations exist to maximize the long-run wealth/profitability to the shareholders.
Marketing	Customers	Corporations should focus on customer satisfaction, so that sales will drive market share and long-term profitability.
Human resources	Employees	Corporations with highly motivated people will produce quality products, which drive repeat sales and long-term profitability.
Strategy and general management	Society	Corporations that do not comply with legal rules and/or fail to include social concerns in decision making will eventually disappear from the competitive scene.

Polarization of Opinion on the Role of Corporations

Corporate management teams are aware of the level of public distrust and are increasingly listening to stakeholder opinions. However, corporate management often moves forward tentatively, even guardedly, in expanding corporate roles and responsibilities due to the uncertainty, conflicts, and dilemmas involved in business integrity commitments.

Corporations are also aware of the risks associated with defining their corporate role too narrowly or too broadly. Defining corporate roles too restrictively may limit corporate responsiveness to business integrity concerns in each operating jurisdiction. Likewise, defining corporate boundaries too expansively may result in a corporation becoming a substitute for governments.

Some corporate managers even disavow a corporate role in defining sustainable development priorities. These managers argue that sustainable development values should be decided on and championed by political processes and not by business leaders.

Other external corporate stakeholders are critical of corporations defining their roles too narrowly, alleging that corporations don't pay their share. Who pays if corporations are not held liable, or if corporations go bankrupt? Arguably, the concept of limited liability means that companies can be sheltered from the full burden of disaster impacts. Do the payments made by corporations to compensate for disasters truly address the full range and extent of environmental and social impacts? Indeed, is money satisfactory recompense to a community if their ancestral lands are confiscated; if their water aquifers are polluted; or if their young people are forced to relocate to find jobs?

Advocacy groups can be harsh in their criticism of narrow corporate mandates. The media is frequently a vehicle for amplification of these criticisms. This advocacy can even become a catalyst for consumer boycotts of targeted corporations. Recall the impacts of consumer boycotts of Shell, Exxon, and Nestlé. Some would argue that the threat of a consumer boycott and its associated negative publicity is more important than the boycott itself.

Corporate stakeholders' activism is not only the mainstay of a few left-wing student radicals—the growth in grassroots alignment of citizens is vigorous and can be quite constructive. For example, in Scandinavia, consumer pressure for environmentally friendly toilet paper and disposable diapers prompted paper producers to do some innovative thinking. As an outcome of this advocacy, Scandinavian paper producers increasingly use unbleached pulp in their paper products.

Boundary Questions

To delineate business integrity values, commitments, and responses, corporate stakeholders must assess the *boundaries* of corporate roles and responsibilities. Boundary questions are the broader contextual questions about the feasible and preferred roles and responsibilities of companies. Defining corporate boundaries, in the context of evolving and emerging stakeholder expectations, requires careful management and committed leadership.

- Should corporations avoid all transactions that raise the risk of perceived conflict of interest?

- Should corporations play a role in political governance issues or in building the capacity of public institutions, or are these issues best left to politicians and international agencies?

- How do corporations design and implement strategies that foster authentic and meaningful communication, dialogue, and partnerships with stakeholders?

- Should corporations attempt to incorporate all stakeholder priorities into their investment plans, and how do corporations do so without operating on a lowest common denominator basis?

- Should corporations exceed compliance with legal requirements in investment jurisdictions and, if so, at what cost?

- Should corporations operate in jurisdictions where corruption is pervasive and, if so, what measures should corporations take to discourage corrupt practices beyond the scope of their own business?

- Are corporations operationally and financially capable of building development capacity in their host communities, and what is the extent of corporations' responsibility in providing basic infrastructure that is normally the responsibility of local governments?

- How should corporations distinguish between cultural sensitivity (understanding that distinct cultures have different perspectives on what is proper and respected) and cultural relativism (concluding that because a different culture does not agree with a particular ethical standard, we should not apply that standard in that culture)?

- Should corporations invest in zones of conflict and, if so, what measures should they adopt to protect their own people and assets, or the personnel and assets of others?

- What is a corporation's feasible and preferred response to human rights violations by host governments or host communities?

- Should corporations invest in a project where economic benefits of investment are not shared equitably? What if the corporate investment contributes to power imbalances?

For corporations operating in several jurisdictions, boundary questions are even more challenging. For example, how do multinational corporations with ties and allegiances to multiple geographical and political jurisdictions determine roles and corresponding business integrity commitments? Should corporate boundaries and corresponding business integrity strategies be standardized or tailored to the unique circumstances of each jurisdiction of investment?

Dilemmas that companies face when operating in multiple projects and multiple jurisdictions are discussed below under the heading "Dilemma: Dual Standards."

Integrity Dilemmas

Integrity dilemmas are inevitable for corporations. There will always be occasions when:

- The right thing to do is unclear.
- Two or more values conflict.
- People may be negatively affected by a corporate decision.

The following sampling of integrity dilemmas that corporations face reflects the range of opinions that corporate leaders must assimilate and understand in defining preferred and feasible corporate boundaries. Dilemmas arise as a result of differences of opinions among stakeholders regarding corporate boundaries and corresponding integrity expectations. The test of civic and corporate leadership is how these dilemmas are managed:

- Corporate conflict of interest
- Balancing stakeholder expectations
- Operating in legal vacuums
- Allocation or sharing of benefits of investment
- Dual standards
- Corporate complicity

Dilemma: Corporate Conflict of Interest

Corporations may be accused of acting in a way that triggers a conflict of interest. For example, by contributing funds to political campaigns or otherwise supporting a government, corporations expose themselves to this potential criticism.

Amnesty International has sharply criticized political parties in the United States for accepting sizable political donations from U.S.–based transnational corporations. In a 2003 news release, Amnesty International questioned the U.S. government's seeming unwillingness to hold U.S.–based transnational corporations accountable to the highest standards of human rights and environmental practices.

If conflicts of interest are perceived, externally or internally, considerable management time may be required to clarify motivations and defend the corporate reputation.

Allegations of conflict of interest are not limited to corporate relationships with politicians. Media headlines also question the coziness of relationships between corporations and academia. For example, relationships between medical researchers and pharmaceutical corporations raise issues about whether the medical community is independent from the design and implementation of corporate marketing strategies and profitability.

Legal and commercial frameworks permit medical researchers to conduct research on pharmaceuticals for drug corporations. Objectively speaking, medically trained researchers with the requisite scientific expertise should conduct this research. However, the media and other critics question the integrity of some of these alliances.

Through this media scrutiny, the legal and commercial boxes defining the scope of engagement between pharmaceutical companies and the medical community are pried open. Pharmaceutical companies and medical researchers are forced to consider their integrity accountabilities outside the strict commercial boundaries of undertakings agreed to in research contracts. Medical researchers may contractually agree to respect the need for objectivity in research, but critics may counter that these commercial undertakings do not sufficiently manage the risk of a conflict of interest. In the critic's opinion, the need for independence in medical research outweighs the importance ascribed to sanctity of the commercial contract.

Dilemma: Balancing Stakeholder Expectations

All corporate investments have stakeholders—individuals and groups affected by, or who can affect (either positively or negatively), a project's outcome. Later in this chapter, the Stakeholder Grid is introduced as a tool to help corporations identify and analyze the perspectives of key stakeholders.

Beyond the challenge of identifying all key stakeholders, corporate management must also balance the wide-ranging stakeholder expectations of corporations, as well as expectations regarding the financial and nonfinancial impacts of the specific corporate project.

Media accounts of development projects provide useful windows to observe the perspectives and interactions of various project stakeholders:

- What do individual stakeholders expect of the corporation in a project?

- What do individual stakeholders expect of the project's financial and nonfinancial impacts?

- How do stakeholders engage to facilitate a balancing of respective priorities?

- What is a corporation's role in managing this stakeholder engagement process, and in resolving potential conflicts in stakeholders' expectations of the corporation, project priorities, and project outcomes?

Managing stakeholder expectations in large-scale multi-party projects is a particular challenge for corporate investors. When a project is situated in an environmentally, politically, and socially sensitive region, these management challenges are exacerbated. To demonstrate these challenges, consider the example of an energy corporation seeking to participate in the construction of a gas pipeline.

To highlight the sensitivities associated with such a project, assume that the pipeline is to be constructed in the Arctic regions of North America. What do stakeholders expect of the corporate investor, and how would the corporation identify and understand these stakeholder expectations? As well, how does corporate management reconcile these different expectations? How can corporations respond to competing demands *within* local communities and how does corporate management balance expectations *between* local and non-local stakeholders? The scenario reviewed in Chapter 10 explores these dilemmas in detail.

As media reports attest, energy corporations seeking to build pipeline projects in the Arctic have encountered resistance for decades from many stakeholder groups, including Aboriginal groups holding interests in treaty and Crown land, and from environmental advocacy groups. Non-local contractors performing services on behalf of corporate investors sometimes find themselves facing off with angry members of local communities along rights of way affected by construction projects. There is an inherent tension between local contractors and "imported" labor and supplies. There is also potential for tension between local communities that may derive direct economic benefit from a development and non-local advocacy groups (for example, wildlife protection agencies) that may see negative consequences of investment.

This insight into the range of stakeholder priorities in a pipeline construction project does not even contemplate the additional expectations of internal corporate stakeholders, including shareholders and corporate employees.

Not surprisingly, identifying stakeholder interests and balancing competing priorities is frequently controversial. Who is "right" and who is "wrong"? Corporate leaders participating in commercial projects struggle to decide how to proceed. How do corporations make decisions when stakeholder interests are so diverse and do not seem capable of being aligned? What is the corporation's role in managing the stakeholder engagement process and in rationalizing competing interests? What should stakeholders reasonably expect of corporations?

Dilemma: Operating in Legal Vacuums

Although legal and commercial gaps can arise in any operating environment, there is a greater risk of encountering these vacuums in the developing world where infrastructure and the rule of law may be catching up to economic development. These omissions pose significant challenges to corporations that are then left to determine the right course of action based on international standards and stakeholder expectations. In the Baku-Tbilisi-Ceyhan oil pipeline, for example, Friends of the Earth and other advocacy groups complained to British Petroleum about the legislative deficiencies in the pipeline right of way, pointing to laws dating back to the Soviet era when fiscal regimes were in place to support a Communist economic structure.

Some of the most daunting legal vacuums that corporations can be forced to fill in the developing world relate to human rights. Since the proclamation of the Universal Declaration of Human Rights in 1948, inherent human rights have been codified in constitutions around the world and endorsed by many organizations, including companies.

For corporations operating in investment jurisdictions that do not recognize human rights, there is an obvious dilemma. Political leaders and judges in some countries do not accept the opinion that human rights are inherent rights, and challenge the view that human rights can be imposed on other cultures. What is a corporate investor to do in a country that does not recognize human rights or, worse, believes that foreign investors are not entitled to impose human rights on other cultures? In his book *The Rights Revolution*, Michael Ignatieff addresses this dilemma head-on:

> This takes us into an important issue of principle. Many people feel that any such override by an international body interferes with the rights of national cultures to define their own laws … in many countries in the Islamic world, in Africa and Asia, human-rights movements are seen as an alien attempt to impose European standards on cultures and norms that have their own legitimacy.

Legal vacuums predictably arise in the context of operations or issues that are not within a single country's jurisdiction—conduct of operations in a maritime region is one such example. Addressing these multi-jurisdictional legal vacuums is not easy for companies.

In the case of a maritime operation, laws governing liability associated with environmental pollution are often unclear. For example, in spite of the acknowledged risk of oil spills by single-hulled tankers, maritime laws still do not require that heavy fuel oil be carried in double-hulled tankers. The European Commission pushed for EU member states to strengthen maritime safety in the wake of the sinking of the *Prestige* oil tanker off Spain in 2002, recommending limits on the transport of dangerous goods by sea within 200 miles (322 kilometers) of a shore and a requirement for heavy fuel oil to be carried in double-hulled tankers.

Even in the absence of legislative mandates, many oil shippers have voluntarily elected to use double-hulled tankers given the magnitude of potential liability for polluters. After the Exxon *Valdez* oil spill, Exxon was ordered to pay U.S. $287 million in actual damages, and a U.S. $5 billion punitive damage award against the company is under appeal. These amounts are in addition to the U.S. $2.2 billion the company spent to clean up Alaska's Prince William Sound.

Dilemma: Allocation and Sharing of Benefits of Investment

Host communities affected by corporate projects derive varying degrees of direct and indirect benefit from these projects. In addition to the potential benefits of capacity building and community investment by corporations, host communities may receive an allocation of the project proceeds, either directly or via a host government.

In cases where the local communities are not satisfied with their allocation of the revenue, corporate investors may find themselves uncomfortably positioned between local or regional interests and national governments. Shell's quandaries in Nigeria and the experiences of mining companies in Latin America exemplify these dilemmas.

Shell's operations in the Delta region of Nigeria have been shut down many times by disgruntled locals who bear the environmental and social burden of investment in their communities, but believe that their allocation of the projects' benefits in terms of jobs, training, and revenue are disproportionately weighted in favor of the federal government in Nigeria. In Bolivia, some communities near the site of mining operations object to foreign investment; at the same time, the national government advocates a pro-investment business climate.

Local communities and regional government representatives may attempt to demonstrate their frustration with the project's revenue allocations by compromising a project in their community or region. It is particularly awkward for corporations to mediate these revenue allocations—the project's operations are physically located in communities, but the corporation's contractual and governance relationships are with the national government. The investors' physical operations and personnel may become a target for local dissenters.

Conversely, when project revenue allocations are adjusted to be responsive to expectations of regional governments and local communities, the corporate investor can encounter different challenges. In Aceh, Indonesia, mineral wealth is substantial. In response to local pressure for autonomy, revenue allocations from resources in Aceh were recalibrated—Jakarta's allocation was reduced in favor of increased distributions to the regional government in Aceh. The challenge for investors in Aceh is to ensure that the allocations of mineral revenues to the regional government are used for the benefit of local communities where the investors operate. This dilemma is not unique to the developing world.

Dilemma: Dual Standards

Another challenge for private sector investors is deciding what technical and operating standards will apply to their projects. This management dilemma is particularly challenging when there is a divergence in legal requirements and regulatory standards within operating jurisdictions (for example, different requirements between communities, regions, states, or host countries).

Operating standards and regulatory practices can vary in terms of a variety of factors, including safety, environmental response, workplace conditions, harassment policy, discrimination policy, gifts, and entertainment requirements. For corporations managing more than one project or operating in more than one investment environment, the challenge is to determine if all projects will be subject to identical technical, operating, and integrity standards. And, will these standards have sufficient flexibility to respond to local conditions?

Environmental standards have evolved over the past two decades to the point where there is some standardization of accepted practice, particularly in the developed world. The developing world continues to define environmental standards frequently, but not always, with reference to some international standards. These evolutions leave the investor with many questions to evaluate from an integrity perspective:

- In a world where operating and technical practices are not standardized, what is the social accountability of a corporation in cases where the host community's environmental compliance requirements are inferior to a corporation's standard operating practices?

- Is an investor ethically obligated to comply with environmental standards at a higher level, even if local competitors do not have such legal or ethical thresholds?

- What if this expectation compromises a corporation's competitiveness?

These questions are not easy to answer. Corporate managers must carefully consider their motivators and the impacts of their strategies. Does a company intend to operate beyond compliance with local standards? It may be tempting for a corporation to boldly declare "We do not have dual standards in environmental practices." But, before making these commitments, corporate managers must be certain of their organizational capacity to ensure that there are no dual standards in their operations.

Oil producers' gas flaring in West Africa is a case in point. Until recently, West African governments did not constrain this practice. Other countries in the developed world constrain gas flaring to varying degrees and apply different motivators. Norway led the campaign to reduce gas flaring, legally mandating nearly zero-tolerance gas emission thresholds. Other countries impose penalties on gas emissions as a way of discouraging the practice.

When a Norwegian corporation or another corporation from a developed country invests in West Africa, what are its stakeholders' expectations when gas is produced in conjunction with oil? Should the corporation be allowed to flare as much gas as is commercially necessary, as long as this flaring does not violate local laws? Or is the corporation expected to find ways to reinject the produced gas or otherwise reduce the emission levels to Western standards? How do corporations decide what standard of practice to apply? What is the primary corporate motivation—compliance or beyond compliance? And how far beyond compliance is a corporation expected to commit itself? Is a corporation ethically obligated to subscribe to the highest standard in all cases, or to follow commercially reasonable standards in the particular circumstances? Who decides within the corporation?

Whenever there are differences in expectations between the host government and a key stakeholder group, corporations are caught in the middle of the dispute. A debate between legally prescribed practices for emission reductions in West Africa and socially accepted practices for gas flaring in the developed world can spark debate that affects an oil producer operating in the developing and developed world. Sometimes the host government is ambivalent to the various arguments or may even be supportive of external standards. In cases where the host government is antagonized by externally imposed standards, corporations have cause to squirm.

In the case of Nike's operations in Southeast Asia, angry American consumers demanded that the corporation operate according to U.S. labor standards in Southeast Asia. By choosing to pay its Southeast Asian workers in accordance with local customs and practices, Nike exposed itself to charges of operating sweatshops. Either alternative created dilemmas. Ultimately, Nike was forced to engage with its key stakeholders and determine how to effectively manage the challenge of dual standards. Nike chose to manage these integrity issues beyond compliance with applicable laws and rules, but did not entirely eradicate dual standards.

Dual standards arise in many operational contexts—dual standards do not just arise when there is a difference in standards between the developed world and the developing world. Corporations may have different levels of regulatory compliance from project to project. Different U.S. states, Canadian provinces, and European countries, even individual cities and municipalities, create independent standards for investors. For example, different operating environments within the same country may have different nondiscrimination laws in support of the rights of Aboriginal communities, health and safety benefits, or consequences of same-sex partnerships. Human resource managers are encouraged to strategically determine how they manage these varying standards—that is, through compliance motivation or beyond compliance—and to consider the project-specific and organizational impacts of dual standards.

Dilemma: Corporate Complicity

Corporate relationships with "unsavory" partners, suppliers, clients, or governments can be problematic if stakeholders label these relationships as complicit. Guilt by association can threaten corporate reputation.

For decades, the public has been legitimately interested in stories of atrocities committed by corrupt political leaders, and implications have been made that a corrupt government's actions are implicitly supported or enabled by private sector investment. Dictators' ability to launch civil wars, suppress their people, and degrade the environment is linked to financial capacity made possible through investors' investment in a country's resources. Corporate complicity in these atrocities may be alleged.

Well-documented examples of allegations of corporate complicity in host government atrocities include:

- Banks investing in South Africa in the 1980s

- Companies' investments in oil and gas development in southern Sudan and Myanmar

- Investments in Nigeria under the reign of General Abacha

More recently, corporate complicity has been alleged against lenders that provide private sector funding to controversial projects or to consumer product manufacturers who depend on child labor in their supply chains. For example, environmental groups have recently asked investment bankers, including Goldman Sachs, Merrill Lynch, and HSBC, not to sell bonds worth more than U.S. $2 billion on behalf of China Development Bank and the China Export Import Bank because they are concerned that the bonds could be used to finance controversial infrastructure projects, including the Three Gorges Dam in China.

These stories and implicit or explicit links to corporate complicity go to the heart of the role of corporations. By investing in emerging democracies, emerging markets, and conflict zones, are corporations complicit in the abuses, violence, and corruption perpetrated by host governments? By providing funding to corporations, is it fair that private sector banks be tarred with the same brush as their clients who borrow monies to fund projects?

Is the question one of zero tolerance, or is there scope for corporate engagement with a host government that violates human rights and tolerates environmental degradation? On one end of the continuum, there are advocates who argue vigorously and publicly that any support given by the private sector to corrupt or unethical governments is not to be countenanced. On the opposite end of the continuum, there are corporations who argue that it is not the investors' role to interfere with matters best left to diplomats and politicians. Applying this reasoning, unless prohibited by law from investment in a jurisdiction, a corporation should then be allowed to participate in commercial opportunities without social accountability conditions attached. The attitude is to let governments govern.

There are many situations where a host government could be criticized for its policy or practices. In these gray zones, a commercial project can become a lightning rod for dissent on government policy. Assessing the potential for complicity allegations is certainly an important legal and ethical question that corporate investors and their lenders and suppliers should ask. However, there is limited precedent to guide a corporation's thinking on these issues.

When faced with these dilemmas, the questions a senior manager should ask include:

- How do we navigate the gaps between stakeholder expectations? What if our shareholders and bonus-seeking managers want us to maximize profitability through increased utilization of lower cost child labor in Country X while some institutional investors want us to exit Country X?

- How does our corporation decide what project is acceptable, and what project is not acceptable? How does our organization define the limits?

- Under what conditions is indirect or direct support for an investment in a repressive regime acceptable?

- How can corporations effectively promote principles and values prioritized by their key stakeholders, including transparency, pluralism, and the rule of law?

- Should corporations be responsible for promoting these principles within or beyond their sphere of investment?

- How can corporations with business integrity practices compete with corporations who either do not value business integrity or do not operationalize business integrity practices?

It can be an arduous corporate experience to manage any of these dilemmas. Look to the experience of Talisman Energy Inc. and the corporation's ultimate decision to sell their Sudanese oil interests for U.S. \$340 million to India's national oil company. Talisman's CEO, Jim Buckee, is quoted as saying, "We simply had Sudan fatigue."

Navigating Frontier 2

The dilemmas reviewed in this chapter are a consequence of evolving expectations about the role of the private sector—differences of opinion among influential corporate stakeholders as to how corporations could assume roles and responsibilities in their areas of influence.

These differences of opinion in corporate mandates are inevitable, as there will always be differences in expectations among key corporate stakeholders. As well, there will always be gaps between legal compliance and best practices. How a corporation manages these decision-making processes—how it assesses and navigates these expectation gaps—affects corporate reputation and management effectiveness, and ultimately corporate profitability.

Corporations are also encouraged to consider if their organization has *proactively* defined their roles and responsibilities. A corporate management team that understands the organization's mandate and key stakeholders' expectations is positioned to proactively identify and manage these dilemmas. A corporation's management team that defines the organization's role only in response to crisis may become vulnerable to external influence. The difference between *proactive* and *reactive* definitions of corporate roles and responsibilities can be pivotal in terms of operational, financial, and reputation impacts.

Defining Corporate Roles Beyond Compliance

Chapter 5 reviews motivations for corporations: Why do corporations decide to assume certain social accountabilities that exceed legal requirements? Why do corporations make voluntary integrity commitments? Why do corporations want to examine their decision-making processes to ensure that internal management frameworks support these integrity strategies and intentions?

A corporation's choice to define its roles and responsibilities beyond compliance is often influenced by the corporation's operating environment.

If the company invests in a jurisdiction where there is a regulatory regime in place, and laws are fairly and expeditiously enforced by an independent judiciary and host government, the company may be predisposed to a compliance strategy. However, even within fully functional states like Canada, the United States, and the European Union, stakeholders may be skeptical that the monitoring of companies' regulatory compliance is adequate. Laws may be in place, but citizens affected by projects may not be comfortable with the state's capacity to inspect operations and verify investor compliance with laws. Corporate stakeholders may encourage companies to create complementary practices and voluntary processes to verify and assure regulatory compliance.

When corporations are invested in quasi-functional or dysfunctional states, corporate stakeholders are more likely to expect that management teams will selectively identify supplementary commitments well beyond compliance with local standards. If corruption compromises the judiciary's enforcement of local laws, it is likely that corporate stakeholders will expect corporate management to define its roles and responsibilities more broadly to supplement legal compliance with voluntary measures.

FUNCTIONAL STATES EXAMPLE: CANADA	QUASI-FUNCTIONAL STATES EXAMPLE: COLOMBIA	DYSFUNCTIONAL STATES EXAMPLE: KAZAKHSTAN
Corporations have option to *complement* legal compliance with voluntary measures	Corporations will need to selectively *supplement* legal compliance with voluntary measures	Corporations will need to *substitute* legal compliance with voluntary measures
Rule of law enforced by judiciary and government	Corruption compromises enforcement of rule of law Host government and judiciary have diminished ability to enforce rule of law	Rule of law is not systematically upheld; corruption is commonplace

Source: Based upon work of Michael Woolcock and Deepa Narayan, "Social Capital: Implications for Development Theory, Research and Policy." *The World Bank Research Observer* 15, no. 2 (August 2000): 225–249.

Business Tools: Stakeholder Grid and Impact Assessment Tool

Most corporations would benefit from an enhanced ability to anticipate stakeholder expectations of the corporation in a project and to strategically respond to dilemmas arising as a result of divergent stakeholder opinions. The Stakeholder Grid and Impact Assessment tool is recommended for this purpose. This business tool helps corporate managers to identify their key stakeholders and evaluate the potential positive and negative impacts of individual stakeholders on the project as part of a risking process. Differences in stakeholder expectations of the corporation in a project can also be anticipated through use of this tool.

STAKEHOLDER CATEGORIES	TYPES OF IMPACT				
	REPUTATION	PHYSICAL ASSETS (HARM OR LOSS)	PERSONNEL (HARM OR LOSS)	TIMELINES	SHARE VALUE
Corporation (parent)					
Employees working on project					
Media					
Regulators					
Investors					
Insurers/ lenders					
Customers					
Suppliers					
Advocacy NGOs					

Nonadvocacy NGOs					
Partners					
Agents					
Host communities					
Host government					
Other relevant governments					

Impact Assessment: −5 = most negative impact potential
0 = no impact
+5 = most positive impact potential

The Stakeholder Grid and Impact Assessment tool must evaluate both the stakeholders' motivation and capability of causing the identified impact to the corporate project.

Further analysis can be incorporated into relevant parts of the assessment and risking matrix to clarify the magnitude of the harmful action. For example, harm or loss to personnel could include a range of impacts from personal injury, detention, kidnapping, or homicide. Impacts to physical assets could include theft, sabotage, destruction of assets, or other types of infrastructure impacts that are unique to a business operation or operating environment.

Reputation impacts can be further refined to identify a variety of triggers, for example: lack of transparency, corruption, unfair sharing of benefits, environmental degradation, social/cultural impacts, discrimination, human rights abuses, and Aboriginal interests.

Share value impacts can be assessed over various timelines: immediate, monthly, financial quarter, annual, life of the project, three to five years or over the long term. Impacts to timelines can be charted against the project timeline.

Beyond the identification of key project/investment stakeholders and the assessment of a project/investment's potential impacts on key stakeholders, the Stakeholder Grid and Impact Assessment tool provides a strategic starting point in anticipating and ultimately reconciling corporate stakeholders' expectations about the company's role in a project. If stakeholders' expectations of a corporation in a project are not aligned, there will be a dilemma that a corporate management team will have to manage.

Not all dilemmas can be anticipated. However, having an appreciation of the potential dilemmas that a corporation may face will allow corporate managers to proactively ensure that decision-making systems and processes are in place to foster a strategic and even proactive corporate response.

Focus on Community Stakeholders

One of the key stakeholder groups for corporations is the community. In order to better understand the impacts of investment to community stakeholders, the Stakeholder Grid and Impact Assessment tool can be tailored for use with community stakeholders as follows:

CATEGORIES OF RISK ARISING IN RELATION TO COMMUNITY	TYPES OF IMPACT				
	REPUTATION	PHYSICAL ASSETS (HARM OR LOSS)	PERSONNEL (HARM OR LOSS)	TIMELINES	SHARE VALUE
Community stakeholder categories:					
Corporate head office					
Corporate local business unit					
Local media					

International media					
Investors					
Insurers/lenders					
Local/global customers					
Local/global suppliers					
Local/ international advocacy NGOs					
Local/global partners					
Local agents					
Local personnel					
Local political leaders					
Host country government					
Indigenous communities					
Local indigenous leaders					
Local regulators					
Representatives of local civil society					
Local disaffected youth					

continued

CATEGORIES OF RISK ARISING IN RELATION TO COMMUNITY	TYPES OF IMPACT				
	REPUTATION	PHYSICAL ASSETS (HARM OR LOSS)	PERSONNEL (HARM OR LOSS)	TIMELINES	SHARE VALUE
Local religious leaders					
Local educators					
Local health care providers					
Communities along transportation corridors					
Communities at export locations					

To focus this Stakeholder Grid and Impact Assessment tool on one key stakeholder group—the community—corporations must thoughtfully consider how to define their "communities":

- Is a community defined as a predetermined geographic radius from the center of operations?

- Can a community include an entire region or country where a corporation is invested?

- Can a community be select groups or populations?

To diminish confusion and the risk of unmanageable expectations, corporations are encouraged to proactively define their communities. This category of corporate stakeholder can be broad, including entire regions or even the populations of a host country. Alternatively, corporations can define communities more narrowly to include only vulnerable groups or people who have a particular need (for example, Aboriginal or indigenous populations).

Some corporate definitions of community are prescribed by reference to geographic parameters, including those populations that live within a certain distance from a project. Some corporations choose to set more fluid parameters for communities, defining their community stakeholders as people directly affected by a project, or considering those people who expect to benefit from a project.

Once a corporation has defined its "community," the next step is for the corporation to assess community stakeholder impacts and priorities. Ultimately, these interests will have to be balanced with the interests of other key stakeholders who may have local, regional, national, or international interests.

A necessary starting point to understanding community stakeholder impacts is research on the community stakeholders, including the characteristics of a corporation's community stakeholders. A social baseline survey is a useful tool to facilitate in-depth corporate understanding of their community stakeholders. If reliable data can be accessed, conducting a social baseline survey allows corporations to understand the characteristics of the communities where they operate. Relevant data to consider include:

- Population numbers
- Livelihoods
- Ages
- Gender distribution
- Income levels
- Ethnic groups
- Languages
- Social and community groups
- Leadership

- Governance structures

- Relationships with regional, national, and international stakeholders

Once corporations have an appreciation of the characteristics of their community stakeholders, it is easier for corporations to anticipate the direct and indirect impacts of their investment on community stakeholders. An understanding of potential impacts of investment fosters more empathetic and trusted engagement, and improves a corporation's ability to proactively manage risks. For example, the impacts of construction and operation of a manufacturing plant in a community can vary depending on the local community's needs. The impacts will differ between a community that has a significant youth population seeking work and a community occupied largely by retirees focused on an affordable lifestyle.

The potential impacts of investment to community stakeholders can be characterized as direct or indirect impacts.

Direct impacts include environmental, economic, and social outcomes caused directly by a project, including:

- Need for imported labor or services

- Adverse environmental consequences

- Resettlement of people

- Allocation of economic share of project benefits

Indirect impacts of a project are more challenging to anticipate, and are caused by broader changes in the community as a consequence of a project, including:

- Increase or decrease in local prices (inflation, deflation)

- Increase or decrease in local traffic

- Increased demands on public goods and services

- Migration to or from the project area

- Increase in contact with community by people from outside the community

- Heightened expectations

- Increase in risk of spread of communicable disease
- Greater public scrutiny of stakeholder interests and practices

Chapter 10 reviews corporate engagement with community stakeholders in detail by analyzing a scenario involving the construction of a pipeline through communities situated in the United States.

Frontier 3:
Aligning Corporate Integrity Values, Commitments, and Action within Individual Corporations

Frontier 3 focuses on how to create, document, manage, and assess alignment of integrity "talk" and integrity "walk" within an organization. Frontier 3 focuses on alignment within individual corporations. This alignment check can be applied to strategic business units, divisions, and departments within individual corporations.

The Integrity Ladder, introduced in Chapter 2, supports an assessment of differences in business integrity values within and among corporations. In order to assess the degree of alignment between business integrity commitments and business integrity action—alignment between corporate talk and walk—this chapter introduces a linked management tool, the Integrity Grid.

Corporations make decisions about their business integrity values. They expressly commit to management policies and operating practices that are intended to reflect expected integrity values of all employees. Corporations then motivate or decide on corporate action to support these business integrity commitments. But, how do corporations create, maintain, and assess alignment between intentions and practices for every employee, in every department, in every strategic business unit or division of the entire corporation?

To navigate Frontier 3, the critical questions to be asked of corporate leaders are:

External corporate stakeholders: What does senior management intend by its express corporate commitments to business integrity? How will senior management create, document, manage, and assess alignment between stated corporate commitments to business integrity and actual practice?

Internal corporate stakeholders: What is our stated corporate commitment to business integrity? How do we create, manage, and assess ongoing alignment between our corporate commitments on integrity and our corporate actions?

The Integrity Grid

The Integrity Grid is a management tool designed to measure alignment between a corporation's business integrity commitments and its actions. This tool can be applied to measure responsiveness to business integrity on a departmental, divisional, or corporate level. Comparative assessment of corporate performance is thus made easier. The *weakest link* in the corporation can be quickly identified and prioritized for action.

In order to assess the integrity alignment (and gaps) between departments within a company, and to identify alignment (and gaps) between individual departments and the organization as a whole, the Integrity Grid tool allows corporate managers to plot individual departmental integrity commitments and integrity actions.

Using the Integrity Ladder, introduced in Chapter 2, overall corporate commitments to integrity, and individual departmental commitments and actions on integrity, are considered and depicted on a grid as follows:

	CODE	COMMITMENT	ACTIONS	DEPARTMENT INTERNAL GAP (DEPARTMENT ACTIONS MINUS DEPARTMENT COMMITMENT)	CORPORATE DEPARTMENT GAP (DEPARTMENTAL COMMITMENT MINUS CORPORATE COMMITMENT)
Overall corporate	C	7	—	n/a	—
Individual departments:					
Security	S	2	2	0	−5
Environment, health, and safety	EHS	3	3	0	−4
Investor relations	IR	4	4	0	−3
Government relations	GR	4	4	0	−3
Operations	O	4	5	+1	−3
Finance	F	6	6	0	−1
Legal	L	6	7	+1	−1
Human resources	HR	8	8	0	+1

To achieve alignment between individual departmental commitments and actions, the preferred departmental internal gap is zero (depicted in the column "Department Internal Gap"). To achieve alignment between the departments and the overall corporate commitments to integrity, the

preferred corporate/department gap is zero (depicted in the column entitled "Corporate/Department Gap").

The data in the chart above (which is based on Integrity Ladder
inputs) can then be plotted on the Integrity Grid as follows:

- Corporate Talk Line (corporation's overall commitment to integrity)

- Equal Alignment Line (a 45-degree reference line that reflects equal
  alignment of department commitments = department actions)

- Plot intersection of individual departmental integrity commitments
  and actions

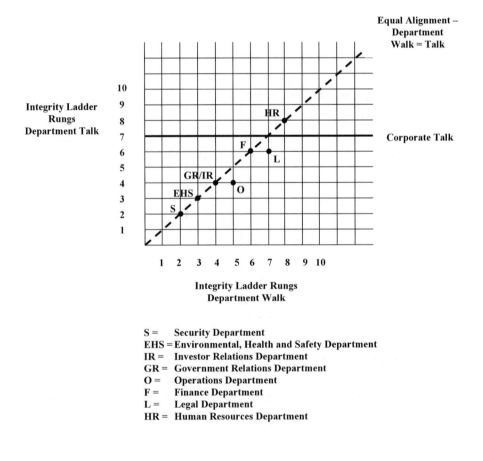

S =   Security Department
EHS = Environmental, Health and Safety Department
IR =   Investor Relations Department
GR =   Government Relations Department
O =   Operations Department
F =   Finance Department
L =   Legal Department
HR =   Human Resources Department

The degree of alignment between integrity commitment and integrity practices can be measured at a corporate, divisional, departmental, or individual level. If the Integrity Grid measures a low degree of corporate commitment and departmental action on business integrity, the corporation may be legally vulnerable. If the Integrity Grid shows a high degree of corporate commitment to integrity but a lower degree of corporate response on integrity, the corporation may be vulnerable to reputation risks.

In this example, this corporation is legally vulnerable for the actions of the Security Department (operating below a compliance threshold), and has significant exposure to reputation risk. The corporate commitment to integrity is at rung 7 on the Integrity Ladder, and departmental commitments and actions fall well below this corporate commitment level (with the exception of the Human Resources Department).

The Weakest Link

Determining corporate and departmental integrity values using the Integrity Ladder, plotting alignment between corporate and departmental integrity commitments on the Integrity Grid, and plotting alignment between departmental integrity commitments and practices on the Integrity Grid involves three distinct phases:

- *Phase 1: Motivation underlying business integrity values:* Use the Integrity Ladder to assess how the corporation values business integrity, as well as the underlying corporate motivations.

- *Phase 2: Creating and managing integrity commitments:* Use the Integrity Ladder to document the status and management of business integrity commitments by the organization and individual departments.

- *Phase 3: Managing integrity practices:* Use the Integrity Grid to assess alignment between business integrity intentions, commitments, and practices.

Motivation for Valuing Business Integrity

It is relatively easy for corporate leaders to ask themselves if their corporation values business integrity. It is more difficult for corporate leaders to comprehensively explain *why* their organization values business integrity. Understanding the business case for integrity within a corporation is critical to the design of corporate *talk* on business integrity and to the demonstration of these values in corporate *walk* on business integrity. Corporate managers who want to make their organizations better corporate citizens can encounter significant obstacles in establishing the business case for integrity.

Many foes of increased business integrity commitments point to competitive disadvantage as a consequence. If corporations undertake costly voluntary initiatives that their competitors don't embrace, these companies may erode competitive advantage. Making a corporate commitment to avoid dual standards in operating practices, regardless of the laws and practices in an investment environment, can be harsh; if a company insists on adopting working conditions and environmental standards that prevail in the world's wealthiest countries, the business rationale for operating in the Third World is eroded.

Some corporations are primarily motivated to adopt integrity commitments to preserve their reputation and will treat integrity commitments as a public relations exercise. Others focus on legal compliance, responding to prescriptives from securities exchange commissions and lawmakers governing their corporate operations. Other corporations are also responsive to their investment environment and will anticipate the expectations of host communities, host governments, and advocacy groups supporting protection of the environment or supporting human rights. Finally, leadership in some corporations will install business integrity management frameworks and systems because it is the right thing to do.

Before drafting business integrity value statements and commitments, or setting expectations for employees in integrity dilemmas, corporations are encouraged to analyze first their motivations for expending resources on these issues. In preparing this cost/benefit analysis, it is important to consider the downside risks and the upside opportunities through this strategic exercise. The Stakeholder Grid and Impact Assessment tool is a useful starting point in this evaluation.

Corporate leaders need to make the *business case* for a business integrity strategy. The first chapter of this book identified several reasons to support business integrity commitments and actions beyond compliance. Rationales to support the business case for business integrity are discussed in detail in Chapter 1 and include the following:

- Benefits of proactive management versus reactive administration
- Management of the weakest link
- Attraction and retention of personnel
- Reputation management
- Competitive advantage
- Business integrity is critical to public and governmental relations messages
- Establish consistency of credibility with local communities
- Enhance corporate ability to balance shorter- and longer-term priorities
- "You do not value what you cannot quantify"
- Link to project and enterprise risk management
- Link to corporate governance
- Correlation to operational and financial integrity
- Assessment of penalties
- Recognition by social funds and socially focused stakeholders
- Assists corporations in defining their sphere of influence
- Response to consumer expectations
- Clarify corporate role in development and in society

The identification of a corporation's strongest and weakest links in business integrity commitment and performance must be seen to have a material impact on the corporation's success and profitability. A business case must first be established *and accepted* within the organization, otherwise corporate commitment to a business integrity strategy will be vulnerable. If a corporation is not willing to pay more than lip service to its business integrity commitments and is not willing to expend the resources necessary to ensure its effective implementation, the strategy will be flawed from the outset and will be predictably unsuccessful.

The downside risks to a corporation embarking on a flawed or unsupported business integrity strategy can be significant. A feeble response, or perceived hypocrisy, could be a powerful disincentive to employees and other stakeholders. For example, at the outset of a large development project, a corporation may announce with great fanfare its commitment to local communities. If that company then stalls, reneges, or underperforms in its undertakings to the community, the company's reputation will be shoddier after making the commitment and failing to perform than if it had not made the commitment in the first place.

Likewise, internal corporate stakeholders will regard the executive team's commitments to integrity with skepticism and even disdain if the corporate commitments to integrity are seen as nothing more than a public relations exercise and there is no demonstrated internal accountability for noncompliance with integrity commitments. Employees who were previously able to function in an organization with vague integrity values may no longer be able to reconcile their personal integrity values with the organization's clearly demonstrated lack of respect for integrity values. A company's announcement of integrity values and its subsequent disregard for these commitments is frequently the proverbial last straw for employees.

Creating the Measuring Stick

Assuming that the business case for designing or revamping a corporation's business integrity mandate has been established, the next step for corporate leadership is to define what this means within the entire corporation. How will the organization expressly and implicitly communicate its commitment to integrity? This process requires considerable dialogue, as there are usually inconsistencies in corporate stakeholders' individual understandings of this mandate.

What a corporation expressly states as its commitment to business integrity becomes the measuring stick against which its performance will be assessed. If the expressed commitments are vague, measurement of performance will be a murky exercise. Corporations' attempts to commit to business integrity are frequently criticized as fluffy, "feel good" undertakings that provide little guidance to internal stakeholders about expected performance and are not helpful to external stakeholders attempting to encourage responsive corporate action.

What guidance can a corporation consider in defining its business integrity commitments? There is a plethora of written standards—some legally binding, some to be adopted voluntarily by corporations—that document stakeholder expectations of corporate integrity. This list of sources includes the following:

- Applicable legislation governing corporate operations, including tax laws, securities laws, corporate laws, environmental laws, competition laws, and employment laws. This legislation may originate in the country where the corporation is based, in the host country where operations are conducted, or in other countries having jurisdiction over corporate activity.

- Specific legislation and guidelines addressing corruption—corporations need to consider host governments' anti-corruption laws, other laws, and regulations with extraterritorial impact, including the U.S.'s Foreign Corrupt Practices Act, the OECD anti-corruption guidelines, and the Canadian Foreign Public Officials Act.

- Voluntary or mandatory guidelines endorsed by advocacy groups, host governments, and key stakeholder groups with an interest in a particular issue or operation. An example is the International Labour Organization's Tripartite Declaration of Principles Concerning Multinational Enterprises and Social Policy.

- Voluntary or mandatory codes of business conduct generated or endorsed by industry associations. One such example is the Responsible Care guidelines generated by the chemical industry in the 1980s.

- Principles recommended by political leaders for adoption by corporations operating in certain jurisdictions. These sources may be unilateral (the International Code of Ethics for Canadian Business promulgated by the Canadian government to be adopted by Canadian corporations operating abroad), or may reflect multilateral political positions (the OECD Guidelines for Multinational Enterprises).

Corporate Culture: Process or Rules?

As a first step in the design of corporate commitments to integrity, corporate managers must evaluate the merits of a rules-based or process-oriented approach to integrity management.

Rules-based approaches to integrity will be more likely to characterize integrity dilemmas as black or white. In organizations facing more complex integrity dilemmas, a process-oriented integrity approach may be more effective in encouraging dialogue about integrity dilemmas and fostering the creation of responsive strategies.

In light of corporate stakeholders' evolving expectations, dilemmas are increasingly more complex. Frequently, there is no obvious *right* answer. Given these evolutions, corporations are encouraged to move away from attempts to enumerate all the rules for internal stakeholders to follow. Instead, corporations are encouraged to move in the direction of clarifying the *process* for analyzing situations that may arise and making corporate decisions that reflect the corporation's values.

Having processes in place cannot negate the risk of crisis. However, corporations with processes in place to navigate integrity frontiers in business are better positioned to mitigate the risk of crises and to respond to unavoidable crises.

A decision-making process to manage business integrity frontiers is best demonstrated through discussion of case scenarios. Part 2 of this book introduces a recommended management process for analyzing integrity dilemmas and developing strategic responses, including how to mitigate downside risks and maximize opportunities. Scenarios then apply the process to real-life situations.

Internal corporate stakeholders, including employees at all levels of the corporation, must be able to understand how their corporation's business integrity values guide and influence management decisions and operational practices. Likewise, external stakeholders have expectations that a corporation's management and decision-making processes will effectively respond to business integrity dilemmas. Pointing to numerous applicable laws, third-party guidelines, or an internally generated code of business conduct—none of which can ever comprehensively address all dilemmas—is an increasingly less acceptable response for internal and external corporate stakeholders.

It is critical for someone or some department within the corporation to be aware and have a working knowledge of all applicable laws and recommended guidelines and relevant industry best practices. It is equally important that employees and corporate contractors understand what to do when a business integrity dilemma arises. In these situations, both internal and external stakeholders need to know that there is a business process in place to support the analysis of the issue and the outcomes. This process will certainly draw on the resources of the corporation, including expertise on applicable laws and industry best practices. However, it is the *process* itself that must be clearly understood by stakeholders and not the rules per se.

Depth and Breadth of Corporate Engagement

When designing a management structure that is responsive to business integrity issues, corporate leaders should consider the intended *breadth* of corporate engagement. What categories of business integrity issues does the corporation wish to proactively address?

The *categories of principles* that a corporation may choose to incorporate in a comprehensive integrity framework are open-ended. The list below identifies some business integrity issues that corporations may choose to address proactively. This list of principles is certainly not exhaustive, as each corporation is encouraged to create its own list of key principles based on its unique circumstances and opportunities.

- Business conduct that often incorporates illegal payments, corrupt business practices, and conflict of interest

- Community engagement, investment, and participation

- Environmental protection, which can include transfer of expertise

- Health and safety

- Labor standards, including international standards prohibiting child labor, forced labor, and discrimination

- Sexual harassment policy

- Gifts and entertainment policy

- Use of confidential information

- Use of corporate assets

- Freedom of association and expression

- Human rights

- Communication

As well, corporations need to consider the intended reach of their business integrity undertakings:

- Do corporations intend to limit the scope of their support for these values to employees and contractors only?

- Or, do corporations intend to extend the applicability of these commitments for the benefit of external stakeholders to include partners, suppliers, agents, the host government, the local community, or others within their sphere of influence?

Corporations' written business integrity commitments should clearly define the intended *scope of applicability* of the corporate value undertaking. Corporations are encouraged to create a grid to depict the integrity issues covered by their written materials and to define the intended scope of application of these values to categories of internal and external stakeholders, including the following:

- Employees

- Corporate directors

- Corporate executives

- Contractors

- Suppliers

- Agents

- Partners

- Local communities

- Host government

- Stakeholders in workplace

- Stakeholders in sphere of influence

- Consumers

When corporations intend to apply corporate values or principles to third parties, corporations must be clear that these third parties will be evaluated and rewarded on their ability and motivation to honor these commitments. These business integrity measures must be clearly defined as a standard for the selection and retention of those who represent the corporation. Third parties may be encouraged to give evidence of their willingness to accept and comply with corporate business integrity policies and procedures.

A few examples to demonstrate possible corporate approaches to depth and breadth of business integrity commitments will be illustrative:

- Corporation A may elect to limit the applicability of its commitments to labor standards to employees only. As a consequence, the corporation would not have an expressed commitment to labor standards of its suppliers in the corporation's supply chain.

- Corporation B may elect to adopt a wide-ranging commitment to human rights, stating that the organization will not be complicit in human rights abuses and will support and respect the protection of human rights within its sphere of influence. As a consequence, this corporation's commitment necessitates that it take a proactive and engaging approach to human rights.

Layers of Corporate Talk on Integrity

A corporation can generate layers of written documents in an effort to communicate its business integrity undertakings. These written commitments are created to introduce integrity commitments into all aspects of corporate activities and operations, thereby embedding a culture of integrity throughout the organization.

The hierarchy of documents intended to communicate these values is presented below from general to specific:

Corporate Vision:

- Corporate vision can expressly include business integrity as a priority.

Corporate Principles:

- Overarching principles for investment and operations can be generated to elaborate on key corporate values, and to guide the corporation in setting appropriate and consistent standards. Independent principles may be generated for domestic and international operations, or for individual regions or projects.

- Corporations may also expressly adopt principles endorsed and recommended by third parties, including:
  - OECD Guidelines for Multinational Enterprises
  - International Labour Organization's Tripartite Declaration of Principles Concerning Multinational Enterprises and Social Policy
  - United Nations Global Compact
  - Universal Declaration of Human Rights

Corporate Policies, Processes, Procedures, Standards, and Guidelines:

- May be consolidated in a guide or code of business conduct

- Specific policies or guidelines may be generated to govern key issues:
  - Conflicts of interest, entertainment, hospitality, and gifts
  - Political donations
  - Stakeholder engagement

- Contracting with agents, suppliers, contractors, procurement
- Contracting with partners
- Community participation
- Government relations
- Confidentiality of information, privacy, intellectual property
- Facilitating payments
- Human rights
- Labor issues
- Competition
- Substance abuse
- Discrimination
- Insider trading
- Cultural sensitivity

Reports to Shareholders and Stakeholders:

- Annual shareholder reports

- Corporate social responsibility or sustainability reports

- Other communications with stakeholders

Divisional Policies, Processes, Procedures, Standards, and Guidelines:

- In some corporations, further elaboration of policies, processes, procedures, standards, and guidelines is documented in regional, jurisdictional, or specific documents.

Departmental Policies, Processes, Procedures, Standards, and Guidelines:

- In some corporations, policies, procedures, standards, and guidelines may be documented on a departmental basis.

Corporate Walk Rests on Corporate Vision

Commitments to integrity are frequently incorporated into a corporation's tiers of principles, policies, reports, and divisional policies and practices. As the layers of corporate commitments cascade from the corporate vision, the detail and volume of the written materials tend to increase. For example, divisional policies and practices are frequently the most substantive and detailed. At the top of the corporate commitment pyramid, the corporate vision can typically be encapsulated in a single sentence or paragraph.

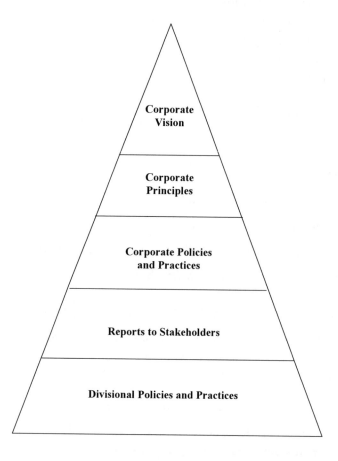

More detailed corporate documentation of policies and best practices are typically located within the corporate operating divisions. The inverted pyramid demonstrates the critical importance of the corporate integrity vision for the rest of the organization. The organization's ability to act on its integrity commitments depends or rests on the corporate vision.

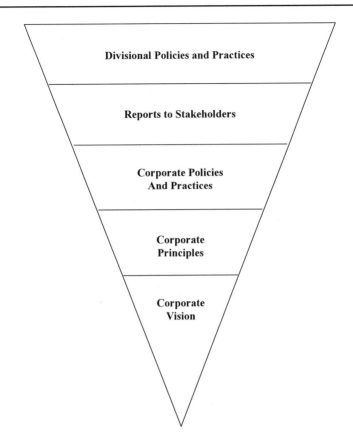

Steps to Proceed with Documentation of Corporate Commitments on Business Integrity

Step 1: The first step for a corporation seeking to ensure effective documentation and communication of business integrity values is to identify and evaluate the corporation's current message.

- What is the corporation currently saying about business integrity to its internal and external stakeholders?

- Review existing internal and external documentation to determine what the corporation is saying about business integrity.

- Check to consider how these messages are understood by stakeholders. Consult with key internal and external stakeholders to understand if commitments are comprehensive and responsive to emerging and evolving stakeholder expectations.

- Check the scope of the message. Does the message overstate the corporate position, creating expectations that are not intended, or does the message understate the corporation's intention?

Step 2: The next step for a corporation to ensure effective communication of business integrity values is to identify the key messages expressing corporate values.

Key messages must be communicated clearly, consistently, and frequently to ensure understanding. A key message may simply be that the corporation's core values include business integrity and that these values are applied consistently wherever the corporation operates.

Step 3: A corporation must also ensure that its overarching policies to ensure business integrity are understood by key stakeholders via effective communication vehicles.

- This may require the creation of a one-page or short form principles document that highlights key categories of issues.

- This concise enumeration of corporate principles that reflect respect for business integrity is a useful document to share with host governments, partners, advocacy groups, the media, and other stakeholders.

- Statements may also become the untouchable cornerstone of internal corporate processes for responding to integrity dilemmas.

Step 4: If the corporation has established *practices* in place, for example, practices that it finds useful in responding to situations where business integrity could potentially be compromised, these practices can also be documented.

- The degree of detail in resulting codes, guidelines, processes, or standards that document these practices should be considered.

- Consider what form of documentation will be the most effective in implementation. This may vary from organization to organization, and from department to department. Some companies prefer to create detailed guidelines and checklists, for example, due diligence checklists on the retention of third-party contractors. Other companies prefer to provide less detailed guidance to personnel, asking them instead to stay within the principles identified by the organization when contracting third-party contractors.

- Evaluate what type of documentation should be updated regularly.

- The autonomy that each operating group or business unit has in the design of these practices and procedures should be discussed. Some corporations prefer to have guidelines that apply across the corporation, while others enable individual business units to generate their own functional control documents as long as the practices endorsed are consistent with corporate principles.

- Consider whether these corporate practices and guidelines are for internal use only, or if they can be shared with external stakeholders.

Corporate commitment to business integrity is not a new phenomenon. As early as 1913, the J.C. Penney Company declared its ethics through principles that guided the corporation for decades, and included the following undertakings that continue to have relevance to corporations nearly a century later:

The Penney Idea (1913)

- To serve the public, as nearly as we can, to its complete satisfaction.

- To expect for the service we render a fair remuneration and not all the profit the traffic will bear.

- To do all in our power to pack the customer's dollar full of value, quality, and satisfaction.

- To continue to train ourselves and our associates so that the service we give will be more and more intelligently performed.

- To improve constantly the human factor in our business.

- To reward men and women in our organization through participation in what the business produces.

- To test our every policy, method, and act in this wise: "Does it square with what is right and just?"

Managing Alignment Between Integrity Commitments and Practices

Once corporate commitments to business integrity are created, the degree of alignment between integrity commitments and actual practices can be assessed and measured with the Integrity Grid.

To create alignment between corporate commitments to integrity and departmental commitments and actions, and within individual departments, business integrity values must be embedded. Managing alignment of business integrity values into action requires commitment. This commitment can be achieved through:

- Leadership
- Education
- Training
- Awareness raising
- Critical need for accountability

Leadership

Internal and external stakeholders increasingly seek to ascertain the authenticity of corporate leaders' commitments to business integrity. If corporate leaders embrace business integrity as a priority and demonstrate these values through their talk and actions, employees will support that leadership and other stakeholders will trust the corporate commitments.

Before the most recent outbreak of integrity breaches, some corporations tended to be authoritarian, sometimes even rigid, in their approach to business integrity. Recognizing the critical need for trust in leadership, CEOs and other corporate leaders are increasingly honest in their communications with key stakeholders. Corporations' annual reports and public statements, even advertisements, frequently acknowledge the challenges of managing integrity dilemmas. For example, in a full-page advertisement in *Economist* magazine, Weyerhaeuser, the forestry company, introduces the dilemmas it faces in reconciling its forestry operations with environmental impacts, and concludes with an endearingly candid statement: "Our system isn't perfect, but we keep getting closer. You can think of it as good business. Or, if you prefer, as a labor of love."

Corporate leaders continue to struggle with integrity dilemmas. However, many corporate leaders are now treating the experience of defining corporate values, including expected corporate undertakings and practices, as an evolutionary process. This honesty is generally well received by stakeholders. In its 2002 Social and Environmental Report, the BG Group indicated that the company had held a series of workshops at senior management levels to debate the meaning and impact of human rights "where answers were not always clear-cut."

Some corporate leaders have adopted the practice of identifying integrity dilemmas in their public reporting as a means of demonstrating to their key stakeholders the challenges in decision making and defining the corporate role. For example, Talisman Energy's 2001 Corporate Social Responsibility report identified the following corporate quandaries: What is the appropriate use of infrastructure in the oil fields, and how much oil revenue is being generated and how is it being used?

Education, Training, and Awareness Raising

Education, training, and awareness raising within the corporation and beyond are critical to a corporation's ability to embed business integrity values into its operations. Corporate employees need to understand the corporate values and talk on integrity, as well as the corporate process for decision making when an integrity dilemma occurs. Employees need to be able to identify and even anticipate integrity dilemmas.

The most effective means of helping employees understand how to implement business integrity values is to use cases or scenarios as a tool for training. Contemporary training workshops that focus on real-life issues and experiences and introduce processes for evaluating and managing integrity dilemmas will assist in an individual employee's response to an integrity challenge.

Education, training, and awareness raising can also be extended to external stakeholders:

- Key contractors and suppliers may benefit from an awareness of corporate expectations of business integrity.

- Host governments may benefit from an understanding of an investor's values and commitments to business integrity.

- Strategic partners should be aware of a corporation's values on business integrity, and of its accountability and reporting expectations.

- Corporate engagement with advocacy groups and not-for-profit stakeholders may be enhanced through dialogue that explains a corporation's commitment to business integrity, including corporate undertakings to monitor, assess, and verify alignment between integrity talk and integrity walk.

It may be useful to expand the Stakeholder Grid and Impact Assessment tool to evaluate methods that can be applied to educate, train, or raise awareness of corporate integrity commitments and expectations with different stakeholder groups. These strategies can form part of the corporate response to integrity dilemmas.

Critical Need for Accountability

Transparency and verifiable reporting by corporations can enhance corporate stakeholders' ability to assess a corporation's integrity commitments and measure alignment between its walk and talk. If corporate accountability structures are weak, stakeholders will not necessarily understand corporate integrity values. Stakeholders' ability to assess the degree of alignment between integrity commitments and action will be compromised.

Chapter 6 provides insight into the critical importance of an accountability structure for corporations. Management systems will be examined to consider how alignment of decision making, governance, and accountability systems are linked to ensure that integrity values are identified and honored in practice. Setting objectives for performance of integrity commitments and measuring performance become imperatives for corporations that intend to respect their integrity undertakings. Setting consequences for employees' and others' failure to comply with integrity commitments is another mandate for corporations that want to promote and demonstrate alignment between corporate commitments and corporate actions.

Frontier 4:
Explaining Differences Between Corporations Regarding Integrity Values, Commitment, and Action

Corporate responses to business integrity should be unique to individual corporations. Cookie-cutter approaches to business integrity strategy or response are not encouraged. Each corporation has unique attributes, objectives, and circumstances that influence its values, vision, and strategy. At the same time, it is important to consider the motivations of individual corporate integrity *values* and the underlying motivations of individual corporate *responses* to business integrity.

This chapter focuses on Frontier 4 and explains differences among corporations with regard to corporate values, commitments, and actions on integrity. Navigation of this new frontier raises the following questions:

- What is the underlying motivation of corporate integrity talk and corporate integrity walk?

- What are the differences in corporate motivators and what are the outcomes of these differences in motivation?

What Are the Motivators?

The following table summarizes some of the major motivations of corporations in managing to the level of compliance and managing beyond compliance.

TO COMPLIANCE LEVEL	BEYOND COMPLIANCE LEVEL
• Corporate culture • Legal requirements • Fear of penalties • Top-down leadership mandate • Financial risk • Reputation • Right thing to do • Corporate code of conduct	• Corporate culture • Benefits of proactive management versus reactive administration • Managing the weakest link • Attraction and retention of personnel • Reputation management • Competitive advantage • Business integrity is critical to public and government relations messages • Consistency of credibility with communities • Enhance ability to balance shorter and longer-term priorities • Triple bottom-line reporting • Equivalent precision for economic and social reporting as with financial reporting • Links to project and enterprise risk management • Links to corporate governance • Correlation to operational and financial integrity • Recognition by social funds and socially minded stakeholders • Assists in defining sphere of influence • Responsive to consumer expectations and hence increase sales • Clarify corporate role in development and in society • Enables strategic giving • Want to be leader • Top-down leadership mandate • Reputation as innovator

Some corporations have a clear vision of their business integrity values and motivation, and have little difficulty in operationalizing their integrity commitments, but these corporations are rare. The vast majority of corporations and their leaders value business integrity, but have not comprehensively assessed corporate motivation. Clarifying motivations makes it easier for corporate leaders to manage business integrity through creation of corporate visions, identifying best practices on integrity, and implementing these practices on a consistent basis.

The ways in which a corporation describes its long-term vision provides clues as to its corporate motivation. For example, there are specific processes by which a corporation, department, or division communicate a long-term vision to internal and external stakeholders.

The Integrity Ladder on the next page was introduced to identify a hierarchy of corporate behaviors and underlying motivation. In this chapter, the Integrity Ladder measurement tool is used to examine corporate motivation in greater detail. In order to gain insight into a corporation's intention, it is useful to look at how a corporation defines its vision.

Where Are We? Where Do We Want to Go? How Do We Get There?

In order to understand corporate motivation regarding integrity, it is important for corporations to ask the following questions:

Where are we? What motivates business integrity values, commitments, and actions in our corporation?

Where do we want to go? Where does our corporation want to be on the Integrity Ladder?

How do we get there? How does our corporation ensure that all employees in all divisions and departments are operating at the same motivation level on our targeted rung of the Integrity Ladder?

The Integrity Ladder

LEVEL	QUESTIONS TO ASK TO REVEAL MOTIVATION (TALK)	PRIMARY MOTIVATION	MANIFESTATION	VISION
10	Will my children and grand-children appreciate my decisions to help others?	Long-term benefit to future generations	Individuals create trusts, foundations, and endow-ments of personal wealth to achieve long-term social impact	Pioneer; visionary
9	Are there ways to leverage our corporate budget to achieve a positive social impact that has sustain-ability?	Both social and financial return on corporate investment are intentionally of substantial importance	Investment by company is intended to result in sustainable positive social impact	Leading edge
8	Are there ways to leverage our corporate budget to achieve a positive social impact?	Social return on corporate investment is a desired and intended by-product of financial investment	Leveraging corporate budgets to achieve positive social impact	In the top three
7	How do we leverage our corporate budget to ensure that we do no harm?	Proactive intention to avoid causing harm to others through financial investment of corporation	Processes to evaluate corpo-rate and societal impacts of investment (not exclusively as a risk management exercise)	Rapid follower of best practices

		Compliance motivation	Minimize financial cost/risk	Top quartile
6	How do we comply with both the letter and spirit of applicable laws and company policy?	Compliance motivation supplemented with proactive risk management to reduce financial variability and vulnerability	Minimize financial cost/risk by proactive management of all risks (including societal impacts)	Top quartile
5	What do we need to do to comply with the letter of the law and company policy?	Compliance with rules	Social impacts are relevant only if they trigger negative financial impacts	Middle of the pack
4	Will this action or inaction detract from my public reputation or private relationships?	Reputation protection; reactive risk management	Practices that reactively minimize financial costs	Good communications will cover a multitude of sins
3	How do I comply with the minimum legal requirements and stay in business?	Minimum compliance	Reactive damage control by company	Not the worst
2	How can I avoid being caught with "dirty hands"?	Personal safety/self-preservation	Outsource the dirty work; minimize the paper trail	Circle the wagons in the face of a threat
1	Will I go to jail?	Personal safety/self-preservation	Plea-bargain; turn in others	Deny, deny, deny
0	How do I cover up?	Personal safety/self-preservation	Reactive damage control by individuals; obfuscate	Integrity doesn't matter

Where Are We?

Where are we? What motivates business integrity values, commitments, and actions in our corporation?

The Integrity Ladder provides insight into corporate motivation underpinning business integrity management. Other clues to understanding corporate motivation can be gleaned through indicators of integrity strengths and weaknesses within the organization. The following chart provides some examples of early indicators of integrity strengths and weaknesses for corporate leaders to observe.

EARLY INDICATOR	INTEGRITY STRENGTHS	INTEGRITY WEAKNESSES
Importance of winning	• Win-win negotiation preferred	• Win-lose negotiation preferred • Personal betting culture that escalates
Interpersonal relationships	• Proactive support for employees at risk • Employer of choice for individuals with integrity • Use first names	• Condoning of harassment • Recognize people by titles, positions, generically by function
Management of promotions, bonuses, perks	• Meritocracy • Objective criteria • Transparency	• Nepotism • Arbitrariness • Political environment
Information flow/access	• Upward/downward/lateral • Transparency	• Top-down flow
Financial focus	• Long-term profitability • Social funds invest	• Short-term earnings • Analyst reports • Social funds divest
Corporate culture emphasis	• Values, mission	• Power, authority

Communication style/objectives	• Focus is on substance of communication	• Focus is on style/spin
Management reporting on personnel	• Report on training, development, succession	• Focus on head count
Relationships with external stakeholders	• Engagement a priority	• Stakeholders not included in decision making
Human rights	• Incorporate into decision making	• Not acknowledged
Health, safety, and environment department standards	• Acknowledged • Global standards	• Minimum compliance

When a company assesses its position on the Integrity Ladder, it is crucial to consider its position on a relative basis—corporate management benefits from understanding the relative position of its competitors on the Integrity Ladder. A corporation's relative position on integrity, particularly with reference to companies in the same industry sector or operating environment, affects its competitive advantage and disadvantage. As well, positive and negative business integrity motivators (and resulting behaviors) of other companies affect a corporation.

Competitors' best practices can be a positive influence for corporations motivated to keep abreast of, or even ahead of, industry practices. As industry practices evolve, what is acceptable changes. There are many catalysts for evolution in what constitutes acceptable standards and best practices. These evolutions affect corporate competitiveness on an ongoing basis. Leading companies must stay abreast of best practices. For example, pulp and paper mills are now expected not just to clean up pollutants at the end of their manufacturing process, but also to remove pollutants in the process from the start. These best practices will soon become acceptable standards for pulp and paper companies.

Conversely, a corporation can be negatively affected by the actions of other corporations. There is the risk of guilt by association in industry sectors, particularly if the negative fallout of an integrity breach is material. The Union Carbide plant disaster in Bhopal, India, in 1984 is a classic example of one corporation's integrity disaster impugning an entire industry's credibility. The Bhopal disaster shocked the entire chemical industry. Many companies realized that although Union Carbide was the plant operator, the same disaster could happen to any chemical company. In response, chemical companies mobilized to audit plants on a global basis so they could respond to stakeholders' predictable questions about the risks: Could a similar event happen at a chemical plant in the U.S. or in Europe?

As companies do business, particularly across jurisdictions, they have integrity choices. These choices affect their competitive advantage or disadvantage. Companies can support the harmonization or melding of standards; they can try to raise their corporate practices to global standards; or they can lower their corporate practices to lowest acceptable local practices. These choices affect their relative competitiveness.

For example, in response to evolving health, safety, and environmental standards, corporations can choose one of the following options:

- Raising their corporate practices to the best practices threshold and applying global standards (for example, standards set by ISO 9000, API) in order to maintain global reputation

- Negotiate or rationalize legitimate differences in standards on a jurisdiction-by-jurisdiction basis

- Lowering their corporate practices to the lowest local practices of the host operating jurisdiction in order to be cost competitive

Companies may even choose different practices in relation to different aspects of their operating practices. For example, a company may:

- Choose to raise corporate practices to adopt global standards for environmental thresholds

- Choose to adopt jurisdiction-by-jurisdiction standards for safety standards

- Choose to lower corporate practices to adopt local standards for health

The outcomes of these choices affect competitiveness. Companies choosing to adopt global standards, wherever they operate, may preserve their global reputation, but may not make the same profit margins as competitors who choose to lower their practices to adopt local standards.

For a corporation invested in several North American operating jurisdictions under the North America Free Trade Agreement (NAFTA) framework, the table below summarizes the options and predictable competitive advantage/disadvantage outcomes. A corporation that chooses to adopt global standards will logically be more competitive in projects requiring global standards, and may be more likely to lose out to competitors in projects where a lowest common denominator approach is encouraged or tolerated by project proponents. Conversely, a company that chooses to move its work to jurisdictions accepting the lowest enforced standards may be competitive only in those environments where project proponents accept these lowered standards.

The thinking on competitive advantage and disadvantage summarized in the table on the next page is only a starting point; there are many aspects to competitive advantage that must be addressed. But clearly, one of the critical elements to evaluate is a corporation's integrity choices. Many companies are able to remain competitive using global standards for environmental, health, and safety in projects where the lowest standards would be acceptable. For example, an investor's decision to adopt the lowest possible standards for health may seem cheaper, but if this decision raises the ire of employees and local communities, this cost efficiency could be quickly swallowed up in the cost of managing these expectations and their impacts on the project's timelines, operating costs, and effectiveness.

CORPORATE STRATEGIES	NAFTA OPERATING ENVIRONMENT: CHOICE AND IMPACTS		
	GLOBAL STANDARDS REQUIRED BY PROJECT PROPONENTS	JURISDICTION-BY-JURISDICTION APPROACH REQUIRED BY PROJECT PROPONENTS	LOWEST COMMON DENOMINATOR APPROACH ENCOURAGED BY PROJECT PROPONENTS
1. Corporation chooses to adopt global standards	Winners	Lose some	Big losers
2. Corporation adopts jurisdiction-by-jurisdiction standards	Lose some	Winners	Win some
3. Corporation chooses to move work to projects with lowest enforced standards	Big losers	Losers	Big winners

Where Do We Want to Go?

Where do we want to go? Where does our corporation want to be on the Integrity Ladder?

The finish line for business integrity is moving. Corporate managers must continuously ask the question: Where does our corporation want to be on the Integrity Ladder?

Corporate leaders face unprecedented pressure to respond to stakeholders' expectations. The expectations of traditional corporate stakeholders are evolving, and new corporate stakeholders are emerging with incremental expectations.

In order to assess this proverbial integrity line in the sand, some corporations benchmark the best practices of other companies and try to emulate or exceed the industry leaders. Other corporations are satisfied with incrementally better management practices that evolve based on proactive or reactive motivations.

Corporate motivation to respond to business integrity values is influenced by stakeholders' evolving and emerging expectations. If corporate motivation for business integrity values and vision is linked to competitive advantage (including access to capital and commercial opportunity), corporations will be motivated to ensure that their reputation with host governments, partners, lending institutions, and international financial institutions remains positive.

If corporate motivation underlying business integrity values and vision is linked to risk management, corporations will be motivated to understand the evolving priorities of advocacy groups and potential critics.

If corporate motivation for business integrity values and vision is linked to being recognized as an industry leader, corporations must ensure that all employees understand and adopt evolving best practices. This requires an enabling corporate culture that allows for innovation and risk taking, and empowers personnel.

If corporate motivation for business integrity values and vision is linked to attracting and retaining qualified and motivated personnel, corporations must ensure that their existing systems are responsive to the evolving priorities of corporate employees.

In order to keep abreast of key stakeholders and their expectations, corporations are encouraged to use the Stakeholder Grid and Impact Assessment tool (see Appendix) and to update key stakeholders' assessments on an ongoing basis. On the basis of these stakeholder assessments and corresponding shifts in industry practices, corporations may even be motivated to move up a rung on the Integrity Ladder.

How Do We Get There?

How do we get there? How does our corporation ensure that all employees in all divisions and departments are operating at the same motivation level on our targeted rung of the Integrity Ladder?

Earlier chapters explain how corporations and their stakeholders identify and measure gaps in corporate values, commitments, and action on integrity. If gaps are identified, it is predictably challenging for corporate managers to effect the organizational changes necessary to fill the gaps, strengthen the weakest link, and be positioned to navigate emerging integrity frontiers.

Motivating and effecting organizational change is difficult. Individuals within organizations must support management's integrity vision or change will be resisted. As the following chart depicts, alignment of individual and corporate values is critical.

When organizations are attempting to move employees or departments from a compliance motivation base to a beyond compliance motivation base, a shift in thinking is required. Moving employees operating at rungs 3, 4, and 5 of the Integrity Ladder to an organizational integrity commitment level that is beyond compliance is challenging. Moving employees operating below rung 3 on the Integrity Ladder to an organizational integrity commitment that is beyond compliance is perhaps even impossible in the absence of a management imperative.

Individuals and corporate departments who do not manage integrity to basic compliance thresholds are often motivated by sheer greed or utter ignorance. Corporate personnel motivated by compliance will have

Individual/Corporate Values Matrix

	MORE ETHICAL CORPORATION	LESS ETHICAL CORPORATION
More Ethical Individual	Recipe for long-term success and high impact	Values conflict Individual likely to leave corporation
Less Ethical Individual	Values conflict Corporation likely to push out the individual	Recipe for disaster

many excuses and rationales to support this motivation. Shifts to beyond compliance integrity commitments and practices will be resisted. It is predictable that individuals within corporations will have excuses that constrain corporate motivation and ability to move ahead on its integrity journey. These integrity anchors can be heavy and challenging for management to loosen.

Management of corporations is both an art and a science. For those focused on compliance motivation, there may be a desire for statistical indications of integrity benefits. Until there is unequivocal proof that beyond compliance motivation is effective in enhancing corporate profitability and effectiveness, shifts beyond compliance may be resisted.

Over the last decade, academics and management advisers have been grappling with quantifying the impacts of integrity for companies. Although there is an acknowledgment that integrity is linked to corporate reputation, and that corporate reputation has an intrinsic value, our inability to assign precise numbers to this value is troubling for people who need statistical evidence. More recently, pieces of the puzzle are moving into place and there are several independent but related efforts to quantify the *value* of companies' adherence to voluntary integrity commitments. For example, studies have been conducted to examine the question of the value of corporations assuming voluntary commitments to reduce pollution beyond legal requirements, and the market response to these voluntary measures. While it is an imprecise science to compare companies' reputations, the research did support the view that there is a positive relationship between environmental performance and the intangible asset value of publicly traded firms on the S&P 500.

Some of the predictable rationales provided by individuals or corporate departments resisting alignment with organizational integrity commitments are enumerated below as integrity anchors:

- "These changes aren't in the budget."
- "Effecting these changes will have no impact on earnings."
- "Resources cannot be allocated—growth corporations are too focused on the day-to-day business of survival."

- "No real commitment from leaders."
- "This is a fad—it will pass."
- "Integrity cannot be taught to people."
- "This isn't the right time."
- "We don't want our corporation to become a lightning rod for dissent."
- "Don't want to get too far ahead of the pack."
- "Where exactly is the corporation headed? We need to know details."
- "We don't have the internal capacity to effect current practices."
- "The status quo is safe for now."

The question of whether integrity and virtue can be taught invites considerable debate. The arguments for and against this proposition are quite compelling, and are best summarized by a quote from Penelope Patsuris, a researcher in this field: "It was Socrates who first said that virtue cannot be taught, yet paradoxically he spent the balance of his life trying to do so anyway." Whether or not integrity can be taught is debatable, but corporate managers do have a management responsibility to ensure that personnel truly understand the integrity thresholds to which their employer is committed.

Embedding business integrity values is a process that requires leaders to educate, reinforce, and internalize values in all personnel. Corporations cannot treat integrity training as a one-time vaccine, inoculating people who have been inclined toward unethical behavior for years. Embedding integrity within organizations evolves from learning to compliance to believing.

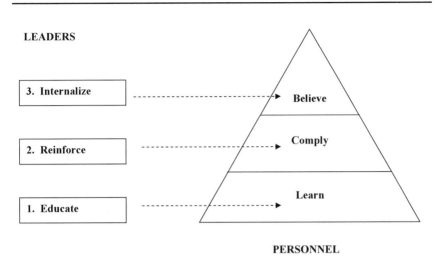

Business Tools

In this chapter, four business tools are introduced to support corporations motivated to align the integrity commitments and actions of their corporate personnel, departments, and divisions at a committed rung on the Integrity Ladder. These four business tools are available to support the operationalization of business integrity strategies:

1. Permeation of Change Model

2. Adapted Best Practices Tool

3. Benchmarking Practices

4. Community Investment Strategy Tool

Permeation of Change Model

Motivating and implementing organizational change is a familiar management practice for corporate leaders. As corporations already know, people within organizations see innovation and change differently. One model for change is the well-known Rogers' Diffusion of Innovations model. This model supports the practice that management inspires changes in response to individuals' innovation styles.

Rogers's Original Model in Diffusion of Innovations (1962)

Innovators	2.5%
Early adopters	13.5%
Early majority	34.0%
Late majority	34.0%
Laggards	16.0%

Strict application of Rogers's Diffusion of Innovations model to integrity commitments and actions in a corporation poses some challenges:

- Rogers's categories involve a continuous normally shaped curve with predictable percentages for each category.

- Employees' attitudes toward change may vary by department within a corporation.

- The percentages of employees in each category are likely to vary between corporations.

When corporate management is motivated to effect organizational change required to align organizational integrity commitments and behaviors, a modified version of the Rogers' model is recommended. The Permeation of Change model, enables companies to identify their Initiators, Interesteds, Wait-and-Sees, Followers, and Non-compliers based on the characteristics in the following table:

GROUPS WITHIN ORGANIZATIONS	CHARACTERISTICS IN INNOVATION DIFFUSION
1. Initiators	• Seek to be first/best • Proceed with change even if no rules • Practical dreamers who implement • Respond to future opportunity
2. Interesteds	• Rely on Initiators • Will proceed if some implementation parameters are established • Respond to present opportunity
3. Wait-and-Sees	• A large group in most organizations • Wait for documentation details • Need safe and detailed plan to proceed
4. Followers	• Will not risk being wrong • Respond to future external threats/risks
5. Non-compliers	• Resist change • Motivated only by direct intervention • Respond to current threats

In most change-management systems and research, change within the Non-compliers group is not a priority. It takes a lot of corporate will and effort to motivate Non-compliers to accept change. It is assumed that Non-compliers, those who most fiercely resist change, will eventually catch up to the rest of the organization with negligible negative consequence for the organization.

However, as early chapters explained, corporations are encouraged to assess alignment of their business integrity values, commitments, and actions in order to identify their weakest link. In many cases, it is imperative that corporations respond first to the weakest link. If there is a significant gap between the organization's Initiators and their Non-compliers on business integrity, the corporation could be exposed to reputation risks. For example, if a corporation is committed to integrity at rung 5 or 6 on the Integrity Ladder, and a Non-complier in the operations group (or even a Non-complier department) is committed to integrity at rung 3 of the Integrity Ladder, the Non-complier's unwillingness to budget for or implement voluntary environmental practices for the benefit of host communities could irreparably harm the corporation's overall reputation.

Given the unique nature of business integrity management strategy, corporate management teams are encouraged to tailor permeation of change practices to be responsive to this unique context. Different responsive strategies for each of the individual groups within the organization are recommended.

GROUPS WITHIN ORGANIZATIONS	EFFECTING CHANGE IN BUSINESS INTEGRITY STRATEGY
1. Initiators	• Manage the risk of Initiators making mistakes that affect the corporation's reputation and/or discourage others. • Encourage Initiators to identify/adopt pilot projects and define success criteria to control risks.
2. Interesteds	• Invite Interesteds to work with Non-compliers on implementation of change to strengthen the weakest links.
3. Wait-and-Sees	• Wait-and-See groups prioritize risk management and are strongly motivated by others. • Recommend that Wait-and-See proactively monitor evolving stakeholder expectations.
4. Followers	• Followers groups prioritize top-down direction to implement change.
5. Non-compliers	• Business integrity Non-compliers become the weakest links in an organization and must be prioritized for change. • Encourage the Interesteds to support the Non-compliers in change. Initiators generally move to the next new idea and may not be effective in supporting change within the Non-compliers group.

Referring back to the Non-compliers in the organization, and the challenges associated with motivating their acceptance of corporate integrity commitments and practices, it is useful to ask: How do managers *manage* Non-compliers?

Those in the Wait-and-See category will generally be won over to change once they appreciate that business integrity standards and expectations are evolving, and that the corporation's integrity commitments are critical to the corporation's effectiveness. The Followers will listen to top-down direction and will implement integrity commitments if they are clearly directed to do so by their supervisors. Non-compliers are often the naysayers in the organization who dogmatically resist any change in historical operating practices on the basis that they have operated this way for years, and their practices have worked, or they may be ideologically opposed to integrity commitments beyond minimum compliance thresholds.

With concerted effort, it may be possible to convince Non-compliers of the merits of evolving integrity commitments, even commitments beyond compliance. The Interesteds is the best group to work with the Non-compliers in this awareness raising, training, and mentoring effort because they are pragmatic implementers. Asking the Initiators to work with the Non-compliers would be problematic because the Initiators are more likely to focus on cutting-edge practices for the future rather than present opportunities and strategies.

Managers should not expect Non-compliers to volunteer for integrity training and awareness raising to better understand stakeholder expectations of corporations. Senior management must *mandate* training for Non-compliers. If a Non-complier refuses to cooperate with this training mandate or with integrity commitments at an organizational threshold, there must be consequences. If this resistance is unrelenting, it may be that an individual's integrity values are not reconcilable with the organizational integrity values, and termination of the employee-employer relationship may be prudent.

Adapted Best Practices Tool

In order to fill integrity gaps within an organization, corporations frequently examine the best practices of other corporations, including their competitors, their partners, and peer group, and identify strategic practices that are effective in impact and feasible to implement.

The Adapted Best Practices tool is intended for use by corporate leaders once a decision has been made to fill an integrity gap in the organization. These are the tool's steps:

Stage 1: Identify business integrity best practices

Stage 2: Assess best practices based on risk/impact and ease of implementation

Stage 3: Select best practices and determine implementation strategy

Stage 1: Identify Business Integrity Best Practices

Corporate management must first identify *which organizations* it would like to include in its best practices review, and the *types of business integrity best practices* that management would like to examine. Corporations may choose to examine the best practices of its peers, partners, or competitors. A corporation may choose to examine the best practices of corporate leaders in integrity identified by independent organizations, such as social investment funds, or corporate leaders identified by business organizations and corporate watchdogs.

Referring back to the Permeation of Change model (see page 101), it is recommended that different groups within a corporation be assigned responsibility for distinct components of the best practices identification and assessment process, as follows:

GROUPS	TASK
Initiators	• Identify emerging and innovative best practices of corporations on the leading edge of business integrity.
Interesteds	• Identify business integrity best practices of competitors.
Wait-and-Sees	• Proactively monitor evolving stakeholder expectations on corporate best practices on business integrity.
Followers	• Top-down directive is likely to produce results.
Non-compliers	• Force to examine and implement best practices within their own department that are consistent with the corporation's lowest acceptable rung on the Integrity Ladder.

Stage 2: *Assess Best Practices Based on Risk/Impact and Ease of Implementation*

Corporate management must then assess and prioritize the best practices for business integrity based on the practices' potential *impact* and *ease of implementation*. A best strategy for one corporation may not provide the same impact for another corporation. And, implementation of best practices will likely be different for each corporation, division, and department.

For example, adoption of a scholarship initiative by Nexen Inc., a Canadian-based oil and gas investor, to support the postsecondary education of students from Yemen, is an award-winning initiative that stakeholders have applauded for its impact and transparency. Notwithstanding the success of this best practice for Nexen, competitors have strenuously resisted adopting scholarship initiatives as part of community participation strategies because of doubts about potential impacts and challenges in implementing objective selection criteria for scholarship candidates.

Corporations are encouraged to work with their obvious strengths in identifying best practices. Companies that employ a majority of female employees are likely better positioned to champion best practices that build on the strength of a female workforce. Avon, a supplier of cosmetics to a largely female consumer base, on the basis of sales by a largely female marketing network, is predictably better able to establish a credible and effective partnership with a breast cancer charity than many other corporations with comparable cash flows or asset ranges.

The range of initiatives that corporate managers will be able to evaluate to fill their organizational integrity gaps may be quite extensive and is growing. To provide focus for this effort, companies may choose to evaluate only the best practices within a narrow band of industry peers (for example, only companies participating in direct marketing to wholesalers in the textile industry) or based on a clearly defined competitor scope (for example, only competitors marketing computer services in a defined geographic region, or only competitors with cash flows ranging between U.S. $500,000 to U.S. $2 million).

To assess and prioritize identified best practices, it is recommended that the options be plotted on a grid. Corporations are encouraged to prioritize action on those best practices that indicate both ease of implementation and high-impact potential (high upside or strength in risk management), as follows:

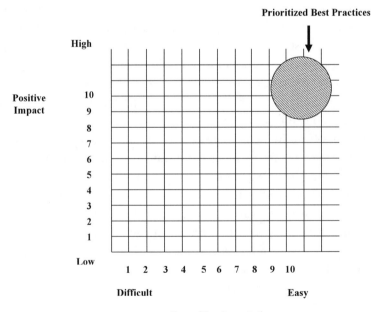

Stage 3: Select Best Practices and Determine Implementation Strategy

On a corporate-wide basis, it is recommended that a few best practices be selected for implementation. Annually, individual departments or divisions can select best practices for implementation as "pilots."

Initiators and Interesteds within an organization may also be encouraged to analyze and possibly select best practices that fall outside the high impact/ease of implementation quadrant of the grid:

- Are there best practices with high impact that rank low on ease of implementation? Can implementation approaches be modified by the corporation to enhance the ease of implementation scoring?

- Are there best practices with ease of implementation that rank low on impact? Can potential impacts to the corporation be enhanced through astute implementation?

Benchmarking Practice

The third management tool introduced in this chapter is benchmarking practice. Benchmarking corporate performance against external performance is a well-understood management practice to measure effectiveness on a relative basis.

In order to maximize the value of benchmarking, corporations can participate in benchmarking surveys conducted by independent organizations. One of many examples of a benchmarking study is a multiclient study undertaken to survey and forecast trends, issues, attitudes, and behaviors related to environmentally friendly procurement and sustainability in markets and technologies in relation to the publishing and printing sector. Internal benchmarking of corporate departments or divisions can also be constructive.

Benchmarking practices need to be focused. What is the benchmarking study attempting to assess? And, by what means and processes is benchmarking to be achieved? Through a review of corporate annual reports? Through dialogue with corporate representatives? Via engagement with corporate stakeholders?

Some of the integrity markers that a benchmarking survey may consider in, for example, a manufacturing company, include the following indicators and practices:

- Child labor

- Harassment or abuse

- Nondiscrimination

- Health and safety

- Freedom of association and collective bargaining

- Wages and benefits

- Hours of work

- Overtime compensation

In some cases, benchmarking studies focus only on a key issue, for example:

- Does the corporation have a human rights policy and supporting practices, and how are these commitments demonstrated in actual practice?

- What are the corporate relationships with host communities, or even with subsets of community groups (for example, Aboriginal groups, visible minorities, women)?

- What are the environmental standards in mining, for example, abandonment and reclamation practices or water-handling practices?

Companies may find benchmarking studies very sensitive. Most of these assessments are conducted within clearly defined parameters, and release of conclusions requires a company's consent.

Community Investment Strategy Tool

A corporation's management team is likely to identify gaps in organizational commitments to community stakeholders. Companies' engagement with host communities is an age-old practice, but the commitments are frequently poorly defined, vaguely managed, and rarely quantified or reported upon in a strategic manner. Designing and implementing management strategies, or best practices, to embed integrity values in corporate relationships with communities can be an elusive exercise, leading to misunderstandings about commitments and intentions.

Before embarking on a community strategy for your company, it is helpful to define what the company intends in its participation with community stakeholders. Corporations' *community participation* is multifaceted and can mean different things to different corporate managers, including:

- Corporate investors' relationships with key stakeholders in the community, including personal relationships between local citizens and corporate project managers and other personnel residing in a community where a company is operating, as well as more formal relationships between the corporation and local community representatives fostered in town hall meetings intended to discuss issues of common interest.

- Investment in capacity-building and infrastructure-building initiatives in the communities where corporations are invested, for example, Magna International's decision to contribute $8 million toward the establishment of a regional cancer center in Newmarket, Ontario, in response to concerns of the 13,000 employees of Magna International who live and work in York Region and South Simcoe County. The center is intended to respond to employees' needs and would also benefit all the residents of the area.

- Corporate response to contractual commitments, including commercial undertakings to provide technical or management training to local personnel, or to share infrastructure benefits such as local roads with local communities.

- Philanthropic donations to beneficiaries in the community, including donations to support a European institution's research for a malaria vaccine or sponsorship of an academic chair at a university.

Corporate departments can define community participation to include some or all of these activities, including stakeholder relations, community investment, contractual compliance, and philanthropy.

In order to fill gaps in community engagement practices, corporations frequently examine the best practices of other corporations to identify strategic practices. In addition to this practice of evaluating other companies' practices, there are also management processes and tools that can guide management thinking on community investment strategy, and to help answer these questions:

- What are the best practice models for community participation available to corporate investors?

- How do corporations decide on an effective best practice?

- How can corporations monitor and measure the impacts of community participation strategies?

When deciding on a strategy or best practice for engagement with community stakeholders, corporations are encouraged to distinguish elements of community participation practices and to clarify their corporate objectives in community participation. The following business tool is useful in defining models of community investment and managing these investments.

Community Investment Strategy Tool

DEFINE THE NATURE OF COMMUNITY INVESTMENT	REGULATORY AND CONTRACTUAL COMMITMENTS TO COMMUNITIES	VOLUNTARY COMMUNITY INVESTMENT	PHILANTHROPIC INVESTMENT
Examples	Technical training commitments; environmental compliance	Capacity-building initiative for community benefit; upgrades to local infrastructure	Donation to support cancer or AIDS research; donation to wildlife protection fund

Corporate motivation	Compliance with laws	Risk management and securing local licence to operate; can incorporate intent to do no harm and/or foster positive social impact; focus is on individual project	Same motivators as voluntary community investment, but less linkage to securing local licence to operate; more corporate focus and less project focus
Short-term and/or long-term impacts	Generally short-term, some long-term	Can be either short-term or long-term impacts, or both	Generally longer term
Stakeholder engagement strategy	Engagement with communities, regulators, commercial partners	Direct engagement with community stakeholders is a priority	May have limited engagement with community stakeholders—act as a funding source
Allocate percentage of corporate community investment budget	Contracts and regulations prescribe level of commitment	Level of commitment can be set by a corporation, generally on a project basis	Level of commitment generally set by corporation on a corporate-wide basis
Corporate approval process	Part of traditional project manage-ment process	Can be managed within an individual project's management process, or within a broader business integrity corporate management system	Routinely managed within a broader business integrity corporate man-agement system rather than on a local project basis

Regulatory and Contractual Commitments to Communities

There is usually limited scope for corporate flexibility in implementing contractual or regulatory commitments to communities. Commercial agreements may dictate the budget for these initiatives, and local or regional governments or regulators may manage the community investment. However, corporations are encouraged to consider their contractual and regulatory commitments and to evaluate how these commitments affect community stakeholders. If feasible, corporations are encouraged to consider how their committed funding can be applied most effectively:

- If there is a legal commitment to provide technical training to identified communities, how can a corporation ensure that its signed checks are directed to this intended objective? Is there a mechanism for direct corporate participation in training? Would corporations have access to a better-qualified local workforce through active engagement in the training mandate?

- Are corporations familiar with, and supportive of, the stakeholder engagement practices supporting the host government's regulations? Is it possible for corporations to participate in stakeholder engagement processes hosted by governmental and regulatory bodies to ensure that community priorities are addressed?

- Contracts with corporations to permit an investment or project may be awarded by regional or national governmental bodies, or may be awarded by the local authority where the project is situated. In cases where the revenues and taxes derived from the project are not shared with the local citizens situated close to the project site, and instead benefit another region or city, corporations may evaluate the benefits of working with local communities to enhance their ability to advocate for an increased allocation of the direct and indirect project benefits. For example, the owners of the OCENSA pipeline in Colombia, championed by BP, were able to support the enhancement of local communities' capacity to advocate for enhanced benefits from the pipeline project with the national government and regulators in Colombia.

Voluntary Commitments to Community Investment

There are a number of motivations for corporations to voluntarily adopt community participation strategies.

Corporations frequently manage engagement with communities beyond compliance with legislative or regulated requirements. Many investors recognize that if the local communities do not benefit from corporate investment, these citizens may not be motivated to intervene in support of a project. Motivations for voluntary initiatives are wide-ranging and include the requirement to obtain a local licence to operate.

Effective engagement with community stakeholders will enable corporations to understand and prioritize community needs, and to assess available resources capable of responding to these needs. This engagement is sometimes referred to as the corporate investor's local licence to operate. This means that a corporation has earned the goodwill of the communities that surround or are affected by a project's operations. Securing a local licence to operate can be critical for projects, including:

Remote operations:

- construction of a pipeline in Alaska
- installation of a manufacturing plant in a rural community

Operations in areas with disputed land tenure or use among local residents or between local residents, corporations, and governments:

- indigenous land claims
- zones of territorial dispute
- corporate investment in rural communities

Projects with significant environmental or social impacts:

- manufacturing processes that utilize or affect local water resources
- projects that involve changes in land use

Projects that form a significant portion of a local or regional economy:

- oil development in West Africa

- coal mining projects in the United States

- corporate agricultural projects in farming communities dominated by family-operated farms

Projects perceived as foreign or from outside the community:

- investments by Western corporations in the developing world

- non-indigenous investment in indigenous regions

- corporate investment in rural communities

Corporations often recognize that effective relationships with host communities constitute a key component in management of risks. If local communities see the benefit in corporate investment, these stakeholders may advocate for projects in the face of nonlocal criticism. In investment scenarios where security is threatened, local communities' support often forms a cornerstone of corporate security practices.

Corporations may also choose to voluntarily invest in their communities as a means of responding to other business issues. Building the capacity of local consultants and contractors to provide goods and services required for a project can save money and time for corporate investors. To this end, corporate investors may promote business transactions between their operations and small or emerging businesses. Capacity building mechanisms include:

- small and medium enterprise training initiatives

- minority equity participation by corporations in emerging businesses

- establishment of partnerships or joint ventures to promote the transfer of business skills to the emerging corporations

Training and educating local personnel on health-related issues, safety, or adult literacy can improve the productivity of a corporation's workforce. For example, Anglo American was a leader in providing its personnel with free AIDS drugs in 2002 in an attempt to stem the region-wide pandemic in Africa.

Tailoring project infrastructure (for example, roads, electricity, water, and health care) to respond to local community priorities need not burden project budgets. Understanding local communities' needs and priorities allows corporate managers to incorporate these priorities into project planning in a cost-efficient manner. Fixing infrastructure problems after the fact are costly and contentious endeavors.

A corporation's ability to tackle business and development issues that directly affect a corporation's operations, in alignment with community stakeholders, can be effective. For example, corporations can support alliances between Transparency International, host communities, and investors to proactively address corruption risks and impacts in the community. Transparency International is an international advocacy organization that champions transparency in business. The organization has an international umbrella organization that provides assessments of corruption risks in investment environments, and supports the capacity of local communities and investors to assess and manage corruption risks. Through a global umbrella, transparency best practices are shared between projects.

Corporations may seek to distinguish their project on the basis of their ability to engage with community stakeholders, thereby establishing competitive advantage. The proven ability to achieve effective relations with communities can make corporations and their projects more attractive to internal and external stakeholders.

Corporate bidders on projects may be directly or implicitly evaluated by host governments, licensing organizations, or general contractors on their track record with local communities. For example, in some West African projects, bidders are formally evaluated on the basis of their proven ability to work effectively with local communities.

Voluntary community investment may also be a means to enhance the morale of internal corporate stakeholders. Employee volunteering is a growing phenomenon and may attract personnel to certain corporate employers. Corporate personnel often reside in the communities affected by investment, and voluntary community investment allows these employees flexibility and latitude in engagement.

In addition to responding to business issues, some corporate investors elect to voluntarily invest in community programs to ensure that their investment does no harm or contributes to the social good. This motivator is identified as rung 7 on the Integrity Ladder.

Philanthropic Investments

The third model of community participation is characterized by corporations' philanthropic contributions to causes or campaigns that are not
necessarily linked to specific investments or projects. These philanthropic donations are generally contributed as financial commitments,
and are usually made by corporate head offices. Philanthropic investments are clearly intended to enhance a corporation's reputation with a
cross-section of stakeholders. Alignment with operational or individual
project strategy is not a prerequisite.

Examples of philanthropic investments include corporate contributions
to United Way campaigns; funding to create a research chair at a university or community college; a foundation to support scholarships; support for
research on cancer; contribution to a women's foundation to support
funding of shelters for battered women.

Understanding Community Stakeholders

In order to understand the priorities and expectations of local citizens,
corporations are encouraged to tailor stakeholder relations practices to
ensure that communication and dialogue with citizens in the community
are effective. Depending on the unique nature of community populations
and interests, the standard corporate approach to stakeholder engagement may need to be refined.

Effective communications with communities may require that corporate messages be targeted to the intended audience. For example, citizens
will have varying literacy levels that may need to be considered. If
younger citizens are a targeted audience, cartoon-style communications
may be best understood. As well, some members of the community may
have unique interests and impacts—for example, local citizens potentially affected by risk of contamination of water aquifers may prefer meetings
to clarify the technical aspects of the project.

Corporations may choose to achieve their community investment
objectives through direct relationships with local communities or through
alliances with other stakeholders or third parties. Philanthropic investments are routinely effected via third parties. Corporations' voluntary
community investments can be implemented through participation with

other corporations in business groups, through contributions to locally developed foundations or nongovernmental organizations, through partnerships with local or international nongovernmental organizations, or through employee volunteer programs.

Each corporation is encouraged to assess its options for community investment, and design a strategy based on its individual corporate capacity and motivation. In cases where the community investment program is long term in nature, and requires complementary skill sets that do not necessarily reside within the corporation, it may be more effective for a corporation to partner with other stakeholders with the requisite capacity. This includes nongovernmental organizations, community-based organizations, national governments, local governments, international donors, other corporations, universities, or multilateral organizations.

Corporate support for a charitable foundation, or even the creation of a corporate foundation as a vehicle for community investment, is not necessarily an effective salve for every wounded relationship with community stakeholders. The Shell Foundation was launched in 2000 as a legally independent charity to foster new social investment programs that would not directly benefit the commercial arm of the corporation. Cynics allege that Shell is using the "independent" nongovernmental organization to disassociate itself from historical controversies and to oil the wheels of new commercial ventures. Others regard the initiative as progressive.

Emerging practices in community investment manifest the diversity of options available for corporations. As discussed earlier in this chapter, corporate managers are encouraged to examine the best practices of competitors and the emerging practices of corporate leaders. Chapter 11 provides details of alliances that have been created by corporations to advance voluntary initiatives intended to respond to a broad range of stakeholder priorities, including community stakeholders. A sampling of co-managed or third party-managed community investment programs includes:

- Alliances among corporate investors in certain jurisdictions, or investment regions, to collectively respond to shared challenges and risks:

- Corporations collaborating on corruption
- Gas producers developing common advocacy strategies such as alternatives to gas flaring
- Oil and gas producers and mining corporations collaborating on abandonment and reclamation alternatives
- Corporate and family farmers collaborating on land-use strategies

• Corporations working with other donors to support community investment programs:

- Alliances by corporations with national or international environmental or social foundations
- Escondida, a copper mine in Chile, created two foundations to address community development needs in surrounding communities and beyond
- Shell Foundation's partnership with Integra, a nonprofit capacity-building group that provides micro-credit support to entrepreneurs in Eastern Europe

• Corporations partnering with local or national governments to implement community investment strategy:

- Rio Tinto Foundation in Indonesia has developed a tuberculosis-control program with the World Health Organization, the government of Indonesia, and a national nongovernmental organization

Due diligence is an imperative to assure integrity in community investment. In a December 2002 initiative of Transparency International and Social Accountability International, "Business Principles for Countering Bribery" were developed with the support of several other stakeholders. These business principles specifically refer to the risk of corruption in charitable giving and caution enterprises to "ensure that charitable contributions and sponsorships are not being used as a subterfuge for bribery," and recommends that enterprises "publicly disclose all its charitable contributions or sponsorships."

Corporate managers are encouraged to apply the same due diligence practices in making donations to charitable foundations and beneficiaries as adopted for other commercial transactions. Managers are discouraged from writing checks to charitable or not-for-profit organizations with which corporations are not familiar. Managers are encouraged to ensure a clear understanding of community investment program beneficiaries and selection processes. Mistakes can compromise corporate integrity and foil the intended corporate objectives. Corporate managers are encouraged to ask the following:

- How are beneficiaries of community investment programs selected and supported?

- Are objective criteria established?

- Are selection processes monitored and measured?

- Are there relationships of influence between charitable foundations and beneficiaries?

Where a corporation's community investment is integrated into a larger humanitarian or development initiative, standards for due diligence cannot be compromised. The experiences of a Canadian engineering company, Acres International Ltd., in an internationally funded water project in Africa are noteworthy. An agent of Acres was found guilty of corruption in this project, and Acres has a U.S. $2.8 million judgment against it lodged by a court in Lesotho. The chief justice in Lesotho expressed anger with the Canadian engineering company working on the development project. Although Acres was recognized as a great name in Canadian engineering, the company was alleged to be remiss in its failure to prevent a local agent from bribing a local official in order to win work on the project.

Succession of Business Integrity Vision

Not only must corporate management teams define the organization's commitment to integrity, and identify and fill integrity gaps, leaders must also ensure the survival of this business integrity vision.

Governance regulations encourage corporations to ensure that business succession plans are in place. Beyond compliance with governance regulations, corporate leaders are also encouraged to ensure that business integrity vision succession plans are prioritized.

Corporations and their key stakeholders need to ask the following:

- What happens to the corporate vision on business integrity when senior leadership changes?

- Does the vision survive leadership change, or is the business integrity vision of the company intrinsically linked to individual leaders?

- How can business integrity vision be embedded into the organization?

If there is a risk that a corporation's business integrity vision may not survive a change in leadership, who then is responsible for ensuring that vision succession is feasible? Arguably, the board of directors of a corporation is in place to ensure continuity on executive or leadership transition and, in this capacity, board members are encouraged to consider these questions.

Raising the Floor on Business Integrity

When corporate managers assess their corporate commitments to integrity and identify their weakest links, they routinely focus on commitments and practices within their own organization. The integrity practices of competitors are largely of relevance for comparative purposes, or as a source for best practices.

However, it is important for corporate managers to keep in mind that the weakest link for their corporation can be their competitors' behaviors. Industry Non-compliers that do not respond to corporate responsibility expectations of key stakeholder groups can compromise the reputation of and opportunities for their peer group.

Some examples will be helpful to illustrate this point; consider the following:

- The impact of Union Carbide's Bhopal disaster on the chemical industry as a whole

- Stakeholders' apprehensive response to environmental risks associated with transporting crude oil and oil products in the wake of the Exxon *Valdez* oil spill

- International financial institutions and development banks' reluctance to fund pipelines in the Amazon in the face of strong environmental advocacy in the region

- Local communities' predisposition to assume that all foreign oil and gas investors operating in communities located onshore in Nigeria would operate in the same manner as Shell

- Consumers' wary response to all diamonds originating from African mines as a result of their inability to distinguish "blood diamonds" from diamonds mined and distributed via credible processes

- Possible tardiness in the identification of mad cow disease in the cattle herd of one Canadian rancher in 2003 resulting in a denial of access to export markets for the entire Canadian beef industry

Although seemingly ambitious for corporations focused on putting their own house in order, it is increasingly relevant for corporations to consider and monitor the integrity commitments and actions of their counterparts in an industry sector. An awareness of the gaps between corporations in business integrity is generally considered valuable in identifying best industry practices and enabling corporations to distinguish behaviors for competitive advantage. Although paradoxical to traditional notions of competitive advantage, it is also important that corporations be aware of the practices of their peer group. As well, the industry's Noncompliers should be identified and industry groups should recognize the collective value of strengthening the weakest links in their sector.

Corporations have traditionally regarded their sphere of influence to include operating partners and, in some cases, other corporations in their direct supply chain. It may now be prudent for a corporation to evaluate the growing relevance of its competitors and peers within an industry sector. As discussed in Chapter 2, distrust of corporations is high; corporations cannot assume that key stakeholder groups will necessarily distinguish between corporate practices within an industry sector.

The onus is on corporations to prove their credibility. Self-policing within industry associations is a growing necessity. Raising the ceiling on business integrity can be driven by the actions of a few industry leaders. Raising the floor on business integrity requires industry-wide action and alignment.

Frontier 5:
Evaluating a Corporation's Accountability for Business Integrity and Measuring Integrity Differences Between Corporations

To objectively assess business integrity, internal and external corporate stakeholders require accountability. Stakeholders must have trust and confidence in a corporation's financial data, products, and services, and also in its publicly stated values, integrity, and leadership. This chapter focuses on Frontier 5 in business integrity management—how to design and implement dependable and strategic corporate accountability systems and processes that manifest business integrity values and build trust.

Corporate managers are under growing pressure to demonstrate competitiveness, not only in terms of market share but also in their corporate governance, corporate integrity, and corporate citizenship. It is expected that the linkages between competitiveness, governance, citizenship, and integrity will grow stronger. This chapter will discuss these linkages and identify ways that corporate managers can reinforce the linkages.

Management components and systems can contribute to the effective accountability and assurance of a corporation's integrity values. These linkages build trust and confidence. Some of the management systems that this chapter will address include:

- Dependable corporate management systems that support integrity values

- Performance measures and monitoring mechanisms to gauge corporate integrity

- Verification processes to affirm the demonstration of integrity intentions, commitments, and actions

- Reporting structures to share integrity intentions, commitments, and outcomes with key corporate stakeholders

Business Integrity Accountability Cycle

This chapter examines the management processes and systems that can be evaluated, fine-tuned, or reconfigured to ensure that business integrity values are measured, monitored, verified, and reported. These processes are continuous and should be incorporated into the continuous improvement cycle of a corporation.

Corporate Management Systems

Is a corporate management system to govern integrity a business imperative?

Many corporations do not have management processes that measure and report on alignment of corporate commitments and corporate responses on business integrity. Also, many corporations have partnerships, joint ventures, and alliances with other organizations that do not measure or report on business integrity.

If management systems within corporations are not directed to *manage* business integrity, how will corporate leaders, employees, shareholders, and others know how and if integrity commitments are being reflected in practice?

Creating a corporate management system that ensures intangible outcomes is challenging. How can this been done?

Corporations motivated to countermand public perceptions of corporate greed are mandating that corporate management systems be designed or refurbished to preserve integrity. Leadership teams within many companies are now setting integrity measures and targets for management on corporate social responsibility and citizenship; these leadership teams can be found within many leading companies and across all sectors: Anglo American, Electricité de France, Diageo, McDonald's, Merck, UBS, and WMC Resources are only a handful of the many companies applauded for this leadership.

As discussed already, defining integrity values and intended management outcomes in tangible and measurable terms is hard work. Creating a management system that ensures integrity outcomes are met is even more difficult, and systematic assessment and verification of integrity outcomes can be daunting.

Corporate leaders have extensive experience in scoping out the parameters of physical projects and in creating management systems to govern project operations. Managers know how to design a manufacturing facility; how to construct a bridge; how to design a catering business; or how to launch a lawn mower repair center. In scoping these physical projects, corporate technical and financial experts can identify the required manpower, services, and materials; can readily point to those in the corporation with responsibility for these tasks; can verify the cost of construction; can estimate project timeframes; can anticipate operating costs on project completion; can measure a competitor's advantages; can quantify risks and costs to manage risks; and can measure technical and financial outputs of the project with confidence.

In contrast, creating and implementing a corporate system that ensures that a corporation manages business integrity is not as clear-cut.

Chapter 5 reviewed the challenges that corporations face in creating change within their organizations. Unlike physical projects and their supporting operational systems, the design and implementation of an integrity system crosses the thresholds of many corporate departments and disciplines. Given the overarching nature of an integrity system and the impact of business integrity on every department within a corporation, everyone within the organization is involved. Within corporations, the responsibilities and processes are not always clear. There is a risk that everyone feels responsible for integrity commitments, but no one feels accountable for integrity performance.

In order to clarify integrity responsibilities and accountabilities within corporations, managers must pose some questions. There are no "right" answers to these questions, but there is a critical need to ask and answer them. If responsibilities and accountabilities for integrity are not clarified within an organization, there is a greater risk that corporate personnel will "feel good" that integrity is an organizational value, but not understand how the corporation manifests integrity in its practices. External corporate stakeholders will be even more unclear of how the corporation embeds integrity values in its practices.

Some questions for managers to ask to clarify internal responsibilities and accountabilities include the following:

- Within our corporation, who has the corporate responsibility to authorize or mandate the creation of an integrity management system? Is it the board of directors, the chief executive officer, the executive team, the human resources manager, or the legal department?

- Which corporate departments in our organization are the strongest integrity links and which are the weakest links? How can our company respond to the risks associated with the weakest links?

- How are integrity outcomes defined in our corporation?

- Who in our company is responsible for assessing and measuring integrity outcomes?

- Should our company independently verify our integrity outcomes and, if so, who should conduct this verification?

- Who is responsible in our corporation for reporting on integrity outcomes? To whom should outcomes be reported?

Alignment of Corporate Management Systems

The evaluation of a business integrity management system frequently coincides with pressure to breathe new life into existing corporate governance compliance systems. We encourage corporate leadership to think beyond compliance in their review and upgrading of management systems, and to maximize their investment of time and resources with a comprehensive evaluation of business integrity accountabilities. Beyond compliance with laws and rules, are your organization's management systems strategically responsive to existing and emerging business integrity frontiers?

Corporate leaders may fumble with the interrelationship of business integrity, governance, and accountability frameworks:

- Where does one system start and another system begin?

- Are these systems linked and, if so, how? Is it one system or three systems?

- Do corporations report separately on each corporate objective— business integrity, governance, and accountability—or should reporting be consolidated?

Governance systems have been around for a long time. Corporate boards of directors routinely discuss corporate governance systems with executive teams, with management advisers, and increasingly with lawyers to ensure that liabilities are understood. Governing bodies are also familiar in other settings—political leaders focus on governance in decision making affecting the allocation of public resources; professional associations focus on governance of their members to assure standardized professional, technical, and ethical expectations; and we depend on governance structures in a host of other organizational settings, including regional or district health boards, Crown or state corporations, not-for-profit boards, and school boards.

In corporations, the focus of governance systems has historically been on the links between the board of directors and the executive team. Governance expectations have come a long way; it used to be acceptable for board members to hire a good CEO and then support him or her to do a good job. Today, governance expectations are weightier. When we talk of governance, we use the language of duties: directors have multiple duties to ensure that governance systems are embedded, including the duty of knowledge; duty of care; duty of skill and prudence; duty of diligence; duty of trusteeship and investment; duty of management and delegation; and fiduciary duty.

Accountability systems were created as part of a management framework intended to guide organizational behaviors, clarify roles and relationships, and enhance performance and transparency of reporting. By clarifying responsibilities for certain management functions, accountability systems make the corporate role and relationship labyrinth more transparent. Accountability systems clarify who is responsible for which functions and outcomes—for example, who values inventory in a manufacturing company; who quantifies reserves in an energy company; who reports on financial outputs in a lending company?

Both governance systems and accountability systems may incorporate integrity outcomes, but it is not likely that these systems will quantify, monitor, verify, or report on integrity outcomes intentionally, and they may not be aligned with the corporation's overall integrity commitments and actions. As a result, corporate managers are encouraged to either create a stand-alone corporate integrity system to quantify, monitor, verify, and report on integrity outcomes, or to ensure that their organizational governance and/or accountability systems are overhauled to incorporate integrity outcomes in an intentional and aligned manner.

Beyond corporate governance and accountability systems, other systems within the corporation may also have a connection to integrity outcomes. In order to streamline assessing, monitoring, verifying, and reporting on integrity, corporate managers are encouraged to ask the following questions:

- What management systems are already in place within the corporation? Examples may include finance, information technology, human resources, risk management, environment/health/safety, public relations, corporate governance, corporate social accountability, and sustainability.

- What values are these existing management systems designed to protect?

- Which individuals or positions within the corporation are responsible for the design and implementation of existing management systems?

- How do existing management systems interrelate, and how effective are these interrelationships?

Existing corporate management systems may already address integrity outcomes at overall corporate or divisional levels. In order to ensure that the corporation's integrity commitments and actions are either "captured" or incorporated into existing systems and reported on with clarity, it is worthwhile for managers to conduct some due diligence to explore existing systems and their performance measures and reporting. Inconsistent reporting on integrity by various corporate management systems would undermine credibility and reliability of outputs. Time is also wasted if multiple management systems report on the same integrity outputs. Streamlined assessment, monitoring, verification, and reporting processes for integrity outcomes should be a priority.

Corporate managers given with the job of assuring corporate commitments to integrity and reporting on this performance can easily get bogged down in corporate management systems. Corporate personnel responsible for administering a well-functioning management system may not welcome changes to their systems. However, in some organizations, it may make little sense to create yet another management system to manage business integrity.

Determining the best way forward to embed integrity management systems in a corporate environment will require thoughtful evaluation of options. Corporate managers are invited to ask the following questions to help them decide on the design of a management system to uphold corporate integrity commitments:

- Can corporate business integrity values be effectively protected (assessed, monitored, verified, and reported on) within the corporation's existing management systems (by incorporating these intended integrity outcomes and processes within an existing framework), or should a stand-alone system to manage business integrity be created?

- Which groups and individuals within the corporation are the most qualified and motivated to design and implement a business integrity management system?

- How can multidisciplinary teams be created to ensure inputs from relevant internal stakeholders? How can external stakeholders' views be effectively incorporated into the integrity management system?

- Does the corporation have the requisite internal expertise, experience, and resources to design and implement an integrity management system, or are external resources required to supplement existing resources or to lend credibility?

- How can efficiencies among related management systems within the corporation be achieved? For example, can committee participation be multidisciplinary, can monitoring and reporting efforts be aligned, and can communication be made more efficient?

- How are links between management systems reinforced? How do management systems communicate with one another? For example, how is reputation risk linked to business integrity management within existing corporate management systems?

Admittedly, these are tough questions for corporate management teams, but corporations have done this work before. Two decades ago, environment, health, and safety commitments were de-linked from operational practices and companies were forced to decide how to manage these evolving environment, health, and safety accountabilities.

Corporations are now increasingly working with enterprise risk processes to manage risks on a corporate-wide basis; these shifts in risking strategy will require shifts in management systems.

Functional Accountability

Systems to assure business integrity do not have to be complicated or elaborate. In fact, clarity of objective and implementation is preferred. Once the overall management system framework to assure business integrity is agreed upon, functional responsibility for business integrity commitments must be clearly delineated. Employees must unequivocally understand who has responsibility for specific roles and functions.

Many corporate codes of conduct will make all employees responsible for adherence to corporate principles, including business integrity values. While it is useful to empower every individual to be responsible for understanding and honoring integrity principles, some further guidance is then required to explain to personnel how these functional responsibilities cascade through the corporation in practice. We know who is responsible for business integrity, but who is accountable?

There are several options available for corporations in designing and implementing functional accountability processes to embed business integrity. These options include adopting a combination of the following processes:

- In most cases, individual employees will be expected to be familiar with corporate business integrity policies and to report violations. To provide assurances of this individual employee comprehension of corporate policy, many corporations require that employees sign off on compliance at least once a year. Some corporations require agents and other third parties acting on the corporation's behalf to sign similar affirmations that they understand the corporation's integrity policies, and undertake to report any suspected or known violations.

- Business unit managers can be directly accountable to ensure that business integrity principles are understood within their respective operational units, and to ensure that practices are aligned to commitments. For example, some multinational companies require that country managers and other business unit managers submit to senior management business assurance letters that are created based on aggregated assurances received from line managers.

- Individual employees may be responsible for reporting suspected or actual integrity violations to their supervisor, and supervisors are then responsible for ensuring that the principles are applied in accordance with corporate policy.

- Employees, supervisors, and business unit managers may be directed to a particular department head or department within the corporation for guidance and direction if an integrity breach is suspected or confirmed. Corporations frequently designate individuals within one or several of the following departments as integrity experts to be consulted: the legal department, human resources, internal audit, environment/health/ safety, and security. Some corporations designate an individual—for example, the general counsel—as the reference point for all integrity issues and questions. Other corporations designate responsibilities on the basis of the issue at hand.

- In this reporting structure, employees must judge who is best qualified to assess the type of integrity breach in question. Is the integrity breach related to environmental practices or a matter of legal compliance? Does the breach have links to financial reporting mandates? Is there need for due diligence?

- To provide better direction to employees, this structure may also provide for further detail as to what types of integrity issues are to be referred to which experts on the basis of clear delineation of functional responsibilities, as follows:

  - *Legal experts* to determine if there is a breach of law or corporate policy
  - *Internal audit experts* to determine if there is any link to fiscal accountability; they may be asked to interpret the policy,

conduct focused audits to assess the situation, provide expertise to operating groups

- *Environment, health, and safety* to assess if there is an integrity breach that has functional impacts on environmental, health, or safety principles or practices of the corporation
- *Human resources* to communicate corporate principles and policies to new personnel; to train personnel or support training; to set performance expectations
- *Corporate security* to conduct due diligence into employees, agents, and other third parties retained by the corporation to perform services; to conduct due diligence in relation to an integrity breach

- In order to provide a "one-window" approach for personnel, corporations may designate a multidisciplinary business integrity management team to be the "champions" of business integrity issues. All reported or suspected violations of business integrity principles can be referred to this integrity team. The team should have a clear reporting relationship with the corporate executive and even the board of directors. As well, the integrity team could be responsible for advising on emerging issues and for advocating changes in corporate practices on business integrity on a proactive or reactive basis.

- Corporations may choose to designate one senior executive to bear ultimate accountability for integrity commitments and performance. In order for this accountability structure to be effective, the designated "point person" in the corporate executive suite must ensure that communication and reporting processes are in place to encourage transparency and disclosure of issues and the discussion, design, and implementation of responsive strategies.

Performance Measurement and Monitoring Systems

Performance measurement and monitoring systems intended to manage business integrity can be:

- Proactive or reactive

- Rules based or process oriented

Chapter 7 and the scenarios introduced in Part 2 of this book consider *proactive* versus *reactive* approaches to integrity management in detail. In a reactive corporate environment, performance measuring and monitoring systems are designed to catch violations. In a proactive corporate culture, these systems will be designed to ensure that the corporation advances or maintains its relative industry position in responding to integrity dilemmas.

Corporate policies on integrity must clearly indicate how policy violations are to be reported. In a rules-based environment, corporate policy will address policy breaches in black-and-white terms.

However, in a corporate culture that acknowledges that more complex integrity dilemmas are inevitable, an organization's expectations on the reporting of policy violations will reflect that it may not always have the answers to all integrity issues. In this open corporate culture, dialogue and access to others would be encouraged as a means of exploring and understanding the integrity dilemma in question and its implications for the corporation. As a first step in the design of corporate policy on integrity, corporate management must consider their intended approach—that is, if it will be rules based or process oriented.

Employees and others subject to corporate policy should understand the consequences of a violation of integrity policy. Performance measurement tools and methods applied by the corporation must have consequences. Personnel must know that breaches of integrity policy will be treated seriously and will, in some cases, result in termination of employment or termination of contracts in the case of third parties. When employees and agents understand the motivation for corporate integrity policies, they are generally better able to appreciate the consequences of noncompliance. Consequences of policy violations should be clearly prescribed in corporate documentation and honored in practice. Corporate management's failure to respond to policy breaches will send conflicting messages to employees and other stakeholders.

The tone adopted by corporations in their engagement with personnel on integrity commitments requires balance. In an open corporate culture, employees must feel comfortable raising and discussing integrity dilemmas, while at the same time respecting the serious consequences of policy violations. Management's objective is to promote a process for decision making that fosters dialogue without fear of retribution. Not surprisingly, many integrity policy violations are an outcome of an employee's independent actions—unilateral decisions made without consultation.

How should employees report policy violations or suspicions of integrity breaches? This question is open to significant debate. Some corporations mandate that breaches be reported to designated corporation personnel. Other corporations allow for reporting of violations to internal personnel or to external contacts. This external reporting arrangement is intended to negate the risk of intimidation that might compromise an individual's willingness to report a violation.

Whistle-Blowing Systems

More progressive corporations have also adopted whistle-blowing help lines or hot lines that allow for anonymity in reporting integrity breaches to an independent third party. Employees are encouraged to use help lines to seek guidance on conflicts of interest; external relationships; environment, health, and safety queries; personnel issues; questions about corporation assets; dealing with meals, gifts, and entertainment; political donations; and even human rights questions.

Corporations are divided on the effectiveness of confidential hot lines. Some corporations resist these measures due to a perceived compromise of corporate culture, while other corporate leaders depend on these reporting systems to ensure effective monitoring of compliance with integrity policy.

Whatever the corporate management philosophy on whistle-blowing, the public is interested. Media accounts of whistle-blowers are being showcased on the covers of newsmagazines. In 2002, *Time* magazine put three women whistle-blowers on its cover as its "Persons of the Year." The April 2002 edition of the magazine hosted three female whistle-blowers—from Enron, WorldCom, and the FBI—on its cover. *Business Week* even declared that it would not be too glib to call 2002 the "Year of the Whistleblower."

The effectiveness of whistle-blowing as a corporate stick to discourage integrity offenders is not yet a perfected management practice. Some employees are legitimately wary of retaliation against whistle-blowers. There is legislation in place in some jurisdictions to impose stiff fines and even jail sentences on those who retaliate against whistle-blowers, and several other governments are assessing the effectiveness of legislation to deter retaliation against whistle-blowers. In other jurisdictions, legislative provisions mandate strengthening the audit committee's role in responding to internal complaints within corporations. Regardless of the legislative environment, a company's adoption of whistle-blowing as part of its integrity management system needs to be coupled with a voluntary and enforceable undertaking to not retaliate against whistle-blowers.

Verification Systems

What systems do corporations have in place to verify that stakeholders are adhering to business integrity policies?

There are several means available to corporations to assess and measure compliance with business integrity commitments. Some methods, such as internal audits, are widely accepted practices and existing processes only need tweaking to ensure that audits embrace the full depth and breadth of corporate integrity policies. Other practices, such as independent verification, are emerging practices that require thoughtful consideration prior to adoption by corporations.

Nonfinancial Audits

One way to assess and measure compliance with corporate integrity policy is to do internal audits. Ensuring that corporate auditors are mandated to examine the full scope of corporate compliance in their audits will provide some after-the-fact assurances that stakeholders can rely upon. However, incorporating nonfinancial considerations into a traditionally financial audit framework will require some definition. Auditors may require additional training to raise their awareness of nonfinancial issues, and their ranks may need to be supplemented with expertise that is more familiar with nonfinancial indicators.

What considerations need to be incorporated into a financial audit to ensure that all business integrity commitments are assessed? Refer back to corporate policy and value statements. What integrity commitments does a corporation make? Consider how the corporation's audit scope can be expanded to ensure that all of these undertakings are evaluated.

In the audit of third-party organizations, including private sector or governmental partners and agency organizations, some explanation of this expanded audit scope will likely be necessary. Contractual language granting audit rights with third parties should also be reevaluated to ensure that the audit scope is sufficiently comprehensive to facilitate audits of nonfinancial criteria.

One way to raise awareness of nonfinancial audit criteria with auditors is to have two-way discussions on the application of the Integrity Grid tool (see Appendix). Audit outcomes provide very useful information that can be plotted on the Integrity Grid to assess departmental, divisional, or corporate performance. This approach works well with internal audits and in navigating integrity frontiers within third-party organizations. This internal evaluation process will assist in identifying weaknesses and also help to highlight corporate strength in responding to business integrity commitments.

Independent Verification

Stakeholders' distrust of corporations has resulted in their growing expectations for independent verification of corporate performance on integrity commitments. Stakeholders do not always wholeheartedly trust corporations' internal assessments and have been quite vocal in their demand for independent assessments.

In response, many corporations are beginning to incorporate reports from objective third parties in their reporting. Identifying a truly objective third party is challenging, but larger public companies rely on public accounting firms, management consultants, academics, and sometimes advocacy organizations to provide verifications. These external verifications of corporate performance are often generated on the basis of site visits, examination of documentation, consultation with key external stakeholders, and discussions with corporate personnel including management.

Benchmarking

Increasingly, corporations are participating in benchmarking surveys to assess their own integrity performance against industry best practices. Benchmarking surveys are generally industry specific. For example, in the energy sector, surveys include the Dow Jones Sustainability Group Index, FTSE4Good, and Business in the Environment Index. Confidentiality of analysis is an important consideration when assessing the merits of participation.

Depending on what is being measured and how, participation in benchmarking surveys can be useful. Corporations can use the Integrity Grid tool to conduct independent benchmarking of their practices and those of their competitors. Consideration of the practices of corporations that rank high in the Integrity Grid assessment is an effective way of identifying methods and options for a corporation to fill integrity gaps.

Reporting Systems

Corporations' financial reporting is largely prescribed by legislation, and practices have been standardized. Expanding the scope of external reporting to include nonfinancial aspects of corporate activity—including a corporation's responsiveness to business integrity commitments—is a relatively new phenomenon.

In the last decade, corporations incorporated environmental, health, and safety indicators in their annual reports. Stakeholders are now challenging corporations to address other less tangible nonfinancial indicators in reporting, including stakeholder relations, government relations, impacts of investment on communities, and human rights. Reporting on nonfinancial indicators is frequently referred to as "triple bottom-line" reporting—reporting on financial, environmental, and social indicators.

Responding to appeals to report on these integrity commitments can be daunting for corporations. How do corporations objectively describe the status of stakeholder relations, community participation, government relations, and human rights context in an investment jurisdiction?

Many corporations are voluntarily reporting on business integrity criteria. According to the 2003 edition of the *Corporation Report*, published by United Kingdom's Prowse & Corporation, corporate ethical reporting has surged in the annual reports of Europe's top 100 corporations.

Some corporations issue social accountability or sustainability reports on a periodic or annual basis to report on nonfinancial objectives and outcomes. As yet, there is no standardized practice for reporting on these integrity commitments and there is little, if any, legislative framework to guide or compel corporations on this reporting. A limited number of countries, including the Netherlands, Germany, and France, have mandated reporting on some "intangibles." Reporting on nonfinancial integrity criteria is an emerging practice.

If a corporation is motivated to report on integrity commitments and outcomes, where can it look for support and guidance? Some practices are beginning to emerge on reporting, particularly for environmental standards. The GRI Index is an example of a sustainability reporting guide that sets out reporting guidelines and protocols. Many public relations groups provide excellent advice in designing reporting documentation. *However, corporations should be cautious.*

Corporations cannot create a reporting document without a management strategy on business integrity. Corporate management must fully understand its corporate commitments on integrity, and must fully appreciate corporate alignment between its commitments on integrity and its practices, otherwise the corporation's reporting vehicle may be regarded as propaganda, and will expose the corporation to criticism from internal and external stakeholders. Corporations can report only on corporate intention and corporate action. The Integrity Grid tool can be applied to test assumptions about the contents and purpose of corporate reporting on integrity.

Reporting on nonfinancial indicators can be an incremental or staged process for corporations. Rather than embarking on an in-depth exposé of corporate integrity practices, it may be more credible and effective for corporations to inform stakeholders of their business integrity intentions, and to progressively report on integrity performance as measuring capabilities are enhanced and made reliable. For example, in response to pressure from advocates against sweatshop labor, Gap Inc. released its first Social Responsibility Report in 2004. The report included an assessment of corporate deficiencies which enhanced company credibility with its critics.

PART 2

Process for Managing Corporate Integrity and Scenario Applications

Process for Proactive Management of Corporate Integrity

Proactive Management or Reactive Tactics

Integrity dilemmas are on the rise and are likely to increase in frequency and complexity. Corporations must anticipate paradox. For some corporations, a wait-and-see attitude may appear to be a less expensive strategy, but actual practice shows that it is more effective from operational, financial, and reputation perspectives to anticipate corporate dilemmas and be positioned to respond.

Corporations and their leaders have choices. Managers can use offensive/proactive management practices or defensive/reactive tactics.

In earlier chapters, we examined sample dilemmas that corporations must manage. To demonstrate the benefits of anticipating and responding to dilemmas in a systematic manner, the management tools introduced in Part 1 will be applied to three case scenarios in Part 2, using both proactive and reactive approaches:

Proactive management practices: A corporation has a proactive evaluation and decision-making process in place to anticipate and respond to dilemmas.

Reactive tactics: A corporation adopts a reactive wait-and-see approach, choosing to respond after a crisis occurs.

Integrity management processes cannot prevent crises, but corporations with processes in place to manage integrity dilemmas are better positioned to mitigate the risk of crises and to manage unavoidable crises. In Part 2, the case studies reviewed will demonstrate the differences in corporate outcomes when companies adopt offensive versus defensive integrity strategies.

Media documentation of corporate behaviors tends to focus on the outcomes of defensive tactics that companies apply in response to crisis. There is less profiling and understanding of the impacts of proactive integrity strategy. When the two strategies are compared, the differences can be fundamental.

For example, in 2003, the international media focused on investment in Argentina by two Canadian gold mining investors—Barrick Gold Corp. and Meridian Gold Inc.—and compared their experiences with Argentinean communities.

According to media accounts, Meridian's project was put on hold in the face of local opposition to its project, while Barrick was able to quietly move forward with construction of a base camp and road network. While both companies were reported to have good intentions, the media accounts drew comparisons between Barrick's proactive management strategies and Meridian's reactive tactics. Barrick is reported to have completed several rounds of community meetings, completed and submitted an environmental impact assessment, and proactively assessed access roads and infrastructure before embarking on their mining project. Meridian's operations were, however, caught up in growing concern over the impacts of cyanide leaching. Media accounts linked Meridian's rush to start production to Greenpeace's ability to exploit Meridian's weak popularity and begin a movement to overhaul Argentina's mining code, banning the use of cyanide leaching and open-pit mining in the whole country. When the local city council organized a nonbinding plebiscite asking residents to approve the Meridian project, an overwhelming 80 percent voted against it.

Embedding Business Integrity Practices through Scenario Training

To embed business integrity practices within corporate management systems, contemporary corporate training models encourage employees to work with real-life scenarios. Working with scenarios affords corporate personnel a nonthreatening opportunity to identify integrity issues and to consider feasible responses within the corporation's decision-making framework.

Part 2 will introduce three fictional scenarios. Business tools introduced in Part 1 are applied to these three scenarios to demonstrate how these tools work. As well, the business tools will be applied to the scenarios on both a reactive and proactive basis to show differences in potential outcomes of reactive versus proactive strategy.

The three scenarios introduced in Part 2 include:

Chapter 8: Scenario A

A business development opportunity for a public European-based high-tech company that manufactures components in Vietnam, an emerging market economy.

Chapter 9: Scenario B

A private company opportunity in a developed market economy (family farm corporation in Canada).

Chapter 10: Scenario C

Construction of a pipeline in the United States by a multinational consortium with a focus on impacts to local communities.

Framework to Apply Business Tools: Evaluation and Decision-Making Framework for Managing Business Integrity

Working though these scenarios, the business tools introduced in Part 1 will be applied in the sequence and within the evaluation and decision-making framework set out below:

Evaluation and Decision-Making Framework for Managing Business Integrity

Phase 1: Establishing the Business Integrity Baseline
- *Phase 1A:* Assess integrity commitments and action (historical) of individual departments within the corporation.
- *Phase 1B:* Apply the Integrity Ladder (introduced in Chapter 2) analysis to the corporation.

Phase 2: Identifying Stakeholders, Assessing Stakeholder Impacts, Anticipating Stakeholder Expectations of a Corporation, Identifying Potential Dilemmas

- *Phase 2A:* Apply the Stakeholder Grid and Impact Assessment tool (introduced in Chapter 3) to identify key stakeholders in a project and assess potential stakeholder impacts.
- *Phase 2B:* Anticipate stakeholders' expectations of the corporation, and identify potential dilemmas arising from project impacts and these expectations.
- *Phase 2C:* Create opportunity for innovation with multidisciplinary brainstorming to identify feasible options to manage dilemmas.

Phase 3: Creating, Managing, and Assessing Alignment between Corporate Commitments to Business Integrity and Actual Practices

- *Phase 3A:* Identify corporate commitments to business integrity.
- *Phase 3B:* Plot departmental integrity commitments and corporate integrity commitments on the Integrity Ladder.
- *Phase 3C:* Apply the Integrity Grid—plot departmental integrity talk and departmental integrity walk on the Integrity Grid (introduced in Chapter 4):
  - *Before* multidisciplinary brainstorming of feasible strategies (reactive)
  - *After* multidisciplinary brainstorming of feasible strategies (proactive)

Phase 4: Identifying, Assessing, and Implementing Best Practices in Business Integrity

- Use the Permeation of Change model, the Adapted Better Practices tool, and Benchmarking Practices (introduced in Chapter 5) to identify, assess, and implement best practices that will enhance strategic management of business integrity frontiers.

Phase 5: Responding to Business Integrity Accountabilities

- *Phase 5A:* Clarify accountabilities with the Business Integrity Accountability Cycle (introduced in Chapter 6).
- *Phase 5B:* Implement tactics.
- *Phase 5C:* Implement continuous improvement.

Evaluation and Decision-Making Framework for Managing Business Integrity

PHASE	INTEGRITY FRONTIER	ACTION	BUSINESS TOOL
1	Understanding different perspectives on corporate integrity	Baseline assessment of corporate integrity commitments and actions	Integrity Ladder (Chapter 2)
2	Clarifying expectations about corporate roles and responsibilities	Identify key stakeholders, assess project impacts, anticipate stakeholder expectations of corporation, identify potential dilemmas	Stakeholder Grid and Impact Assessment tool (Chapter 3)
3	Aligning corporate values, commitments, and actions	Creating, managing, and assessing alignment between integrity talk and integrity walk	Integrity Ladder and Integrity Grid (Chapter 4)
4	Understanding differences between corporations in business integrity	Identify, assess, and implement best practices in business integrity	Community Investment Strategy Tool Permeation of Change model Adapted Best Practices tool Benchmarking Practices (Chapter 5)
5	Assessing corporate accountability for business integrity	Clarify accountabilities; implement strategy; continuous improvement	Business Integrity Accountability Cycle (Chapter 6)

Community Participation Dilemmas

The Evaluation and Decision-Making Framework for Managing Business Integrity will be slightly modified in Chapter 10 to address community stakeholders' expectations and resulting dilemmas. As well, Chapter 10 will apply the Community Investment Strategy tool.

Evaluation and Decision-Making Process for Managing Community Participation

Phase 1: Establishing the Community Participation Baseline in a Corporation

- *Phase 1A:* Assess individual corporate departments/divisions' commitments to community and historical actions.
- *Phase 1B:* Apply the Integrity Ladder (introduced in Chapter 2) analysis in relation to community participation.

Phase 2: Identifying Community Stakeholders, Assessing Community Stakeholder Impacts, Anticipating Stakeholder Expectations of a Corporation, Identifying Potential Dilemmas with Community Stakeholders

- *Phase 2A:* Apply the Stakeholder Grid and Impact Assessment tool (introduced in Chapter 3) to key community stakeholders in a project and assess potential stakeholder impacts.
- *Phase 2B:* Anticipate stakeholders' expectations of the corporation, and identify potential integrity dilemmas arising from project impacts and expectations of community stakeholders.
- *Phase 2C:* Create opportunity for innovation with multidisciplinary brainstorming to identify feasible options to manage dilemmas.

Phase 3: Creating, Managing, and Assessing Alignment between Corporate Commitments to Community Participation and Actual Practices

- *Phase 3A:* Identify the corporation's commitments to community participation.

- *Phase 3B:* Plot departmental/divisional commitments to community participation and corporate commitments to community participation on the Integrity Ladder.
- *Phase 3C:* Apply the Integrity Grid—plot department/division talk and department/division walk regarding community participation on the Integrity Grid (introduced in Chapter 4):
  - *Before* multidepartment brainstorming session on feasible alternatives (reactive)
  - *After* multidepartment brainstorming session on feasible alternatives (proactive)

Phase 4: Identifying, Assessing, and Implementing Best Practices for Community Participation
- *Phase 4A:* Apply the Community Investment Strategy tool.
- *Phase 4B:* Apply the Permeation of Change model.
- *Phase 4C:* Apply the Adapted Best Practices tool.
- *Phase 4D:* Apply the Benchmarking Practices.

Phase 5: Accountability for Community Participation
- *Phase 5A:* Clarify accountabilities with the Business Integrity Accountability Cycle.
- *Phase 5B:* Implement accountability strategy for community participation.
- *Phase 5C:* Develop continuous improvement.

Scenario A:
Applying Business Integrity Tools to a Business Development Opportunity for a European-based Investor in Vietnam, an Emerging Market Economy

Corporate Background

ABC Corporation Ltd. is a European-based company that manufactures and assembles primarily high-tech components used in the automotive industry and is publicly traded on the London and New York stock exchanges. In order to reduce its costs of production, the corporation's business development department has proposed that a new corporate division be established in Vietnam, an emerging market economy, to reduce the cost of goods sold (of which the labor component is 55 percent). The strategic objective of the marketing department is to become the lowest-cost producer in order to maintain market share within the highly competitive industry segment.

ABC Corporation has limited experience with investment in emerging market economies. The majority of its operations are located in Europe and North America, although there are some Asian suppliers for components used in its manufacturing processes. To date, ABC Corporation has not investigated supply chain labor issues in any detail and plans to address these issues on a reactive basis. Some advocacy groups have complained about working conditions for laborers in the factories of ABC Corporation's Asian suppliers, but advocacy groups have not complained directly to the headquarters of ABC Corporation.

The corporation has a good reputation with European and North American governments and seeks to maintain this reputation. In order to appear to be responsive to the European Union government priorities for companies operating abroad, ABC has recently committed to principles for international operations, including commitments to human rights and standards for labor, environment, health, and safety. The company has expressly stated in its Principles and Code of Conduct that corruption is not condoned and that all laws (including labor practices) will be respected.

ABC Corporation generally does not consider that it has a responsibility to build local community infrastructure capacity in developing countries. By "keeping its own nose clean," ABC Corporation believes the company can be a good corporate citizen and model best practices. The company is aware of anti-corruption laws, but does not have an employee training program in place.

Evaluation and Decision-Making Framework for Managing Business Integrity

Navigating Frontier 1 in Corporate Integrity: Understanding Perspectives Related to the Integrity of Corporations

Navigating Frontier 1 requires that the following questions be addressed:

- Do corporations truly care about stakeholders or is integrity merely a public relations exercise?

- How can corporate stakeholders measure integrity?

Phase 1: Establish the Business Integrity Baseline in ABC Corporation
- *Phase 1A:* Assessing integrity commitments and actions (historical) of individual departments within ABC Corporation in relation to the Vietnam investment opportunity.
- *Phase 1B:* Applying the Integrity Ladder analysis to ABC Corporation.

Phase 1A: Assessing Integrity Commitments and Actions (Historical) of Individual Departments within ABC Corporation

The following vignettes provide insight into the integrity commitments and actions of individual departments of ABC:

Business Development: The last time that the business development department at ABC Corporation recommended that the corporation invest in an emerging market jurisdiction (Romania), senior management was very frustrated by the lengthy time (two years) it took to conclude the investment transaction. The business development department did not clearly communicate to other departments that twenty-four months of lead time was required to negotiate the manufacturing contracts and to establish operations in Romania. Senior management ultimately withdrew the funds budgeted for the Romanian investment and applied the monies to an opportunity in another European country. The business development manager responsible for the proposal to invest in Romania was not officially demoted, but now supports nonpriority projects and is contemplating other employment offers.

Operations: The operations department believes that application of patented corporate processes to manufacturing of component parts in Vietnam will create operational efficiencies and reduce vulnerability to third-party suppliers. There are concerns that the host government in Vietnam may not strictly enforce copyright and patent laws, thus potentially compromising the corporation's patented processes. The operations department intends to pressure the government of Vietnam to ensure that these patents are protected, as release of this patented information and corporate manufacturing know-how may compromise corporate competitiveness. The operations department intends to comply, to the extent that laws are clear, with anti-corruption laws to which the corporation is subject in the European community and in Vietnam.

Finance: Operating and labor costs to produce less sophisticated components in Vietnam would be cheaper than producing the products in Europe or North America. However, managers in the finance department have niggling concerns about Vietnam's reputation for corruption. They recommend that the corporation consider adopting a policy in Vietnam of not paying facilitating payments, which finance defines as relatively small payments, much like restaurant tips, paid to government employees to expedite administrative decisions and paperwork.

Even if facilitating payments are legal, the finance department wants to demonstrate internal leadership in corporate commitment to combat corruption and to reduce the risk that employees wrongfully make any payments that could be construed as bribes.

Legal: Due diligence checks with Transparency International and other advocacy groups focused on business integrity issues suggest that there are some concerns with corruption and judicial independence in Vietnam.

Although there are foreign investment laws in place, these laws are relatively untested in the emerging Vietnamese judicial systems. ABC Corporation's legal department questions whether the judicial system in Vietnam can enforce the laws that concern ABC Corporation. Thus, the legal department strongly recommends adopting a very clear business integrity strategy and internal training to ensure that ABC Corporation does not contribute to a corrupt business environment in Vietnam.

Human Resources: Managers in ABC Corporation's human resources department are very concerned about managing personnel in an emerging market economy. Imported skilled labor may be required in Vietnam for the first few years to ensure quality products. At the same time, building local capacity in Vietnam is a priority for many local stakeholders.

The human resources department encourages the other ABC departments to apply the same labor standards in Vietnam as applied to the corporation's operations in Europe, even if additional costs may erode corporate competitiveness.

Environment, Health, and Safety: The environment, health, and safety managers are keen to produce the lower-cost materials and assembly components in Vietnam as environmental requirements are less stringent than in Europe. Water handling is needed for process cooling and is a costly and environmentally sensitive process in European plants. The more "flexible" environmental requirements set out in the contracts and laws of Vietnam will be much easier and cheaper to satisfy.

Investor Relations: The number of European corporations investing in Vietnam is relatively small and the investor relations department is uncertain of market reaction to an investment in this emerging market economy. Further, the investor relations group has concerns about corruption in Vietnam: Will perceptions of corruption cloud investor confidence in ABC Corporation as a whole? The investor relations department would prefer to keep the investment in Vietnam off the investor "radar screen" as long as possible.

Government Relations: The government relations department believes that ABC Corporation should consider the effects of these international operations with reference to voluntary integrity commitments made by the industry within the European Union and legal integrity requirements by governments in the European Union.

Security: The security department believes that ensuring security of personnel and property will be manageable in Vietnam. The security department intends to hire local "enforcers" to protect the company's people and property. However, the security department believes that ensuring the integrity of intellectual property in Vietnam may be challenging.

Phase 1B: Plotting ABC Corporation's Departments on the Integrity Ladder

The Integrity Ladder business tool was introduced and explained in Chapter 2.

Using the insights in the short vignettes provided for each department, intended integrity commitments in relation to the Vietnam project are assessed for each department and plotted on the Integrity Ladder under the heading "Integrity Commitment."

In order to create this baseline, there is a need to refer to historical departmental practices. Thus, individual departments' historical practices in other projects (for example, individual departmental actions in the Romanian project) are considered and plotted on the Integrity Ladder under the final column "Integrity Action (Historical)," as follows:

INTEGRITY LADDER RUNG	PRIMARY MOTIVATION	INTEGRITY COMMITMENT	INTEGRITY ACTION (HISTORICAL)
10	Future generations		
9	Sustainable positive social impact		
8	Leverage budget to achieve positive social impact	*Human resources:* Seek international application of labor standards (no dual standards) and prioritize local capacity building	*Human resources:* consistent in motivation and practice
7	Leverage budget to do no harm	*Legal:* Mandate policy/training to avoid corrupt business practices	
6	Compliance, plus proactive risk management	*Finance:* Recommend practice of no facilitating payments	*Finance:* Generally adopt a proactive approach *Legal:* A somewhat proactive approach in other operations
5	Compliance with rules	*Operations:* Intend to comply with laws and policies	*Operations:* complies with local laws
4	Reputation and reactive risk management	*Investor relations and government relations:* Will make integrity commitments if pressured	*Operations:* Romania project was reactive to risks, not proactive *Investor relations and government relations:* Reputation focus

		Environment, health, and safety: Dual standards in environmental practices	Environment, health, and safety: Always regard international operations as minimum compliance standards
3	Minimum legal compliance		
2	Avoid being caught with "dirty hands"	Security: Intends to hire enforcers to do "dirty work"	Security: Has hired agents in past
1	Avoid jail		
0	Self-preservation		

The Integrity Ladder baseline assessment shows there are significant differences within ABC Corporation with regard to integrity commitments and integrity action. Departments' commitments to integrity and responses in practice range from rung 2 (the weakest link) to rung 8. Further in-depth analysis would likely identify any gaps between walk and talk within individual departments.

Navigating Frontier 2: Defining the Proper Role of Corporations

To navigate Frontier 2 in business integrity the following questions are posed:

The external corporate stakeholder asks: What do I expect of this corporate investor?

The internal corporate stakeholder asks: What do stakeholders expect of our corporation? Does our corporation have the motivation and capacity to effectively respond to these stakeholder expectations?

Phase 2: Identify Stakeholders, Assess Stakeholder Impacts, Anticipate Stakeholder Expectations of a Corporation, Identify Potential Dilemmas

Phase 2A: Applying the Stakeholder Grid and Impact Assessment tool to the project in Vietnam.

Phase 2B: Anticipating stakeholders' expectations of ABC Corporation and potential dilemmas arising from project impacts and stakeholders' expectations.

Phase 2C: Creating opportunity for innovation with multidepartment brainstorming to identify feasible alternatives

Phase 2A: Applying the Stakeholder Grid and Impact Assessment Tool

The Stakeholder Grid and Impact Assessment tool is introduced and explained in Chapter 3.

ABC Corporation must first identify its key stakeholders in the Vietnam project and list these stakeholders in the grid. Specifically, it is necessary to identify who is affected by this project or has the motivation and ability to affect the project.

In general, once key project stakeholders are identified, an assessment is made to determine the potential impacts of the project to and by these stakeholders (positive and negative impacts). The magnitude and range of potential impacts is assessed and quantified in the assessment tool.

In order to ensure a comprehensive stakeholder identification and assessment process, ABC Corporation should ensure that this tool has inputs from multiple disciplines and corporate departments. Independent expertise should be sought if the company does not have internal expertise to assess the potential impacts.

SHAREHOLDER GROUPS	TYPES OF IMPACT				
	REPUTATION	PHYSICAL ASSETS (HARM OR LOSS)	PERSONNEL (HARM OR LOSS)	TIMELINES	SHARE VALUE
ABC corporate	−5 to +5	0	0	−5 to +5	−5 to +5
Employees supporting Vietnam project (by individual departments; local and head office)	−5 to +5	0 to +3	0 to +5	−5 to +5	−5 to +5
Media	−4 to +4	0	0	0	−4 to +4
Regulators	0	0	0	−5 to +5	0
Investors	−5 to +5	0	0	0	−5 to +5
Insurers/lenders	−3 to +3	0	0	0	−3 to +3
Customers	−5 to +5	0	0	−3 to +3	−5 to +5
Suppliers	−5 to +5	0	0	−5 to +5	−5 to +5
Advocacy NGOs	−5 to +3	−3 to 0	0	−4 to 0	−5 to +3

SHAREHOLDER GROUPS	TYPES OF IMPACT				
	REPUTATION	PHYSICAL ASSETS (HARM OR LOSS)	PERSONNEL (HARM OR LOSS)	TIMELINES	SHARE VALUE
Partners	−4 to +4	0	0	−5 to +5	−4 to +4
Agents	−4 to +4	0	0	−5 to +5	−4 to +4
Host communities	−4 to +4	−5 to +5	−5 to +5	−5 to +5	−4 to +4
Host government	−4 to +4	−4 to +4	−5 to +5	−5 to +5	−4 to +4
E.U. governments	−4 to +4	0	0	0	−4 to +4

Impact Assessment Scale: −5 = most negative impact potential
                                      0   = no impact
                                    +5   = most positive impact potential

The Stakeholder Grid and Impact Assessment tool must evaluate both the stakeholders' motivation and capability of causing the identified impact to the corporate project.

Further analysis and details can be incorporated into relevant parts of the matrix to clarify the magnitude of the harmful action. For example, harm or loss to personnel could include a range of impacts from personal injury, detention, kidnapping, and homicide; impacts to physical assets could include theft, sabotage, destruction of assets, or other types of infrastructure impacts that are unique to a business operation or operating environment.

Reputation impacts can be further refined to identify a variety of triggers, for example: lack of transparency, corruption, unfair sharing of benefits, environmental degradation, social/cultural impacts, discrimination, human rights abuses, or Aboriginal interests.

Share value impacts can be assessed over various timelines: immediate, monthly, financial quarter, annual, life of the project, three to five years, or longer term. Impacts to timelines can be charted against the project timeline.

Phase 2B: Anticipating Stakeholders' Expectations of ABC Corporation and Potential Dilemmas Arising from Project Impacts and Stakeholders' Expectations

Beyond the identification of key project stakeholders and the assessment of potential impacts of a project on the key stakeholders, the Stakeholder Grid and Impact Assessment tool provides a strategic starting point in anticipating and ultimately reconciling corporate responses to stakeholders' expectations of ABC Corporation in this endeavor. To the extent that key stakeholders' expectations of ABC Corporation in this project are not aligned, there is a dilemma that the corporate management team will likely encounter.

It is not possible to anticipate every possible dilemma. However, having an appreciation of the potential dilemmas that ABC Corporation may face will allow corporate managers to proactively ensure that decision-making systems and processes are in place to foster a strategic and even proactive corporate response.

The following three potential dilemmas can be identified by ABC Corporation in this process by examining the range of project impacts to key stakeholders and considering stakeholders' expectations (internal and external stakeholders) of ABC Corporation.

Potential Dilemma A-1: Differing Perspectives on ABC Corporation's Role in Advocating for Transparent Business Practices and Enforcement of Laws in Vietnam

In assessing various stakeholder impacts of this project, several potential impacts are linked to corruption risks in Vietnam. These impacts are particularly acute for certain corporate stakeholder groups—advocacy groups, media, and investors.

Internal stakeholders (including the individual departments within ABC Corporation) have differing perspectives on corruption and ABC

Corporation's role in advocating for transparency and enforcement of laws in Vietnam. The range of internal stakeholder perspectives on ABC Corporation's preferred role in advocating for transparent business practices in Vietnam is reflected in the following positions:

- *ABC Corporation's security department:* Maintain corporate competitive edge by using agents to enforce patent protection and intellectual property.

- *ABC Corporation's finance department:* Declare a policy of no facilitating payments as a means of mitigating risk.

- *ABC Corporation's operations department:* Demand that the Vietnamese government enforce its patent laws as a condition of the investment.

- *ABC Corporation's legal department:* Proactively support advocacy against corruption in partnership with Transparency International.

Potential Dilemma A-2: Different Perspectives on the Role of ABC Corporation in Supply Chain Issues

Historically, ABC Corporation has not concerned itself with supply chain issues. However, the Stakeholder Impact and Assessment tool and process reflects that some of the corporation's stakeholders (internal and external) identify supply chain–related impacts resulting from ABC Corporation's Vietnam project. For example, advocacy groups' concerns about the labor practices of Asian suppliers used by ABC Corporation are anticipated in this assessment. Clearly, there are links to the corporate reputation, which can affect financial performance and market capitalization.

Corporate stakeholders recognize that while the company is concerned with its environmental practices in Europe and North America, there is no monitoring or reporting of its Asian suppliers' environmental practices. An investment in Vietnam is expected to raise the risks of ABC Corporation being associated with supply chain issues, thereby raising the potential for impacts to reputation and financial outcomes.

The internal perspectives on the possible role of ABC Corporation regarding supply chain management are quite wide-ranging and include the following perspectives:

- *ABC Corporation's investor relations department:* Continue to ignore such issues until forced to react as a result of a direct attack on ABC Corporation's reputation.

- *ABC Corporation's human resources department:* Use the investment in a Vietnamese manufacturing plant as a means of emulating best labor and environmental practices.

- *ABC Corporation's environmental department:* Continue to apply local standards and do not rock the boat in the Vietnamese manufacturing sector by applying international labor and environmental standards.

Potential Dilemma A-3: Different Stakeholder Perspectives on the Role of ABC Corporation in Building Local Capacity and Balancing Stakeholder Expectations

The Stakeholder Impact and Assessment Tool identifies a range of stakeholder impacts for this project that relate to sharing in the benefits of the investment.

ABC Corporation must determine the composition of its labor force and local suppliers in Vietnam. To ensure quality products, expatriate workers may be required, but local Vietnamese communities will want to benefit from the investment by ABC Corporation and likely expect training benefits, supply contracts, and service contracts.

ABC Corporation's stakeholder impacts will be significantly influenced by the company's strategy in responding to local expectations for sharing project benefits—in particular, local access to training and jobs. In responding to this anticipated dilemma, the departments of ABC Corporation see two mutually exclusive strategic choices for ABC Corporation:

- Emphasize the financial cost/benefit analysis with a focus on the ABC Corporation share price, ignore the local community, and ignore the local Vietnamese community priorities and expectations until the plant is profitable, *or*

- Engage local communities in up-front dialogue on their priorities and capabilities, with a proactive view to building local capacity.

Either choice has significant downside risk.

Phase 2C: Creating Opportunity for Innovation with Multidepartment Brainstorming to Identify Feasible Alternatives

ABC Corporation decided that a multidisciplinary, multidepartment task force could help to deal with the growing number of anticipated dilemmas arising from the range of stakeholder impacts anticipated in this project, and the wide range of stakeholder expectations (internal and external) of the corporation's role in responding to identified issues.

The terms of reference for this multidisciplinary task force included consideration of stakeholder impacts and brainstorming feasible strategies for management of anticipated dilemmas.

Multidisciplinary Task Force Analysis of Potential Dilemma A-1: The Role of ABC Corporation in Advocating Transparent Business Practices and Enforcement of Laws in Vietnam

Guided by additional information on ABC Corporation's integrity values and commitments, the multidisciplinary task force agrees that the following alternatives for ABC Corporation are feasible responses to this dilemma:

- Establish guidelines and practices to ensure that agents are not used by the company's security department or others to do ABC Corporation's dirty work. All Vietnamese and European laws must be respected.

- Create a finance subcommittee to evaluate the feasibility of a policy of no facilitating payments to mitigate risk, based on consultation with other corporations and key people in the legal and operations departments.

- Discuss means to work collaboratively with other foreign investors in Vietnam to ensure that patents, know-how, and other intellectual property are respected by meeting with appropriate Vietnamese business leaders, government leaders, and other companies operating in Vietnam. These discussions would stress the financial impact to foreign investors if patents, confidential information, or intellectual property were violated.

- Ensure that all employees of ABC Corporation respect the applicable laws and corporate policy governing business practices and evaluate ways to work with others to influence against corruption. However, due to budget constraints at ABC Corporation, senior managers decide that costs to participate in any advocacy work on corruption must be minimal.

Multidisciplinary Task Force Analysis of Potential Dilemma A-2: Define ABC Corporation's Response to Supply Chain Issues

Although ABC Corporation has not historically concerned itself with supply chain issues, it realizes that due diligence is required to better understand the issues and risks. As well, the senior managers of ABC Corporation must decide if the environmental and labor practices adopted for Europe are to be applied to international operations.

As an outcome of these discussions, the multidisciplinary task force recommends implementing all the following policies and tactics:

- Create corporate guidelines recommending how due diligence on all suppliers is to be conducted based on defined criteria. Suppliers will be expected to comply with the same integrity commitments as ABC Corporation as reflected in ABC Corporation's codes and guidelines. Discussions with suppliers will be prioritized to ensure their understanding of these integrity commitments and the consequences of breaches in practice.

- In communications with all internal and external stakeholders, ABC Corporation will clarify that its reputation is international, as behaviors in one division affect the corporate reputation worldwide.

- To ensure that its activities are consistent with sound environmental management and conservation practices on a global basis, ABC Corporation will examine water effluent practices in Vietnam to assess how practices need to be modified to be consistent with sound environmental practices and associated costs will be incorporated into the project analysis. The corporation will also evaluate its commitments on environment and labor practices to assess its intention and ability to commit to universal standards. In this evaluation, best practices of competitors throughout the world will be considered.

Multidisciplinary Task Force Analysis of Potential Dilemma A-3: How Will the Company Reconcile Competing Expectations for Local Benefits?

The multidisciplinary task force agrees that the company's stakeholder consultation methods for international operations need to be adapted to incorporate local inputs. As well, local expectations must be managed.

To this end, the multidisciplinary task force recommends that ABC Corporation engage local communities in up-front dialogue on their priorities and capabilities on building local capacity. Through this direct engagement, the newly appointed managing director (Vietnam) can better evaluate local skills and costs. To the extent that foreign expatriates are required in start-up to train locals, expectations should be clarified.

Navigating Frontier 3: Aligning Corporate Integrity Values, Talk, and Walk

In order to navigate Frontier 3 in business integrity, the following questions are posed:

The external corporate stakeholder asks: What do you intend by your commitment to integrity? How do you create, assess, and manage alignment between corporate commitments with integrity and actual corporate practices?

The internal corporate stakeholder asks: What is our corporate commitment to integrity? How do we create, manage, and assess ongoing alignment between our corporate commitments and our corporate actions?

Phase 3: Create, Manage, and Assess Alignment between Corporate Commitments with Business Integrity and Actual Practices

Phase 3A: Identifying corporate talk on business integrity in ABC Corporation.

Phase 3B: Plotting departmental integrity talk and corporate integrity talk on the Integrity Ladder for ABC Corporation.

Phase 3C: Applying the the Integrity Grid—plot departmental integrity talk and departmental integrity walk on the Integrity Grid:
- *Before* best alternative tactics decision
- *After* best alternative tactics decision

Phase 3 involves application of the Integrity Ladder and the Integrity Grid. The Integrity Ladder is introduced and discussed in Part 1: Chapter 2, and the Integrity Grid is introduced and discussed in Part 1: Chapter 4.

Phase 3A: Identifying ABC Corporation's Corporate Commitments to Business Integrity That May Be Relevant to the Three Identified Integrity Dilemmas

The multidisciplinary task force within ABC Corporation established to address integrity dilemmas anticipated in relation to the Vietnam project identifies the following relevant corporate principles and values:

- ABC Corporation has publicly declared support for business integrity principles that apply to the corporation's international operations in a Code of Business Conduct.

  The vision of the company's internal code is values based. Specifically, ABC Corporation acknowledges in writing that: its business has a global presence that is recognized by all stakeholders as economically rewarding to all parties; acknowledges being ethically, socially, and environmentally responsible, welcomed by the communities in which it operates; and that the company facilitates economic, human resource, and community development within a stable operating environment.

- The code enumerates key values commitments, including commitments to labor standards, human rights, environment standards, health standards, and safety standards.

- Corporate management and accountability structures require that employees report violations of corporate policy and integrity commitments to their supervisors.

- Corporate practices to guide corporate conduct are extensive, but are not necessarily consistent. Guidelines are issued by individual departments and frequently overlap in content.

- Stakeholder engagement and community investment and participation guidelines for international operations have not yet been designed. The corporation has extensive guidelines for European operations, but the applicability to international operations is not yet clear.

- Pertinent industry-wide guidelines are generally assumed by the company to apply to European operations only.

Beyond corporate commitments, the legal department has identified applicable legislation and guidelines (European, Vietnamese, and OECD) and has enumerated legal commitments. These commitments include anti-corruption laws, reporting obligations, competition laws, labor codes, financial and tax laws, corporate laws, and commercial laws.

Phase 3B: Plotting the Departmental Integrity Talk and Corporate Integrity Talk on the Integrity Ladder

In Phase 3B, the objective is to identify alignments and gaps between the corporation's commitments to integrity and the commitments of individual departments within ABC Corporation. Using the Integrity Ladder, applied as set out below, the corporation's integrity commitments are identified in the column "Integrity Commitments (as a Corporation)" and individual departments' commitments are plotted in the column "Integrity Commitments (Individual Departments)."

In order to identify the corporation's integrity commitments, refer back to the outcomes of Phase 3A. In order to identify individual departments' integrity commitments, refer to the integrity commitments previously plotted on the Integrity Ladder for each department as set out in Phase 1B.

INTEGRITY LADDER RUNG	PRIMARY MOTIVATION	INTEGRITY COMMITMENTS (INDIVIDUAL DEPARTMENTS)	INTEGRITY COMMITMENTS (AS A CORPORATION)
10	Future generations		
9	Sustainable positive social impact		
8	Leverage budget to achieve positive social impact	*Human resources:* Seek international application of labor standards (no dual standards) and prioritize local capacity building	ABC Corporation
7	Leverage budget to do no harm	*Legal:* Strategy to ensure no corporate contribution to corruption	ABC Corporation
6	Compliance, plus proactive risk management	*Finance:* Recommend practice of no facilitating payments	
5	Compliance with rules	*Operations:* Intend to comply with law and policy	
4	Reputation and reactive risk management	*Investor relations and government relations:* Will make commitments if pressured	

continued

INTEGRITY LADDER RUNG	PRIMARY MOTIVATION	INTEGRITY COMMITMENTS (INDIVIDUAL DEPARTMENTS)	INTEGRITY COMMITMENTS (AS A CORPORATION)
3	Minimum legal compliance	*Environment, health, and safety:* Dual standards in environmental practices are acceptable	
2	Avoid being caught with "dirty hands"	*Security:* Intends to hire "enforcers" to do dirty work	
1	Avoid jail		
0	Self-preservation		

Plotting corporate and departmental integrity commitments on the Integrity Ladder clearly shows the wide gaps in integrity commitments among individual corporate departments, and the wide gaps between the corporation as a whole and individual departments. Although ABC Corporation has written integrity commitments that could be responsive to the dilemmas identified in the Vietnam project, organizational alignment with these commitments is very inconsistent. Thus, there are significant integrity gaps.

Phase 3C: Plotting Departmental Integrity Commitments, Departmental Integrity Actions, and Corporate Integrity Commitments on Integrity Grid

In order to assess the integrity alignment (and gaps) between departments within ABC Corporation, and to identify alignment (and gaps) between individual departments and the organization as a whole, Phase 3C uses the Integrity Grid tool to plot individual departmental commitments and actions.

Plotting individual departmental commitments and actions on integrity is done twice in this phase to reflect differences between proactive and reactive business integrity management practices.

The first plotting is done on the basis of departmental positions prior to the multidisciplinary brainstorming on feasible options (Phase 1 Integrity Ladder outcomes). This plotting reflects the state of ABC Corporation's department integrity commitments and actions in a *reactive mode*.

The second plotting is done on the basis of departmental positions after the multidisciplinary brainstorming on feasible options (Phase 2 Stakeholder and Dilemma Analysis outcomes). This second plotting reflects the state of ABC Corporation's departmental integrity commitments and actions in a *proactive* mode.

First Plotting on Integrity Grid: Departmental Commitments and Departmental Actions *before* Stakeholder Grid and Impact Assessment Process

Overall corporate and the individual departmental commitments and actions are considered based on the discussion set out in Phase 1 of this process, and depicted on the grid as follows:

	CODE	COMMITMENT	ACTIONS	DEPARTMENT INTERNAL GAP (DEPARTMENT ACTIONS MINUS DEPARTMENT COMMITMENT)	CORPORATE DEPARTMENT GAP (DEPARTMENT COMMITMENT MINUS CORPORATE COMMITMENT)
Overall corporate	C	7	—	—	—
Individual departments:					
Security	S	2	2	0	-5
Environment, health, and safety	EHS	3	3	0	-4
Investor relations	IR	4	4	0	-3
Government relations	GR	4	4	0	-3
Operations	O	4	5	+1	-3
Finance	F	6	6	0	-1
Legal	L	6	7	+1	-1
Human resources	HR	8	8	0	+1

To achieve alignment between individual departmental commitments and actions, the preferred department internal gap is zero for the column "Department Internal Gap (Actions Minus Commitment)." There are five departments within ABC Corporation that have alignment in their own departmental commitments and actions. Two departments (operations and legal) have variances where the alignment gap is not significant—in both cases, the departmental practices exceed the rung of the Integrity Ladder of ˙ departmental commitments. Operations and legal departments in the company are exceeding their stated department's commitments.

The data in the chart above (which is based on Phase 1 Integrity Ladder inputs) is plotted on the Integrity Grid to depict the following:

- Corporate Talk Line (ABC Corporation's overall commitments to integrity, based on Phase 3B plotting)

- Equal Alignment Line (a 45-degree reference line that reflects equal alignment of departmental talk and walk)

- Plot intersection of individual departmental commitments and actions

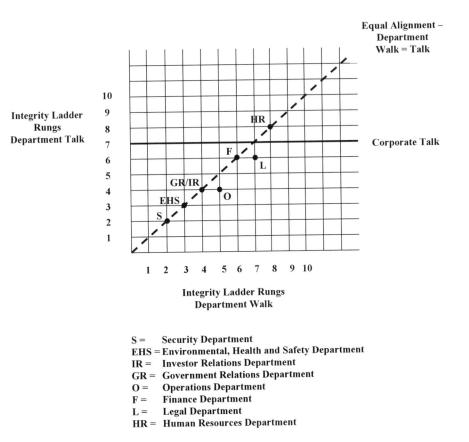

S =   Security Department
EHS = Environmental, Health and Safety Department
IR =   Investor Relations Department
GR =   Government Relations Department
O =   Operations Department
F =   Finance Department
L =   Legal Department
HR = Human Resources Department

Observations from the Integrity Grid Plotting Exercise

Security: Although the security department is aligned in its departmental commitments and practices, the department's level of commitment and actions (rung 2) is not aligned with the organization's integrity commitments (rung 7). This department is one of the company's weakest links and should be a priority for action within the organization.

Environment, health, and safety: This department's commitments and actions are marginally stronger than the security department. However, there is a wide disparity between this department's commitments and actions (rung 3) and the commitments of the organization (rung 7). Given this differential between departmental commitments/actions and corporation commitments, this department should also be identified as a weak link requiring attention.

Investor relations and government relations: These two departments' integrity commitments and actions are at rung 4; this is inconsistent with the corporate commitment to rung 7.

Operations: The operations department commits to rung 4 in integrity performance, but performs at rung 5. This misalignment in departmental commitments and actions should be addressed. As well, the department's commitments/actions are several levels lower than the organizational level of commitment.

Finance: The finance department is aligned in its commitments and actions at rung 6, very close to the organizational commitment level. With some additional focus, this department could be aligned with the organizational expectations.

Legal: This department commits to integrity at rung 6, but its practices are at rung 7 in alignment with overall corporate commitments. By refining the legal departmental commitments, this department could achieve alignment within the department between commitments and actions, and alignment of commitments and actions with the organization's expectations.

Human resources: The human resources department is at rung 8 in its departmental commitments and actions, but the department's integrity commitments and practices are higher than the overall corporate level of commitment. This higher level of performance could be quite misleading to external stakeholders, raising expectations of corporate commitments and practices and exacerbating differences within the corporation as a whole between integrity commitments and practices. This department's integrity commitments and practices should be adjusted downwards to align with the overall corporate commitments at rung 7.

Second Plotting on Integrity Grid: Departmental Commitments and Departmental Actions *after* Stakeholder Grid and Impact Assessment Process

The second plotting is done on the basis of departmental positions after the multidisciplinary brainstorming on feasible options (Phase 2 Stakeholder and Dilemma Analysis outcomes). This second plotting reflects the state of ABC Corporation's integrity commitments and actions in a *proactive* mode for each department.

Individual department commitments and actions are considered based on the discussion set out in Phase 2 of this process, and depicted on the grid as follows:

To achieve alignment between individual departmental commitments and actions, the preferred department internal gap is zero for the column "Department Internal Gap (Actions Minus Commitment)."

	CODE	COMMITMENT	ACTIONS	DEPARTMENT INTERNAL GAP (DEPARTMENT ACTIONS MINUS DEPARTMENT COMMITMENT)	CORPORATE DEPARTMENT GAP (DEPARTMENT COMMITMENT MINUS CORPORATE COMMITMENT)
Overall corporate	C	7	—	—	—
Individual departments:					
Security	S	5	5	0	-2

continued

	CODE	COMMITMENT	ACTIONS	DEPARTMENT INTERNAL GAP (DEPARTMENT ACTIONS MINUS DEPARTMENT COMMITMENT)	CORPORATE DEPARTMENT GAP (DEPARTMENT COMMITMENT MINUS CORPORATE COMMITMENT)
Environment, health, and safety	EHS	4	4	0	-3
Investor relations	IR	4	4	0	-3
Government relations	GR	4	4	0	-3
Operations	0	5	5	0	-2
Finance	F	6	6	0	-1
Legal	L	7	7	0	0
Human resources	HR	7	7	0	0

On the basis of processes set out in Phase 3B of this framework, the legal and operations departments have achieved internal alignment in their commitments and actions. This is a very critical and positive first step in building alignment in business integrity and reducing gaps.

Beyond achieving alignment in individual departmental actions and commitments, some of the departments within ABC Corporation have also moved up the Integrity Ladder:

- The security department has moved from rung 2 to rung 5, a substantial improvement.

- The environment, health, and safety department has moved up only one rung to rung 4, and remains one of the organization's weakest links, which is likely to attract unwanted attention from critics.

- The investor relations and government relations departments remain unchanged at rung 4.

- The operations department has aligned its commitments to be consistent with its actions at rung 5.

- The finance department is unchanged at rung 6.

- The legal and human resources departments have become aligned with the organizational level of integrity commitment at rung 7, a commendable objective.

The first priority was to identify misalignments within individual departments between commitments and actions. The next priority was to work within the individual departments to achieve alignment between the departmental commitments, departmental actions, and the overall corporate commitments.

The data in the chart above (which is based on Phase 2 Stakeholder Impact and Dilemma Analysis outcomes) is plotted on the Integrity Grid to depict the following:

- Corporate Talk Line (ABC Corporation's commitments to integrity based on Phase 3B plotting)

- Equal Alignment Line (a 45-degree reference line that reflects equal alignment of departmental talk and walk)

- Plot intersection of individual departmental commitments and actions

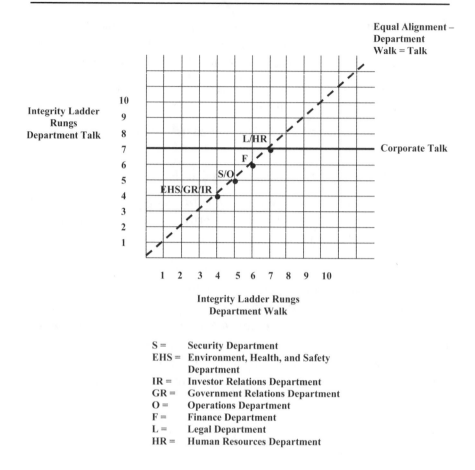

S =   Security Department
EHS =   Environment, Health, and Safety
         Department
IR =   Investor Relations Department
GR =   Government Relations Department
O =   Operations Department
F =   Finance Department
L =   Legal Department
HR =   Human Resources Department

Observations from the Second Integrity Grid Plotting Exercise

Security: This department must still work to reach the organizational commitment level at rung 7, but has moved significantly from its earlier position as the weakest link through proactive management practices.

Environment, health, and safety: Proactive management practices moved this department up one rung on the Integrity Ladder, but the department still has work to do to reach rung 7.

Investor relations and government relations: Proactive business strategies did little to alter the practices of these two departments.

Operations: Proactive practices created alignment between the department's commitments and actions.

Finance: Proactive management practices caused no change within this group.

Legal: This department is a star performing group. Through proactive business practices, the department aligned its commitments and actions and also achieved alignment with the organizational level of commitment to integrity. This department is qualified to speak for the company.

Human resources: Proactive management practices supported the human resources department in bringing its departmental commitments in line with the company as a whole. Commitments and actions at a departmental level were reduced by a level to rung 7. Although it is commendable that the department has high ethical aspirations, it is challenging for the organization to have individuals or departments that are overcommitting and overperforming. This can be misleading. This department is now qualified to speak for the entire organization.

Navigating Frontier 4: Understanding Differences Between Corporations Regarding Corporate Values, Commitments, and Action

To navigate Frontier 4 in business integrity, the following questions are posed:

- What motivates corporate behavior to value integrity? How are these commitments and values manifested in practice?

- What are the differences in corporate motivations in relation to integrity values, commitments, and practices? What are the outcomes of these differences in motivation?

Phase 4: Evaluation and Decision-Making Framework for Business Integrity Management

Using the Permeation of Change model, the Adapted Best Practices tool, and Benchmarking Practices, identify, assess, and implement best practices that will respond to the weakest links within a corporation.

Applying the Permeation of Change model introduced in Chapter 5, ABC Corporation's management team identifies its corporate Initiators, Interesteds, Wait-and-See, Followers, and Non-compliers. Each group is assigned a distinct task in the identification and assessment of best practices:

GROUPS	EFFECTING CHANGE IN BUSINESS INTEGRITY STRATEGY
Initiators: Human resources department	• Manage the risk of Initiators making mistakes of exuberance or overcommitment that affect the company's reputation and/or discourage others • Encourage Initiators to identify/adopt pilot projects and define success criteria to control risks • *Sample initiative:* Explore the possibility of aligning with other investors in an industry association or organization to identify opportunities for collaboration on local capacity building and training opportunities in Vietnam
Interesteds: Legal, finance	• Invite Interesteds to work with Non-compliers on implementation of change to shore up the weakest links • *Sample program:* Legal and finance could work with the environment, health, and safety department to create EHS standards and incorporate them into the corporation's project-risking model and overall enterprise-risking model
Wait-and-Sees: Operations, security	• Wait-and-Sees prioritize opportunity management and are strongly motivated by others • Recommend that Wait-and-See groups proactively monitor evolving stakeholder expectations • *Sample monitoring objective:* The operations department can be responsible for monitoring local stakeholders in Vietnam
Followers: Investor relations, government relations	• Followers groups prioritize risk management • *Sample risking strategy:* Ask these groups to monitor impacts to corporate reputation

Non-compliers: Environment, health, and safety	• Business integrity Non-compliers become the weakest links in an organization and must be prioritized for change
	• Encourage the Interesteds to support the Non-compliers in change. Initiators are not likely to be effective in supporting change within the Non-compliers group
	• *Sample program:* Legal and finance can work with environment, health, and safety to create EHS standards and incorporate into the corporation's project-risking model and overall enterprise-risking model

Next, the ABC Corporation applies the Adapted Best Practices tool in the following stages, as described in Chapter 5.

Stage 1: Identifying business integrity best practices

Stage 2: Assessing best practices based on risk/impact and ease of implementation

Stage 3: Selecting best practices for ABC Corporation and determine implementation tactics

Stage 1: Identifying Business Integrity Best Practices

Based on its analysis of the Integrity Grid outcomes, ABC Corporation recognizes that it will be helpful to evaluate the business integrity best practices of other corporations, preferably competitors and leaders in the sector, in relation to the following key issues:

- ABC Corporation recognizes the need to fund and implement training programs for local personnel. If the corporation determines that environmental practices in its Vietnamese operations are to conform to European standards, additional training costs for local personnel should be anticipated.

- The corporation recognizes the need to enhance its operational capacity to conduct due diligence on agents, suppliers, and partners. Due diligence guidelines must be created and personnel trained to perform these tasks.

- ABC Corporation also acknowledges that there is a wide divergence in understandings within the corporation in managing corporate commitments to business integrity. Some departments ignore the corporate undertakings. Other departments observe but do not fully understand intended corporate consequences. Training internal personnel is identified as a priority. Working with employees and contractors to review scenarios and corporate decision-making processes will increase management's capacity to respond more effectively when dilemmas occur.

- As well, from an operational perspective, ABC Corporation recognizes that the timelines for international operations, particularly in an emerging market like Vietnam, need to be adjusted. ABC Corporation's operational teams in Vietnam and the management team in Europe recognize the need for flexible implementation strategies and realistic expectations in their investment timeframes. Vietnam is an emerging market economy and economic shifts will trigger social and political impacts that must be factored into decision-making and operational strategies and timelines.

Referring back to the Permeation of Change model, the management team then decides to assign different groups within the corporation responsibility for distinct components of the best practices identification and assessment process:

GROUP	TASK
Initiators: Human resources	• Identify emerging and innovative best practices of corporations on the leading edge of business integrity • *Method:* Participate in industry benchmarking initiatives • *Deliverable:* Benchmarking study
Interesteds: Legal, finance	• Identify business integrity best practices of competitors

	• *Method:* Monitor what other manufacturing companies are doing to report on supply chain dilemmas • *Deliverable:* Review of reporting practices of competitors
Wait-and-See: Operations, security	• Proactive monitoring of evolving stakeholder expectations on corporate best practices on business integrity • *Method:* Set up process for engagement with Transparency International and industry associations • *Deliverable:* Report on developments at monthly meetings
Followers: Investor relations, government relations	• Monitor implementation of new company policies • *Method:* Set up quarterly meetings with those in company responsible for due diligence on suppliers and agents in Vietnam • *Deliverable:* Quarterly compliance reports
Non-compliers: Environment, health, and safety	• Force to examine and implement lowest acceptable level and best practices within ABC Corporation • *Method:* Training programs implemented by human resources • *Deliverable:* Mandatory attendance in training

Stage 2: Assessing Best Practices Based on Risk/Impact and Ease of Implementation

Best practices for business integrity must then be assessed and prioritized by corporate management based on the practices' potential impact and ease of implementation for ABC Corporation.

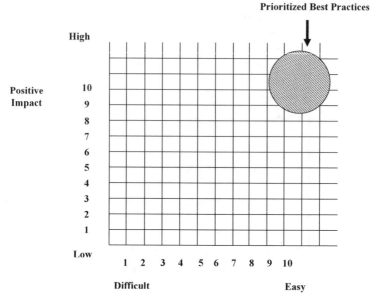

Ease of Implementation

Stage 3: Selecting Best Practices for ABC Corporation and Determine Implementation Tactics

On a corporate-wide basis, ABC Corporation selects three best practices in the upper right quadrant of the grid for implementation. Also, it encourages individual departments or divisions to select best practices for implementation within their groups as "pilots."

Initiators and Interesteds within ABC Corporation are also encouraged to consider best practices that fall outside the High Impact/Ease of Implementation quadrant of the grid. Initiators and Interesteds are encouraged to ask the following questions:

- Are there any best practices with high impact that rank low on implementation? Can the corporation modify implementation approaches to enhance the ease of implementation scoring?

- Are there any best practices with ease of implementation that rank low on impact? Can potential impacts to the company be enhanced through implementation?

Benchmarking Practices

ABC Corporation is evaluating the benefits of participation in a benchmarking survey conducted by a reputable organization in relation to their sector. Internal benchmarking of corporate departments or divisions is also being evaluated.

Navigating Frontier 5: Accountability

Key challenges to be navigated in Frontier 5 are the design and implementation of dependable and strategic corporate accountability systems and processes that manifest integrity values and build trust.

> **Phase 5: Evaluation and Decision-Making Process for Business Integrity Management**
>
> *Phase 5A:* Clarifying accountabilities with the Business Integrity Accountability Cycle
>
> *Phase 5B:* Implementing responsive strategies monitoring outcomes
>
> *Phase 5C:* Improving continuously

Phase 5A: Clarifying Accountabilities with the Business Integrity Accountability Cycle

- Each department or defined group is assigned responsibility for functions within the overall corporate system that manages business integrity.

- Responsibilities are defined within the existing corporate management systems.

- Performance measures and monitoring mechanisms are agreed upon based on outcomes of the Integrity Grid, Permeation of Change model, the Adapted Best Practices tool, and the Benchmarking Practices.

- Verification and reporting structures are agreed upon.

The strategies adopted by ABC Corporation align with the steps along the Business Integrity Accountability Cycle. Work is required to delineate responsibilities for monitoring performance, assessing outcomes, and reporting on these outcomes. The company is evaluating the need to create a business integrity strategy team on an ongoing basis to assume responsibility for setting performance indicators, monitoring accountabilities, and reporting.

Phase 5B: Implementing Responsive Strategies and Monitoring Outcomes

- Implement strategies to address dilemmas/issues.
- Monitor/measure outcomes as described in Chapter 6.
- Measure outcomes on Integrity Grid at defined intervals (at least quarterly).
- Verify and report on outcomes.

Phase 5C: Continuous Improvement

The first priority is to identify misalignments within individual departments between commitments and actions; the next priority is to work within the individual departments to achieve alignment between the department commitments/practices and the organizational commitments.

As stakeholder expectations evolve, the general manager (Vietnam) should immediately report major variances between walk and talk to the senior managers in Europe. The weekly meetings of the managers in Vietnam should highlight any changes in integrity walk. The monthly communications and reports to and from corporate headquarters should identify any needed changes or adjustments related to integrity deficiencies. Further, ABC Corporation could benefit by applying rigorous business integrity analysis used for Vietnam to its other divisions.

Observations for ABC Corporation: Impacts of Reactive or Proactive Management of Business Integrity

Outcomes vary when a corporation decides to adopt a proactive or reactive approach to business integrity management.

If ABC Corporation had applied a reactive approach to this opportunity in Vietnam, the company would not be positioned to:

- recognize the wide gaps in department understandings of corporate business integrity values

- identify the security and environment, health, and safety departments as the weakest links

- identify the impacts of the operations and legal departments misalignment in walk and talk on integrity

- recognize the wide gaps between its corporate talk and corporate walk on integrity

A wait-and-see approach may save money in the short term, but would reduce the benefit of early assessment of dilemmas and adoption of cost-effective and strategic responses.

The corporation's reluctance to proactively report on international operations may trigger a shift in the burden of proof. Limited reporting will not negate the risk of advocacy groups becoming aware of the corporation's specific operations in Vietnam or supply chain dilemmas in other global operations. By failing to proactively report, the corporation allows third parties to make a pre-emptive strike. European governments and other key stakeholders will not be impressed by negative allegations. The corporation might find itself having to defend its reputation and actions.

Corporate personnel, including third-party contractors and agents, may not understand how to manage corruption in Vietnam. Limiting the payment of facilitating payments in Vietnam may not be a practical reality, until effective training of personnel is in place to ensure understanding of best practices to avoid facilitating payments.

The security department's planned methods to reduce the risk of patent infringement are likely to be problematic and may compromise the corporation's reputation. If corruption allegations are made that affect the corporation's global reputation, corporate management may shut down the Vietnam project prematurely.

Negative domino effects could affect the marketing/sales department as ABC Corporation's high-tech automotive products may be less competitive. Moreover, key customers who expect lower-cost components may temper their confidence in ABC's credibility, which will have a negative impact on market share, profitability, earnings per share, and stock price.

Internally, investment timelines are likely to become problematic for the business development team. Corporate management's expectations about investment in an emerging economy have not been well managed. Based on corporate precedent in Romania, the progression of careers within the Vietnam business unit may also be jeopardized.

From a corporate governance perspective, accounting for business integrity is still not well defined. The board of directors and the executive team must depend on the judgment of individuals within the business development and operations units. Given their competencies, these individuals may not be well equipped to discern the breadth and depth of potential integrity dilemmas, and may inadvertently fail to advise superiors on the risks.

Scenario B:
Applying Business Integrity Tools to Private Company Opportunity for a Family Farm Corporation in Canada, a Developed Market Economy

Corporate Background

Family corporations and other private companies are particularly vulnerable to the risk of personality conflicts among key stakeholders on integrity commitments. Frequently, the corporation's founder sets the integrity course. Beyond the founder, the clarification and embedding of integrity commitments at a corporate level can be challenging. Clarifying the integrity expectations on an organizational basis as a supplement to personal relationships reduces the risk of decision making and dilemmas escalating into family and shareholder feuds. Succession of the integrity vision is also a priority with smaller corporations.

Against this generic backdrop, Family Farm Corporation was originally incorporated as a means for Joe White Sr. and his wife, Lily White, to manage their agricultural holdings more effectively, and was largely motivated to generate tax efficiencies. Joe and Lily White have owned farmland in the province of Ontario, Canada, for decades. When their children, Joe Jr. and Anna, expressed interest in farming, shares in the Family Farm Corporation were transferred to Joe Jr. and Anna as a means for the family to clarify roles, responsibilities, and finances in the family farm operations.

Family Farm Corporation has diversified interests, including cash cropping and the management of a beef feedlot. As well, the corporation provides custom contract work for other farmers in the community. More recently, Joe Jr. has been invited to construct and manage a substantial hog operation for a very large consortium that will agree to purchase fattened hogs over a defined contract period.

The family is divided on the investment in the hog operation. Joe Sr. and Lily are satisfied with the current mix of farming pursuits. They are also concerned about how a large hog operation would be accepted by their neighbors and friends. Anna's husband, Michael, is an environmental lawyer and is concerned about an investment in a large, factory-style hog operation. Joe Jr. is excited by the financial upside of a hog management operation and wants to act quickly on the initiative before regional and local laws are revised to preclude such operations.

The four shareholders of Family Farm Corporation meet to discuss the proposal, but consensus cannot be reached. Ultimately, Joe Jr.'s parents support his appeal for this opportunity, and agree that Family Farm Corporation should apply to the county for zoning approvals required to proceed with the construction of a very large hog barn.

Anna objects to this decision, fearing that an intensive livestock operation could become a lightning rod for rural discontent. This important corporate decision risks escalating into a bitter battle between the White siblings.

Evaluation and Decision-Making Process for Managing Business Integrity

Navigating Frontier 1 in Corporate Integrity: Understanding Perspectives Related to the Integrity of Corporations

Navigating Frontier 1 requires that the following questions be addressed:

- Do corporations truly care about stakeholders or is integrity merely a public relations exercise?

- How can corporate stakeholders measure integrity?

Phase 1: Establish the Business Integrity Baseline for Family Farm Corporation

Phase 1A: Assessing integrity commitments and actions (historical) of individual shareholders within Family Farm Corporation

Phase 1B: Applying Integrity Ladder analysis to Family Farm Corporation

Phase 1A: Assessing Integrity Commitments and Actions of Individual Shareholders of Family Farm Corporation

The following vignettes provide insight into the integrity commitments and actions of individual shareholders of the Family Farm Corporation.

Joe White Sr.: Joe White Sr. accepts that family farming is evolving, and that to be globally competitive, traditional farming structures must be responsive. Although he is not interested in personally managing a factory farm, he appreciates that his children may have to accept these emerging farm practices if they wish to earn their livelihood in agricultural pursuits.

Joe White Sr. has always insisted that his farming practices comply with minimum legal standards. However, he has little empathy for nonfarming members of the local community. Land use in the local community has evolved over the years, and many of the Whites' neighbors are hobby farmers and former city dwellers who prefer to live on country acreages. Joe White Sr. has encountered criticism in the past for his abrupt response to these new rural community members who turn up their noses when Joe White Sr. spreads manure from his feedlot onto the Whites' farmland.

Lily White: Lily White has always supported her husband's business decisions, but is sometimes uncomfortable with their family's reputation within the community. Nearly half of the congregation of the local church to which the Whites belong do not farm, and Lily White feels defensive, even apologetic, about the impact of her family's farming operations. Several years have passed since the public health calamity in Walkerton when seven residents of the Ontario town died from drinking E. coli–infected water. More than 2,500 residents became ill, and many of them still struggle with health-related problems. Since this tainted-water catastrophe in the province, Lily White has been vigilant about ensuring that their beef feedlot runoff is kept to a minimum. She is aware that the predictable noise and air pollution generated by their farm expansions are likely to negatively affect the upside potential of land values for residential acreages.

Joe White Jr.: Young and ambitious, Joe White Jr. chose to farm instead of pursuing academics. Prices of cash crops have been volatile, which has resulted in a direct impact on the farm incomes and an indirect impact on custom work opportunities in the area. In order to diversify risk, Joe sees the offer to have access to funding and a market for hogs as a unique window of opportunity. Joe believes that only one such factory hog operation will be approved for construction in their community. He would prefer to profit himself, rather than have one of his competitors build a barn and benefit from this opportunity.

Joe realizes that other farmers are aware of this opportunity, and may try to block approval of the Whites' application for zoning approval. In order to minimize this risk, Joe has talked to the zoning bylaw official and asked for special treatment, as Joe has known the official and his family for years. Joe has tried this tactic with county councils in the past and the practice has proven effective, particularly when the bylaws were not entirely clear on intention.

Anna White: Anna White's passion for farming is focused on the breeding of purebred cattle. Anna is not involved in the cash crop or custom work operations. She has a veterinarian degree and recently married a lawyer practising environmental law.

Anna is supportive of the Family Farm Corporation's farming pursuits, but has always been concerned about compliance with rules and best practices. She is aware that the county's zoning bylaws are not geared to managing factory-farm operations, and believes that the county officials are not sufficiently qualified to conduct an evaluation of the impact of a large hog operation. The bylaws' requirements for environmental assessments are cursory, and Anna is concerned that water aquifers may be negatively affected by the corporation's inability to manage the liquid manure storage tanks required for a large hog operation. Liability is a concern for Anna, and she is motivated to cause no harm, even if it means that barn construction will cost more, or if project delays are required to ensure that risks are thoroughly assessed.

Phase 1B: Plotting Family Farm Corporation's Shareholders on the Integrity Ladder

The Integrity Ladder business tool is introduced and explained in Chapter 2.

Using the insights in the short vignettes provided for each shareholder, individual shareholders' intended integrity commitments in relation to the new project are assessed and plotted on the Integrity Ladder under the heading "Integrity Commitment."

In order to create this baseline, there is a need to refer to historical shareholder actions. Thus, individual shareholder practices in other projects and issues are considered and plotted on the Integrity Ladder under the final column "Integrity Action (Historical)," as follows:

RUNG	PRIMARY MOTIVATION	INTEGRITY COMMITMENT	INTEGRITY ACTION (HISTORICAL)
10	Future generations		
9	Sustainable positive social impact		
8	Leverage budget to achieve positive social impact		
7	Leverage budget to do no harm	Anna White	
6	Compliance plus proactive risk management		
5	Compliance with rules		Anna White

continued

RUNG	PRIMARY MOTIVATION	INTEGRITY COMMITMENT	INTEGRITY ACTION (HISTORICAL)
4	Reputation and reactive risk management	Lily White	Lily White
3	Minimum legal compliance	Joe White Sr.	Joe White Sr. Joe White Jr.
2	Avoid being caught with "dirty hands"	Joe White Jr.	
1	Avoid jail		
0	Self-preservation		

The Integrity Ladder baseline assessment shows there are significant differences within Family Farm Corporation with regard to integrity commitments and integrity practices. Individual shareholders' commitments to integrity and responses in practice range from rung 2 (the weakest link) to rung 7.

Integrity Ladder outcomes suggest that the unique opportunity to invest in a large hog operation has the result of widening perspectives among shareholders. The investment opportunity has exacerbated historical differences in approach taken by the White children. Joe Jr. sees the opportunity as one that may be lost if not pursued vigorously. Anna is concerned about the potential negative impacts and wants risks to be well managed to ensure that no harm will be done.

Navigating Frontier 2: Defining the Proper Role of Corporations

Navigating Frontier 2 requires that the following questions be addressed:

The external corporate stakeholder asks: What do I expect of this corporate investor?

The internal corporate stakeholder asks: What do stakeholders expect of our corporation? Does our corporation have the motivation and capacity to effectively respond to these stakeholder expectations?

Phase 2: Evaluation and Decision-Making Framework for Business Integrity Management, as applied to Family Farm Corporation

Phase 2A: Applying Stakeholder Grid and Impact Assessment tool to new factory-farm project

Phase 2B: Anticipating stakeholders' expectations of Family Farm Corporation and potential dilemmas arising from project impacts and stakeholders' expectations

Phase 2C: Creating opportunity for innovation—shareholder brainstorming to identify feasible alternatives

Phase 2A: Applying Stakeholder Grid and Impact Assessment Tool

The Stakeholder Grid and Impact Assessment tool is introduced and explained in Chapter 3.

Family Farm Corporation must first identify its key stakeholders in the proposed factory-farm project, and list these stakeholders in the grid. *Who is affected by this project, or has the motivation and ability to affect the project?*

Once key project stakeholders are identified, an assessment is made to determine the potential positive and negative impacts of the project to and by these stakeholders. The magnitude and range of potential impacts is assessed and quantified in the assessment tool.

In order to ensure a comprehensive stakeholder identification and assessment process, the company is encouraged to ensure that this tool has inputs from all shareholders. Independent expertise should be sought if the company does not have internal expertise to assess the potential impacts.

STAKEHOLDER GROUPS	TYPES OF IMPACT				
	REPUTATION	PHYSICAL ASSETS (HARM OR LOSS)	PERSONNEL (HARM OR LOSS)	TIMELINES	SHARE VALUE
Family Farm Corporation	−5 to +5	0	0	−5 to +5	−5 to +5
Farm employees	−5 to +5	0 to +5	0 to +5	−5 to +5	−5 to +5
Media	−4 to +4	0	0	−4 to +4	−4 to +4
Regulators	−5 to +5	0	0	−5 to +5	−3 to +3
Investors	−5 to +5	0	0	0	−5 to +5
Insurers/lenders	−3 to +3	0	0	0	−3 to +3
Customers	−3 to +3	0	0	0	−5 to +5
Suppliers	−3 to +3	0	0	−5 to +5	−5 to +5
Advocacy NGOs	−5 to +3	−5 to 0	−2 to 0	−5 to 0	−5 to +3
Partners	−3 to +3	0	0	0	−3 to +3
Agents	0	0	0	0	0
Host communities	−5 to +5	−5 to +2	−2 to 0	−5 to +5	−5 to +5
Provincial government	−3 to +3	0	0	−3 to +3	−3 to +3
County council	−4 to +4	0	0	−4 to +4	−4 to + 4

Impact Assessment Scale: −5 = most negative impact potential
                              0 = no impact
                             +5 = most positive impact potential

The Stakeholder Grid and Impact Assessment tool must evaluate both the key stakeholders' motivation and capability to cause the identified impact to the corporate factory-farm project.

Further analysis can be incorporated into relevant parts of the matrix to clarify the magnitude of the harmful action. For example, impacts to physical assets could include theft, sabotage, destruction of assets, or other types of infrastructure impacts that are unique to a business operation or operating environment. Reputation impacts can be further refined to identify a variety of triggers, for example: lack of transparency, corruption, unfair sharing of benefits, environmental degradation, social/cultural impacts, discrimination, human rights abuses, and Aboriginal interests. Share value impacts can be assessed over various timelines: immediate, monthly, financial quarter, annual, life of the project, three to five years, or longer term. Impacts to timelines can be considered against the project timeline.

Phase 2B: Anticipating Stakeholders' Expectations of Family Farm Corporation and Potential Dilemmas Arising from Project Impacts and Stakeholders' Expectations

Beyond the identification of key project stakeholders and the assessment of potential project impacts on the key stakeholders, the Stakeholder Grid and Impact Assessment tool provides a strategic starting point in anticipating and ultimately reconciling corporate responses to stakeholders' expectations of Family Farm Corporation in this endeavor. To the extent that key stakeholders' expectations of Family Farm Corporation in this project are not aligned, there is room for a dilemma that the corporate management team will have to manage.

Not all dilemmas can be anticipated. However, having an appreciation of the potential dilemmas that Family Farm Corporation may face will allow shareholders to proactively ensure that decision-making systems and processes are in place to foster a strategic and even proactive corporate response.

The following potential dilemmas can be identified by Family Farm Corporation in this process by examining the range of project impacts to key stakeholders, and considering internal and external stakeholders' expectations of Family Farm Corporation:

Potential Dilemma B-1: Regional and provincial governance and bylaw structures are not sufficiently sophisticated to identify and respond to environmental and other risks associated with intensive livestock operations.

Should the corporation:

- Push for approval of the hog operation by the local council on an expedited basis before the laws are changed, and threaten litigation for loss of opportunity if the local municipal council stalls in its decision making?

- Encourage examination of the bylaws to ensure that they are adequate to manage the risks associated with intensive livestock operations?

- Initiate an independent evaluation of environmental risks to ensure that the project can respond to identified risks?

Potential Dilemma B-2: Local community stakeholders are expected to be divided by the issue of an intensive livestock operation in the community. How can the local community stakeholders be engaged in the issue, and how can differences in stakeholder opinions be bridged?

Should the corporation:

- Ignore complaints from the local community and proceed as quickly as possible with the commercial opportunity?

- Undermine the credibility of dissenters by pointing to their self-interest? For example, the smell factor will erode property values for nonfarmers. Emphasize that this community's first priority is farming, and that farming must be allowed in Canada or food will have to be imported.

- Depend on local regulations to facilitate opportunity for stakeholder engagement?

- Encourage public meetings to gain an appreciation of local stakeholder priorities, and to educate these stakeholders on risk management strategies to respond to these concerns?

Phase 2C: Creating Opportunity for Innovation: Brainstorming to Identify Feasible Alternatives

Family Farm Corporation decides that a shareholder meeting is required to deal with the growing number of anticipated dilemmas arising from the range of stakeholder impacts anticipated in this project, and the wide range of internal and external stakeholder expectations of the corporation's role in responding to identified dilemmas.

The terms of reference for this meeting include considering stakeholder impacts and creating an opportunity for innovation in the brainstorming of feasible strategies for management of anticipated dilemmas.

Innovation Outcomes by Shareholders re: Potential Dilemma B-1

Regional and provincial governance and bylaw structures are not sufficiently sophisticated to identify and respond to environmental and other risks associated with intensive livestock operations. What is the role of Family Farm Corporation?

Guided by additional information on Family Farm Corporation's integrity values and commitments, the shareholders agree that the following alternatives for Family Farm Corporation are feasible responses to this dilemma.

Lily White is increasingly uncomfortable with the nervousness of neighbors and friends in the community, and fears that their concerns about contamination of water aquifers may be legitimate. Joe Jr.'s wife is expecting their first grandchild and Lily White has niggling concerns about the legacy that she is leaving her grandchildren.

Anna is adamant that the Family Farm Corporation should not proceed on a path that could result in legal liability for water contamination, even if the local council is willing to approve the barn's construction. Anna wants to be certain that the risks are well understood, and that an investment in an intensive farming operation will not harm the local environment.

Joe Jr. is equally adamant that early approval of the zoning application by the local council is of strategic value.

After many heated family debates, including presentation of documentation of factory-farm impacts elsewhere in North America by Anna's husband, the family elects to proceed in a manner that secures Family Farm Corporation's "rights" to the commercial opportunity *and* ensures that risks are thoroughly assessed.

On this basis, the family decides to proceed with the zoning application. However, a decision to proceed with the project will be conditional on the corporation's assessment of environmental and other risks, and satisfaction that the risks can and will be effectively managed.

Innovative Outcomes by Shareholders re: Potential Dilemma B-2

The local community stakeholders will be divided on the issue of an intensive livestock operation in the community. How can the local community be engaged in the issue, and how can differences in opinions be bridged?

The family recognizes that local community stakeholders will have the motivation and capacity to enlist support from nonlocal stakeholders, including environmental advocacy groups and political opposition. If the local stakeholders cannot be engaged in a manner that is respectful of their concerns, the entire project may be jeopardized. Local politicians and council members may be vulnerable to pressures from the media and external stakeholders.

The stakeholder engagement consultation process prescribed by local regulation is not sufficiently comprehensive to respond to issues arising from intensive farming operations. These processes were designed to manage issues arising from traditional farming operations.

In order to ensure that the community stakeholders' concerns are understood, and to educate these stakeholders on risk management strategies to be adopted in this project, the Family Farm Corporation will encourage the local council to support an enhanced stakeholder engagement consultation process managed by professionals.

The family concurs that Family Farm Corporation is committed to acting proactively in anticipating stakeholder concerns, rather than responding reactively when stakeholder criticisms escalate beyond the local community.

Navigating Frontier 3: Aligning Corporate Integrity Values, Talk, and Walk

In order to navigate Frontier 3 in business integrity, the following questions are posed:

The external corporate stakeholder asks: What do you intend by your commitment to integrity? How do you create, assess, and manage alignment between corporate commitments to integrity and actual corporate practices?

The internal corporate stakeholder asks: What is our corporate commitment to integrity? How do we create, manage, and assess ongoing alignment between our corporate commitments and our corporate actions?

Phase 3: Create, Manage, and Assess Alignment between Corporate Commitments to Business Integrity and Actual Practices

Phase 3A: Identifying corporate talk on business integrity in Family Farm Corporation

Phase 3B: Plotting departmental integrity talk and corporate integrity talk on the Integrity Ladder for Family Farm Corporation

Phase 3C: Applying the Integrity Grid: Plot departmental integrity talk and departmental integrity walk on the Integrity Grid:
- *Before* best alternative tactics decision
- *After* best alternative tactics decision

Phase 3 involves applying the Integrity Ladder and the Integrity Grid. The Integrity Ladder is introduced and discussed in Chapter 2 and the Integrity Grid is introduced and discussed in Chapter 4.

Phase 3A: Identifying Family Farm Corporation's Corporate Commitments to Business Integrity That May Be Relevant to the Two Identified Integrity Dilemmas

Like most private corporations, the Family Farm Corporation has no express corporate talk on integrity. Private companies do not have public disclosure requirements. It is not uncommon for a private company to be informal in its definition of business integrity commitments. Private companies' corporate commitments to integrity routinely reflect the personal integrity commitments of the majority shareholders or founders.

Phase 3B: Plotting Shareholder Integrity Commitments and Corporate Integrity Commitment on the Integrity Ladder

In Phase 3B, the objective is to identify alignments and gaps between the corporation's commitments to integrity, and the commitments of individual shareholders of Family Farm Corporation. Using the Integrity Ladder, applied as set out below, the corporation's integrity commitments are identified in the column "Integrity Commitments (as a Corporation)" and individual shareholders' commitments are plotted in the column "Integrity Commitments (Individual Shareholders)."

In order to identify the corporation's integrity commitments, look to the outcomes of Phase 3A; in order to identify individual shareholders' integrity commitments, go back to the integrity commitments plotted on the Integrity Ladder for each shareholder as set out in Phase 1B.

RUNG	PRIMARY MOTIVATION	INTEGRITY COMMITMENTS (INDIVIDUAL SHAREHOLDERS)	INTEGRITY COMMITMENTS (AS A CORPORATION)
10	Future generations		
9	Sustainable positive social impact		
8	Leverage budget to achieve positive social impact		

7	Leverage budget to do no harm		
6	Compliance plus proactive risk management	Anna White	
5	Compliance with rules		
4	Reputation and reactive risk management	Lily White	
3	Minimum legal compliance	Joe White Sr.	
2	Avoid being caught with "dirty hands"	Joe White Jr.	
1	Avoid jail		
0	Self-preservation		

Plotting corporate and shareholder integrity commitments on the Integrity Ladder clearly shows the problems in measuring alignment between integrity commitments at an individual shareholder level and integrity commitments at a corporate level.

Phase 3C: Plotting Shareholder Integrity Commitments and Shareholder Integrity Actions on the Integrity Grid

In order to assess the integrity alignment and gaps between shareholders within Family Farm Corporation, and to identify alignment and gaps between individuals and the organization as a whole, Phase 3C uses the Integrity Grid tool to plot individual shareholder commitments and actions.

Individual shareholder commitments and actions on integrity are plotted twice in this exercise to reflect differences between proactive and reactive business integrity management practices.

The first plotting is done on the basis of shareholder positions prior to the innovative brainstorming on feasible options (Phase 1 Integrity Ladder outcomes). This plotting reflects the state of Family Farm Corporation shareholders' integrity commitments and actions in a *reactive* mode.

The second plotting is done on the basis of shareholder positions after the innovative brainstorming on feasible options (Phase 2 Stakeholder and Dilemma Analysis outcomes). This second plotting reflects the state of Family Farm Corporation shareholders' integrity commitments and actions in a *proactive* mode.

First Plotting on Integrity Grid: Shareholder Commitments and Shareholder Actions before Stakeholder Grid and Impact Assessment Process

Individual shareholder commitments and actions are considered based on the discussion set out in Phase 1 of this process, and depicted on the grid as follows:

INDIVIDUALS	CODE	COMMITMENTS	ACTIONS	INDIVIDUAL SHAREHOLDER GAP (ACTIONS MINUS COMMITMENTS)
Joe White Jr.	J	2	3	+1
Joe White Sr.	Mr.	3	3	0
Lily White	Mrs.	4	4	0
Anna White	A	7	5	−2

To achieve alignment between individual shareholder commitments and actions, the preferred differential set out in the column entitled "Individual Shareholder Gap (Actions Minus Commitments)" is zero. There are four shareholders in Family Farm Corporation. Two shareholders—Joe White Sr. and Lily White—are aligned in their commitments and actions. Two shareholders (Joe Jr. and Anna) have variances. In Joe Jr.'s case, his actions exceed commitments by one rung of the Integrity Ladder; in Anna's case, her commitments exceed her actions by two rungs.

The data the chart above (which is based on Phase 1 Integrity Ladder inputs) is then plotted on the Integrity Grid to depict the following:

- Equal Alignment Line (a 45-degree reference line that reflects equal alignment of shareholder talk and walk)

- Plot intersection of individual shareholder commitments and actions

The individual shareholder commitments and actions are plotted on the Integrity Grid, as shown below:

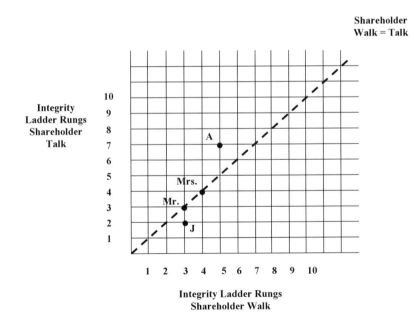

Observations from the Integrity Grid plotting exercise:

Family Farm Corporation: The company does not have a clear commitment to integrity so there is no corporate commitment to measure against shareholder commitments.

Joe White Sr.: Although Joe White Sr. is aligned in his commitments and practices, his level of commitment and actions (rung 3) is not in alignment with the commitments or actions of other shareholders (others range in commitments from rung 2 to rung 7). Joe White Sr.'s actions are aligned with his son's actions.

Lily White: This shareholder's commitments and actions are aligned at rung 4 and are marginally higher than her husband's commitments and actions. However, there is a wide disparity between this shareholder's commitments and actions (rung 4) and the commitments and actions of other shareholders.

Joe White: Joe Jr.'s commitment level is at rung 2 and actions are at rung 3. Joe is the Family Farm Corporation's weakest link.

Anna White: Anna's commitment level is very high at rung 7, and her actions are closer to that of the other shareholders at rung 5. Anna's overstatement of commitments is likely to be problematic for the company. Her level of commitment and action is higher than the other shareholders'. This higher level of talk and action could be misleading to external stakeholders, raising expectations of corporate commitments and practices, and exacerbating differences within the corporation as a whole between integrity commitments and practices. This shareholder's integrity commitments should be adjusted downwards to align with the other shareholders' commitments and practices.

Second Plotting on the Integrity Grid: Shareholder Talk and Shareholder Walk *after* Stakeholder Grid and Impact Assessment Process

The second plotting is done on the basis of shareholders' positions after the innovative multidisciplinary brainstorming on feasible options (Phase 2 Stakeholder and Dilemma Analysis outcomes). This second plotting reflects the state of Family Farm Corporation shareholders' integrity commitments and actions in a proactive mode.

Individual shareholder commitments and actions are considered based on the discussion set out in Phase 2 of this process, and depicted on the grid as follows:

	CODE	COMMITMENT	ACTIONS	INDIVIDUAL SHAREHOLDER GAP (ACTIONS MINUS COMMITMENT)	CORPORATE/ INDIVIDUAL GAP (SHAREHOLDER COMMITMENT MINUS CORPORATE COMMITMENT)
Corporate	C	5	—	—	—
Individual Shareholders					
Joe White Jr.	J	4	5	+1	−1
Joe White Sr.	Mr.	4	5	+1	−1
Lily White	Mrs.	5	6	+1	0
Anna White	A	5	6	+1	0

To achieve alignment between individual shareholder commitments and actions, the preferred differential set out in the column entitled "Corporate/Individual Gap (Shareholder Commitment Minus Corporate Commitment)" is zero.

On the basis of processes set out in Phase B of this framework, Joe Jr. has moved significantly up the Integrity Ladder rungs (from rung 3 to rung 5 in action and from rung 2 to rung 4 in commitment). There is still work to be done to increase Joe Jr.'s public commitments, but he is no longer the weakest link in the company.

Joe Sr. and his wife, Lily, have each shifted up the rungs of the Integrity Ladder. Joe Sr. is committed to integrity at rung 4 and his actions are at rung 5; Lily has committed to integrity at rung 5 and her actions are at rung 6. Both Joe Sr. and his wife have lost their individual alignment in commitment and practices. Each of these shareholders needs to work on achieving alignment in their personal commitments and practices.

Anna has reduced her very high integrity commitment from rung 7 to 5, and her actions have increased from rung 5 to 6. These adjustments reduce her differential significantly. Anna will need to continue to work to bring her personal commitments and actions in alignment.

Another important outcome is the alignment between shareholders. Joe Jr. and his father have become more aligned in their commitments and actions—both now being at rung 4 in commitments and rung 5 in action. The same is true of Lily and her daughter, Anna. There are two approaches that are emerging.

When the level of corporate commitment is not clear, the first priority is to identify and agree on a targeted organizational commitment level. The next priority is to address the weakest link—Joe Jr.—and that priority has been addressed.

In a company with a small number of shareholders, the corporation is encouraged to focus on reducing the gaps between individual shareholders, and then to ask each shareholder to address alignment in his or her individual commitments and practices.

The data in the chart above (which is based on Phase 2 Stakeholder Impact and Dilemma Analysis outcomes) is plotted on the Integrity Grid to depict the following:

- Corporate Talk Line (Family Farm Corporation's commitment to integrity based on Phase 3B plotting)

- Plot intersection of individual shareholder commitments and actions

The second plotting of the Integrity Grid is depicted below, which shows the Shareholder talk and Shareholder walk *after* the Stakeholder Grid and Impact Assessment process.

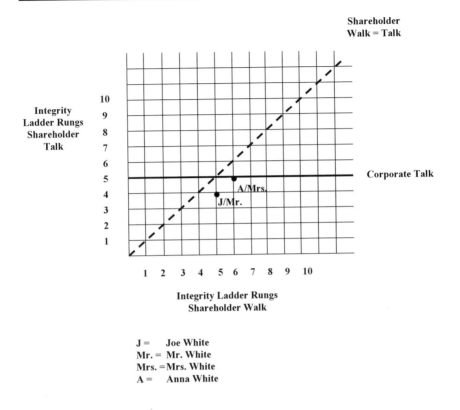

J =   Joe White
Mr. = Mr. White
Mrs. =Mrs. White
A =   Anna White

Observations from the Second Integrity Grid plotting exercise:

Joe Jr.: This shareholder had some work to do to bring his commitment level from rung 2 to rung 4 and closer to the corporate commitment level of rung 5, but he has moved significantly from its earlier position as the weakest link through proactive management practices. Coaching Joe Jr. on how he talks about the corporation's commitments to integrity will help.

Joe Sr.: Proactive management practices moved this shareholder up from rung 3 to rung 4 on the ladder, but he needs to work on aligning commitment and actions.

Lily White: Proactive business strategies resulted in Lily moving from rung 4 (commitment and actions) up to rung 5 (commitment) and rung 6 (action). Her commitment level is now aligned with the organization as a whole, but her integrity actions will have to be managed down to rung 5.

Anna White: Proactive practices significantly reduced her level of commitment from rung 7 to rung 5 in line with organizational commitments. Like her mother, Anna's actions will have to be aligned with the company.

It is possible that with such a small company, stakeholders will be more likely to approach Lily or Anna with issues. Likewise, Joe Jr. and his father may seem to be insensitive in discussions with stakeholders. This could be problematic if corporate messages on integrity commitments are unclear.

More importantly, decisions on actions/implementation will require discussion and agreement on implementation to ensure that Lily and Anna do not act in a way that is not aligned with the organization's commitment at rung 5. Lily and Anna may talk the corporate line, but may act in a way that oversteps their commitments. This will create expectations with stakeholders. Although it may be commendable that Anna and Lily have higher integrity aspirations, it is challenging for the organization to have individuals overperforming. Over time, Lily and Anna may be able to work with the other shareholders to commit to higher integrity levels.

Navigating Frontier 4: Understanding Differences between Corporations Regarding Corporate Values, Commitments, and Action

To navigate Frontier 4 in business integrity, the following questions are posed:

- What motivates corporate behavior to value integrity? How are these commitments and values manifested in practice?

- What are the differences in corporate motivations in relation to integrity values, commitments, and practices? What are the outcomes of these differences in motivation?

Phase 4 in the Evaluation and Decision-Making Framework for Business Integrity Management

Using the Permeation of Change model, the Adapted Best Practices tool, and Benchmarking Practices, identify, assess, and implement best practices that will enhance Family Farm Corporation's strategic management of business integrity frontiers.

Applying the Permeation of Change model introduced in Chapter 5, Family Farm Corporation's management team characterizes its shareholders as Initiators, Interesteds, Wait-and-Sees, Followers, and Non-compliers. Each individual is assigned a distinct task in the identification and assessment of best practices:

INDIVIDUALS	EFFECTING CHANGE IN BUSINESS INTEGRITY STRATEGY
Initiator: Anna White	• Manage the risk of Initiators making mistakes that affect the corporation's reputation and/or discourage others • Encourage Initiator to identify/adopt pilot projects and define success criteria to control risks • *Example:* Creation of a local citizens group to monitor water quality in the area
Interested: Lily White	• Invite Interested to work with Follower on implementation of change to shore up the weakest links • *Example:* Lily can work with her son, Joe Jr., to clarify corporate commitments in writing through preparation of corporate vision, mission, and values statements
Wait-and-See: Joe White Sr.	• Wait-and-See prioritizes risk management, and is strongly motivated by others • Recommend that Wait-and-See proactively monitor evolving stakeholder expectations • *Example:* Joe Sr. can clearly assume responsibility for meeting with farming and nonfarming neighbors and local government representatives to understand their expectations
Follower: Joe White Jr.	• Encourage the Interested to support the Follower in change. Initiator is not likely to be effective in supporting change in Follower's practices • *Example:* Joe Jr. can work with his mother, Lily, to define corporate commitments to integrity, and can be encouraged to speak on the corporation's behalf only in a manner consistent with these values

Next, the Family Farm Corporation applies the Adapted Best Practices tool in the following stages, as described in Chapter 5.

Stage 1: Identify Business Integrity Best Practices

Stage 2: Assess Best Practices Based on Risk/Impact and Ease of Implementation

Stage 3: Select Practices for Family Farm Corporation and Determine Implementation Tactics

Stage 1: Identification of Business Integrity Best Practices

In the case of intensive livestock operations, it is easier for the Family Farm Corporation to identify worst practices within the industry that should not be replicated. The introduction of factory farms into traditional farming communities is not an easy one, and best practices are only just beginning to emerge.

What can the Family Farm Corporation learn from the experiences of other intensive farming operators and key stakeholders?

- Legal liability for environmental contamination of water aquifers is increasingly a deterrent for some local municipal councils. The fear of liability is motivating caution. In some cases, moratoriums on intensive livestock operations are being imposed by local governments to provide breathing space for assessment of the risks and to engage stakeholders. The Walkerton tainted-water disaster demonstrates the horrific consequences of ineffective risk management of bacteria. The negative impacts to a family farm corporation complicit in such loss can be enormous.

- Although traditional farmers may be supportive of the position that farming be allowed in rural communities (the "right to farm" lobby), traditional farmers are increasingly distinguishing their activities from those of factory farmers. Polarization of opinion among farming and nonfarming stakeholders in local communities will be further fragmented by distinctions drawn between traditional family farm practices and intensive livestock operations.

- It has been constructive for some intensive livestock operators to demonstrate to host communities the benefits of the investment to the local stakeholders in terms of taxes, jobs, and infrastructure.

- Density of intensive farming operations is a growing issue. When approvals are granted by local counties or districts, local decision makers must evaluate location and density of proposed operations on a regional basis given the collective impact of intensive farming operations.

What can Family Farm Corporation learn from the experiences of other industry sectors?

Best practices from other industries and sectors within North America and globally may be useful guides. Family Farm Corporation decides to examine best practices within the industry sector to understand:

- Stakeholder engagement models

- Environmental and social impact models

- Environmental protection practices

Referring back to the Permeation of Change model (see Appendix), the corporation decides that different groups within the corporation be assigned responsibility for distinct components of the Best Practices identification and assessment process:

INDIVIDUALS	EFFECTING CHANGE IN BUSINESS INTEGRITY STRATEGY
Anna White	• Identify emerging and innovative best practices of organizations inside the sector • *Example:* Anna can partner with North American and European agriculture sector groups to keep abreast of best practices in management of environmental impacts of farming

continued

INDIVIDUALS	EFFECTING CHANGE IN BUSINESS INTEGRITY STRATEGY
Lily White	• Identify business integrity best practices of competitors • *Example:* Lily can join a provincial industry association to keep abreast of best practices as they evolve locally
Joe White Sr.	• Do proactive monitoring of evolving stakeholder expectations on corporate best practices on business integrity • *Example:* Joe Sr. can be responsible for reporting back to the other shareholders on discussions with neighbors
Joe White Jr.	• Be forced to examine and implement best practices within the Family Farm Corporation • *Example:* Joe Jr. can work with his mother, Lily, in reviewing materials from the provincial industry association

Stage 2: Assessment of Best Practices

Best Practices for business integrity must then be assessed and prioritized by corporate management based on the practices' potential impacts and ease of implementation for Family Farm Corporation.

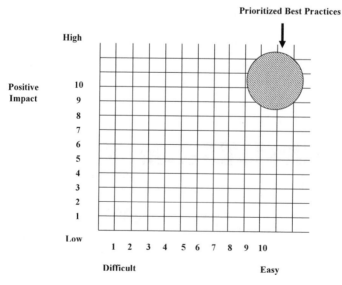

Stage 3: Select Best Practices for Family Farm Corporation and Determine Implementation Tactics

Family Farm Corporation selects for implementation one best practice for engaging with stakeholders that is plotted onto the upper right-hand quadrant of the grid. Additionally, Family Farm Corporation encourages Anna and Lily White to select one additional best practice for the environment as a pilot.

Anna is also encouraged to identify and assess a best practice for environmental and social impact assessment that fell outside the High Impact/Ease of Implementation quadrant of the grid. Anna will see if the implementation challenges with this model can be reduced.

Benchmarking Practices

Family Farm Corporation intends to evaluate the benefits of benchmarking their intensive livestock operations once the operation is operational.

Navigating Frontier 5 in Business Integrity: Accountability

Key challenges to be navigated in Frontier 5 are the design and implementation of dependable and strategic corporate accountability systems and processes that manifest integrity values and build trust.

Phase 5: Respond to Business Integrity Accountabilities

Phase 5A: Clarifying accountabilities with the Business Integrity Accountability Cycle (introduced in Chapter 6)

Phase 5B: Implementing strategy

Phase 5C: Implementing continuous improvement

Phase 5A: Business Integrity Accountability Cycle

Family Farm Corporation is a privately owned corporation with minimal public reporting obligations. Notwithstanding its status as a private corporation, Family Farm Corporation is encouraged to clarify accountabilities. Performance measures and monitoring mechanisms are agreed based on outcomes of the Integrity Grid, Permeation of Change model, the Best Practices tool, and the Benchmarking Practices. Each individual shareholder is assigned responsibility for functions that are responsive to business integrity expectations of key stakeholders.

Although certainly less formal than larger or public corporations, Family Farm Corporation is encouraged to consider how it defines and accounts for integrity values to its key stakeholders. The family shareholders are encouraged to formally discuss their integrity values, and to assign responsibilities for ensuring that these values are reflected in corporate commitments and action. Corporate decisions and strategy should be superimposed on their corporation's "integrity lens." On a quarterly basis, strategies should be reevaluated to consider their implementation status and to assess their alignment with corporate integrity intention.

Phase 5B: Implementing Responsive Strategy and Monitoring Outcomes

- Implement strategies to address identified dilemmas/issues

- Monitor/measure outcomes as described in Chapter 6

- Measure outcomes on Integrity Grid at defined intervals (at least quarterly)

- Verify and report on outcomes

Phase 5C: Continuous Improvement

Now that the corporate integrity commitment level is clarified, the ongoing priority is to align commitments and actions of individual stakeholders with the corporate commitment level. As the company examines best practices and stakeholder expectations, the company may choose to move its integrity commitments further up the Integrity Ladder. However, such talk must balance the risk of committing beyond personal comfort.

Observations for Family Farm Corporation: Impacts of Reactive or Proactive Management of Business Integrity

Outcomes vary when a corporation decides to adopt a proactive or reactive approach to business integrity management.

Prior to reassessing corporate integrity values (as a collective as contrasted to individual shareholder positions) Family Farm Corporation did not present itself as a corporate entity. Rather, the individual shareholders projected their personal values and priorities, frequently in a misaligned manner. This projection of individual shareholder values and strategies is confusing to corporate stakeholders. With smaller corporations, shareholders' interests and opinions can dominate and blur corporate strategy and values.

In the absence of a proactive strategy, it is likely that the investment in the intensive farming opportunity would have been severed from the Family Farm Corporation's interests, to be pursued by Joe White Jr. on an independent basis. This strategy would have jeopardized existing relationships and operations. As well, Joe White Jr.'s independent operation of a hog farm could well have harmed the reputation and relationships of the Family Farm Corporation.

By proactively addressing the risks and issues, the shareholders of Family Farm Corporation have averted a potential disaster, and have positioned the corporation to responsibly pursue an opportunity. The gaps between the corporate and shareholder talk on integrity are closed, and there is clarity on corporate integrity values. Beyond corporate interests, the risk of sibling rivalry has been averted.

Scenario C:
Applying Business Integrity Management Tools to Community Stakeholders

Corporate Background

DEF Corporation Inc. is a U.S.-based corporation producing oil and gas on a worldwide basis and is listed on the New York Stock Exchange. Although it is not one of the major energy corporations, DEF is an ambitious explorer and producer with producing assets in Texas, Colorado, Canada, and Indonesia.

DEF's producing assets in the United States are quite important in light of the U.S. economic dependency on fossil fuels and production disruptions caused by tensions in oil-producing countries. The company's present oil and gas output in the U.S. is in decline. Without incremental drilling, the company's petroleum reserves are expected to be unprofitable within five to seven years. DEF Corporation is keen to evaluate enhanced recovery for oil, step-out exploration for oil, and exploring for gas at deeper zones based on revised economic terms made available by the local regulators, and encouraged by high energy prices.

Drilling for gas in Colorado is a priority for DEF Corporation. As operator of a joint venture consortium, DEF Corporation is recommending that substantial drilling budgets for gas exploration and development be approved for Colorado. DEF is also recommending in its annual budget that a pipeline be constructed to link its producing gas fields in Colorado. DEF's joint venture partners in the multinational consortium include three companies—one is a small local producer well known in Colorado; one is a large multinational with a head office in Europe; and the third partner is a mid-sized Latin American producer.

Local communities in Colorado are familiar with the surge in oil and gas drilling and operations in their region of the country. Drilling activity is not a new phenomenon; however, the level and pace of activity is troubling some locals. Local community organizations are banding together, sharing experiences, and identifying means to collaborate to discuss and proactively manage development impacts. Local politicians and regulators are challenged to keep abreast of the requests for drilling permits and must keep hiring personnel to ensure regulatory compliance with local legislation. Local landowners are growing frustrated and, in some cases, angry with the density of drilling activity and the aggressive timeframes and ambitions of investors.

DEF Corporation has some written policies to guide its global operations. For example, the company has consistent guidelines on environment and safety that include commitments to the safety of corporate personnel, and undertakings not to flare gas in its operations. The company provides very limited public reporting on its assets, does not have a formal process for stakeholder engagement, and has no guidelines for participation with local communities. Decisions to contribute to local charities are made by DEF Corporation's chief executive officer.

Evaluation and Decision-Making Process: Focus on Managing Community Participation

Phase 1: Establish the Community Participation Baseline in a Corporation

Phase 1A: Assessing commitments to community made by individual corporate departments/divisions and historical actions

Phase 1B: Applying the Integrity Ladder (introduced in Chapter 2) analysis in relation to community participation

Phase 2: Identify Community Stakeholders, Assess Community Stakeholder Impacts, Anticipate Stakeholder Expectations of a Corporation, and Identify Potential Dilemmas with Community Stakeholders

Phase 2A: Applying Stakeholder Grid and Impact Assessment tool (introduced in Chapter 3) to key community stakeholders in a project and assessing potential stakeholder impacts

Phase 2B: Anticipating stakeholders' expectations of the corporation, and identifying potential integrity dilemmas arising from project impacts and expectations of community stakeholders

Phase 2C: Creating opportunity for innovation with multidisciplinary brainstorming to identify feasible options to manage dilemmas

Phase 3: Create, Manage, and Assess Alignment Between Corporate Commitments and Community Participation and Actual Practices

Phase 3A: Identifying a corporation's commitments to community participation

Phase 3B: Plotting departmental/divisional commitments to community participation and corporate commitments to community participation on the Integrity Ladder

Phase 3C: Applying the Integrity Grid—plotting department/division talk and department/division walk regarding community participation on the Integrity Grid (introduced in Chapter 4):
- *Before* multidepartment brainstorming session on feasible alternatives (reactive)
- *After* multidepartment brainstorming session on feasible alternatives (proactive)

Phase 4: Identify, Assess, and Implement Best Practices for Community Participation

Phase 4A: Applying the Community Investment Strategy tool

Phase 4B: Applying the Permeation of Change model

Phase 4C: Applying the Adapted Best Practices tool

Phase 4D: Applying Benchmarking Practices

Phase 5: Accountability for Community Participation

Phase 5A: Clarifying accountabilities with the Business Integrity Accountability Cycle

Phase 5B: Implementing accountability strategy for community participation

Phase 5C: Developing continuous improvement

Navigating Frontier 1 in Corporate Integrity: Understanding Perspectives Related to the Integrity of Corporations in Responsiveness to Community Stakeholders

Navigating Frontier 1 requires that the following questions be addressed:

- Do corporations truly care about community stakeholders or is integrity merely a public relations exercise?

- How can corporate stakeholders measure integrity with regard to relations with communities?

Phase 1: Evaluation and Decision-Making Process: Establishing the Community Participation Baseline in a Corporation

Phase 1A: Assessing commitments to community made by individual corporate departments/divisions and historical actions

Phase 1B: Applying the Integrity Ladder (introduced in Chapter 2) analysis in relation to community participation

Phase 1A: Assessing Integrity Commitments and Actions (Historical) of Individual Departments within DEF Corporation

The following vignettes provide insight into the integrity commitments and actions of individual departments of DEF Corporation:

Operations: The operations department looks at each phase of the project to explore for, develop, and produce gas independently.

Instead of looking at the joint venture's intention to accelerate drilling and production, and build a pipeline to gather the produced gas, the operations department compartmentalizes the various project aspects into work programs, budgets, and timeframes for each phase. The operations team is technically very qualified, but underestimates the reaction of the local communities to accelerated timeframes for drilling. As well, the team vastly underestimates local furor about the prospects for yet another gas pipeline dissecting their communities.

This operations team is very quick to respond to a citizen complaint about gas flaring or any safety or environmentally focused question or concern. However, the group does not consider the impacts to the host communities on a full-cycle project basis or on a cumulative basis in light of drilling and production activities of other investors in the state. As well, the group does not factor into the pipeline project any process for engagement with key stakeholders, including local community stakeholders.

When the operations group encounters queries or challenges from host communities that it cannot respond to (which is quite frequently), the queries are passed along the management line to the corporate head office located out of state.

Environment, health, and safety: The environment, health, and safety managers in DEF Corporation are proud of their worldwide gas management strategies—their practices are consistent globally, regardless of local regulations. As well, the company prides itself on its safety record for employees. The aggressive timelines on the gas development project in Colorado have, however, resulted in the need to hire more consultants, and the company's record for safety with consultants and contractors is not nearly as good as their record with employee safety. These risks are of concern to the environment, health, and safety managers responsible for this project in Colorado.

Local communities are legitimately concerned about the environmental impacts of gas development in their state, and the environment, health, and safety group anticipates the need for significant dialogue with local stakeholders in order to ensure their understanding of the environmental risks associated with accelerated gas drilling and construction of a gas pipeline.

Public relations: Gas prices have never been higher. DEF's ability to produce gas in the United States is an enormous competitive advantage. The public relations group based in the company's head office wants to maintain a low profile on the project—"Stay below the radar screen" is their motto. Whenever the public relations group encounters any expertise or advocacy group that could be perceived as being critical of the company's practices, it discredits the would-be critics. The public relations group has a stable of "supportive technical experts" on call to reinforce the corporation's position on potentially contentious issues.

Government relations: The government relations group is familiar working with regulators and officials in several oil and gas producing jurisdictions. The group encourages the Colorado legislative and regulatory bodies to allow accelerated gas development for the benefit of the country, and encourages closer drilling spacing units so that more wells can be drilled at a faster pace. When the local regulators express concerns about the impacts to local communities, including owners of surface rights where operations are conducted, the government relations group is dismissive of the impacts on the basis that the benefits to the nation should prevail over concerns about local impacts.

In the face of stiff challenge, the government relations group has been known to let legislators know, by innuendo and inference, that DEF Corporation has many investment opportunities and the company is positioned to refocus its investment in another jurisdiction if cooperation with legislators is not feasible in Colorado. If necessary, the government relations group provides tacit approval for the company to adopt divide-and-conquer tactics with local community stakeholders.

Finance: The finance group is concerned with raising funds necessary to finance, on a fast-tracked basis, a gas development project, including a pipeline system. The group is aware that the company's and joint venture's reputation and ability to manage risks will be relevant to lenders. More recently, the finance group is aware that their private lending institutions have signed on to the Equator Principles, a series of commitments to environmental and social standards for projects exceeding U.S. $40 million in costs. If the pipeline project exceeds this threshold, it is likely that DEF's lenders will expect an integrated impact assessment of the project to be completed before the project can begin. This process will set back the project timelines.

DEF's joint venture partners in this project are not aligned in their appreciation of the need for an integrated impact assessment to understand impacts of the pipeline project. As well, the finance group is wary of the reputation of one of its joint venture partners. This partner has participated in a gas pipeline project in Latin America that has attracted negative attention.

Human resources: The human resources group applies the same organizational and motivational practices globally. In the Canadian Arctic, Indonesia, and the United States, corporate operations are conducted with as little direct engagement with communities as possible. Corporate personnel reside in compounds sheltered from local communities, and personnel are put on rotation schedules so they can focus full-time on their work and then return to their homes every twenty-one days. Relationships between corporate personnel and local citizens are not encouraged.

The manager in this human resources group was originally responsible for corporate operations in Indonesia where these types of practices were encouraged in the 1980s. Hiring and training locals is not encouraged, particularly for the pipeline project. Expertise is flown in on an as-needed basis to keep costs to a minimum. Besides, the technical and operating groups know each other well and work well together as a team. In the opinion of the human resources group, it would be difficult to incorporate local thinking into their practices.

Legal and land: The DEF corporate group responsible for negotiations with surface landowners and contract negotiations/administration is headed by a lawyer. This legal and land group focuses on compliance with local regulations and strict adherence to corporate precedents and standard form contracts. Any deviations from these rules or precedents require the approval of a vice president located at head office; this individual is quite annoyed by these requests and rewards individuals who can function within the rules.

Chief executive officer (CEO): The chief executive officer of DEF Corporation is a resident of Texas. He is directly involved in deciding the company's contributions to charity, and often donations to charities are made on the basis of the CEO's personal relationships. For example, the company recently donated U.S. $1 million to establish an engineering chair at the local college in Dallas (where the CEO's daughter is studying engineering), and funded a wing of a cancer research facility in Houston because the CEO is concerned with cancer patients' access to facilities (his son-in-law has recently been diagnosed with cancer).

The CEO is not supportive of contributions to local communities unless these contributions are mandated by law or contracts. However, the CEO has authorized a discreet and undisclosed payment to the tribal leader of an Aboriginal reservation situated in the pipeline right-of-way as a way of expressing the corporation's good faith.

Phase 1B: Plotting DEF Corporation's Departments on the Integrity Ladder

In order to assess a corporation's current state of commitment and response to community participation, it is useful to establish the organization's community participation baseline. Thus, it is important to consider a corporation's individual departments/divisions' commitments to community stakeholders. Also, it is important to consider the historical actions (or inactions) of individual departments/divisions.

These assessments can be plotted on the Integrity Ladder to provide a snapshot of the community participation baseline within the corporation. The Integrity Ladder business tool is introduced and explained in Chapter 2.

Using the insights in the short vignettes for each department, individual departments' intended integrity commitments in relation to the Colorado gas development project are assessed and plotted on the Integrity Ladder under "Integrity Commitment."

In order to create this baseline, there is a need to refer to historical departmental practices. Thus, individual departments' historical practices in other projects (individual department actions in other projects) are considered and plotted on the Integrity Ladder under "Integrity Action (Historical)," as follows:

The Integrity Ladder

RUNG	PRIMARY MOTIVATION	INTEGRITY COMMITMENT	INTEGRITY ACTION (HISTORICAL)
10	Future generations		
9	Sustainable positive social impact		
8	Leverage budget to achieve positive social impact		
7	Leverage budget to do no harm	*Environment, health, and safety:* Concern with safety record for employees and contractors	*Environment, health, and safety:* Global standards for environment, health, and safety (e.g., gas-flaring practices)
6	Compliance plus proactive risk management		
5	Compliance with rules	*Operations:* Comply with legal/commercial rules within individual project phases (not whole project)	*Finance:* Acknowledge that lenders may require an integrated impact assessment on the pipeline project
4	Reputation and reactive risk management	*Finance:* Corporate reputation and risk management skills linked to access to funding	*Operations:* React to risks/community expectations as they arise

continued

RUNG	PRIMARY MOTIVATION	INTEGRITY COMMITMENT	INTEGRITY ACTION (HISTORICAL)
		CEO: Voluntary contributions to charities based on personal relationships	
3	Minimum legal compliance	*Government relations:* Exert influence with regulators *Legal/human resources:* Comply with local regulations to the letter of the law—no voluntary engagement with communities	*Government relations:* Divide and conquer community stakeholders *Legal/human resources:* Apply corporate rules and local laws rigidly
2	Avoid being caught with "dirty hands"	*Public relations:* Do not want poor relations with communities reported in public media	*Public relations:* Discredit critics *CEO:* Has agent pay undisclosed bonus to Aboriginal leaders to diffuse indigenous community concerns
1	Avoid jail		
0	Self-preservation		

Integrity Ladder outcomes reflect enormous differences within the corporation in terms of commitments and related responses to community stakeholders. Departments range from rung 2 (the weakest link) to rung 7. In some cases, there are wide gaps between commitments and actual performance within individual departments. Community stakeholders will be confused about the authenticity of any of the corporation's commitments to the community.

Navigating Frontier 2: Defining the Proper Role of Corporations in Relation to Community Stakeholders

To navigate Frontier 2 the following questions need to be addressed:

The external corporate stakeholder asks: This corporation has invested in a project in our community or is conducting operations within our community. As a citizen of this community, what do I expect of this corporate investor? What is the corporation's role in our community?

The internal corporate stakeholder asks: What do citizens of this community, individually and collectively, expect of our corporation? Does our corporation have the motivation and capacity to effectively respond to these individual or collective expectations of local citizens?

Phase 2: Identify Community Stakeholders, Assess Community Stakeholder Impacts, Anticipate Stakeholder Expectations of DEF Corporation, and Identify Potential Dilemmas with Community Stakeholders

Phase 2A: Applying the Stakeholder Grid and Impact Assessment tool (introduced in Chapter 3) to key community stakeholders in the gas development project and assess potential stakeholder impacts

Phase 2B: Anticipating stakeholders' expectations of the corporation, and identifying potential integrity dilemmas arising from project impacts and expectations of community stakeholders

Phase 2C: Creating opportunity for innovation with multidisciplinary brainstorming to identify feasible options to manage dilemmas

---

Phase 2A: Applying the Stakeholder Grid and Impact Assessment Tool to Key Community Stakeholders in the Gas Development Project and Assessing Potential Stakeholder Impacts

The Stakeholder Grid and Impact Assessment tool is introduced and explained in Chapter 3.

Earlier chapters highlighted the importance of identifying and defining key corporate stakeholders and their priorities. The Stakeholder Grid and Impact Assessment tool is designed for this purpose. This scenario tailors the tool to focus on one key stakeholder group—the community.

DEF Corporation must first consider how they are going to define their "community" in the context of the gas development project:

- Is a community defined as a predetermined geographic radius from the drilling operations and the pipeline right-of-way?

- Should the community include an entire region (e.g., the state of Colorado) or the county where DEF Corporation is invested?

- Can "community" be defined as selected groups or populations, for example, Aboriginal communities along the pipeline right-of-way?

To reduce confusion and the risk of unmanageable expectations, DEF Corporation is encouraged to thoughtfully consider the definition of their community stakeholders affected by, or having the ability and motivation to affect, the gas project.

After much discussion, DEF Corporation agrees to define its communities as a predetermined geographic radius from the drilling operations and the pipeline right-of-way.

Stakeholder Grid and Impact Assessment Tool: Focus on Community Stakeholders

CATEGORIES OF RISK ARISING IN RELATION TO COMMUNITY	TYPES OF IMPACT				
	REPUTATION	PHYSICAL ASSETS (HARM OR LOSS)	PERSONNEL (HARM OR LOSS)	TIMELINES	SHARE VALUE
Community stakeholder categories:					
Corporate head office	−5 to +5	−3 to +3	−2 to +2	−5 to +5	−5 to +5
Corporate local business unit	−5 to +5	−3 to +3	−3 to +3	−5 to +5	−5 to +5
Local media	−5 to +5	0	0	−5 to +5	−5 to +5

International media	−5 to +5	0	0	−5 to +5	−5 to +5
Project lenders	−5 to +5	0	0	−5 to +5	−5 to +5
Local suppliers	−5 to +5	0	0	−5 to +5	0
Local advocacy NGOs	−5 to +5	−3 to +3	−3 to +3	−5 to +5	−5 to +5
Local partners	−5 to +5	0	−3 to +3	−5 to +5	−5 to +5
Local agents	−5 to +5	−5 to +5	−5 to +5	−5 to +5	−5 to +5
Local personnel	−5 to +5	−5 to +5	−5 to +5	−5 to +5	−5 to +5
Local political leaders	−5 to +5	0	0	−5 to +5	−5 to +5
State government	−5 to +5	0	0	−5 to +5	−5 to +5
Indigenous communities	−5 to +5	−5 to +5	−5 to +5	−5 to +5	−5 to +5
Local indigenous leaders	−5 to +5	−5 to +5	−5 to +5	−5 to +5	−5 to +5
Local regulators	−3 to +3	0	0	−5 to +5	−5 to +5
Representatives of local civil society	−5 to +5	−5 to +5	−5 to +5	−5 to +5	−5 to +5
Local disaffected youth	−5 to +5	−5 to +5	−5 to +5	−5 to +5	−5 to +5
Local religious leaders	−3 to +3	0	0	0	−3 to +3

continued

CATEGORIES OF RISK ARISING IN RELATION TO COMMUNITY	TYPES OF IMPACT				
	REPUTATION	PHYSICAL ASSETS (HARM OR LOSS)	PERSONNEL (HARM OR LOSS)	TIMELINES	SHARE VALUE
Local educators	−2 to +2	0	0	0	0
Local health care providers	−2 to +2	0	0	0	0
Communities along transportation corridors	−5 to +5	−5 to +5	−5 to +5	−5 to +5	−5 to +5

Impact Assessment Scale: −5 = most negative impact potential
0 = no impact
+5 = most positive impact potential

The Stakeholder Grid and Impact Assessment tool must evaluate both the community stakeholders' motivation and capability of causing the identified impact to the corporate project.

Further analysis can be incorporated into relevant parts of the matrix to clarify the magnitude of the harmful action. For example, harm or loss to personnel could include a range of impacts from personal injury, detention, kidnapping, homicide; impacts to physical assets could include theft, sabotage, destruction of assets, or other types of infrastructure impacts that are unique to a business operation or operating environment.

Reputation impacts can be further refined to identify a variety of triggers, for example: lack of transparency, corruption, unfair sharing of benefits, environmental degradation, social/cultural impacts, discrimination, human rights abuses, and Aboriginal interests.

Impacts to share values can be assessed over various timelines: immediate, monthly, financial quarter, annual, life of the project, three to five years, or longer term. Impacts to timelines can be charted against the project timeline.

Given the phases of the gas development project, DEF Corporation is encouraged to plot impacts over the life cycle of the development project. Through this process, the operations group realizes that impacts vary depending on the project phase, but they must be assessed for the full project cycle. Project life cycles for the gas development project and pipeline are defined by DEF Corporation:

Oil and gas project:

- project planning
- right-of-way negotiations
- appraisal and seismic operations
- drilling or mining operations
- production operations
- marketing
- abandonment

Pipeline project:

- project planning
- pipeline route selection
- right-of-way negotiation
- construction and operation

Phase 2B: Anticipating Stakeholders' Expectations of the Corporation, and Identifying Potential Integrity Dilemmas Arising from Project Impacts and Expectations of Community Stakeholders

Some managers within DEF Corporation realize that the company does not really understand the priorities and expectations of local citizens. The Stakeholder Grid and Impact Assessment tool helped the company to identify community stakeholders' potential impacts to the company. As well, the tool helped DEF Corporation to understand the impacts of the gas project on local communities. This understanding enhanced

DEF Corporation's ability to anticipate stakeholders' expectations of DEF Corporation, and to identify and characterize dilemmas.

DEF Corporation can characterize these impacts to the community stakeholders as direct or indirect impacts.

Direct impacts to community stakeholders include environmental, economic, and social outcomes caused directly by a project, including:

- Need for imported labor or services

- Adverse environmental consequences

- Resettlement of people along the pipeline right-of-way

- Allocation of economic share of project benefits to local citizens

Indirect impacts to community stakeholders of the gas development project are more challenging to anticipate, and are caused by broader changes in the community as a consequence of the project, including:

- Increase or decrease in local prices (inflation, deflation)

- Increase or decrease in local traffic

- Increased demands on public goods and services

- Migration to or from the project area

- Increase in contact with community from people outside the community

- Heightened expectations

- Increase in risk of spread of communicable disease

- Greater public scrutiny of stakeholder interests and practices

DEF Corporation recognizes that it is difficult for the company to design community participation strategies without a better knowledge of the community. The company agrees that it should develop some type of stakeholder relations practices to foster dialogue with citizens in the community. Finance in particular is concerned that their project lenders will want more details on community expectations of the project.

The legal group considers it prudent to ensure that the company and its joint venture partners are not liable for any environmental or other liabilities that predate their operation of the gas fields. In addition to assessing legal liabilities, the legal group recommends (contrary to head office) that the joint venture conducts a social baseline survey to facilitate in-depth corporate understanding of their community stakeholders. The finance group endorses this strategy.

DEF Corporation recognizes that different engagement practices will be necessary for individual community groups. In some cases, town hall meetings will be effective to discuss the impacts of a development project with local companies, local citizens, and local government officials. In other cases, DEF Corporation acknowledges that meetings and interviews with local citizens may need to be tailored to be responsive to the community group's culture and impacts. For example, Aboriginal communities may prefer private meetings between their band leader and the company's senior representatives if there are unique project impacts to discuss, such as the need for the company to respect Aboriginal cultural sites in the project design.

As the finance group recognized early, education may be necessary to dispel inaccurate myths about the potential impacts of the gas development project. Some landowners may expect too much from the project, and some landowners may anticipate extreme environmental impacts (e.g., water contamination, noise pollution, heavy traffic, sour gas).

DEF Corporation also realizes that community members have mixed understanding of the risks associated with a gas development project. If exploration activity is not as successful as anticipated, a pipeline may not be constructed. Some members of the corporate management team are tempted to wait until there is undisputed exploration success before engaging with community stakeholders. Other members of the team disagree.

Phase 2C: Creating Opportunity for Innovation with Multidisciplinary Brainstorming to Identify Feasible Options to Manage Dilemmas

The multidepartment team responsible for designing and implementing the corporation's gas development project in Colorado is encouraged to brainstorm and evaluate the potential dilemmas identified by applying the Stakeholder Grid and Impact Assessment tool, and to proactively identify feasible options for strategic response by the corporations. An understanding of the corporation's baseline for community participation established in Phase 1 of this evaluation and decision-making process is helpful in evaluating corporate capacity and motivation to respond to these dilemmas.

This opportunity for innovation cultivates responses to the identified dilemmas as follows:

> *Dilemma:* How can the corporation balance the benefits of early engagement with local stakeholders (in order to better understand community stakeholders and potential project impacts) with the need to manage community expectations?

- Educate local communities about gas development projects so these two objectives can be aligned.

- Design stakeholder engagement practices across the company to ensure consistency in approach for this project.

- Design a community participation strategy for this project, which contemplates voluntary investments in the community. It is particularly critical that the board of directors of DEF Corporation direct the CEO to give the local project managers the authority to make these community investment decisions independently.

- Discuss community engagement strategies with joint venture partners—consider the Colorado-based joint venture partner's direct participation in community engagement; try to garner support for strategies from all partners.

- Encourage an empowerment model in the company to enable corporate personnel to engage with stakeholders and make decisions on the spot (without referral to head office).

- Clarify corporate commitments to community stakeholders, and define corporate personnel's responsibilities and budgets for this work.

> *Dilemma:* An enhanced appreciation of the impacts of the gas development project and pipeline on local communities will be important to

private lenders and, arguably, the company, but what if the analysis takes too much time and slows down the fast-tracking of the project?

- Accept the fact that the project timelines will be slowed down by local communities if an impact assessment is not conducted and impacts are not managed proactively.

- Acknowledge that it is easier and cheaper to incorporate community priorities into project plans on a proactive basis—for example, community preferences for the location of access roads can easily be incorporated into the development plan, but would be costly to revise after development is in place.

- Working with local regulators and community groups to define the scope of assessment can reduce the joint venture's exposure to liability.

Dilemma: Local citizens groups that are not supportive of gas development do not distinguish between investors, so what is the advantage of operating with integrity in relationships with communities?

- Acknowledge that DEF Corporation's corporate reputation is global. Even if some stakeholder groups do not at first distinguish DEF Corporation's practices and commitments to the community, these commitments and practices are relevant to the company's reputation and effectiveness at a local and global level.

- Employ more local personnel; reduce reliance on third-party contractors; encourage employees to reside in the communities and thus develop personal relationships with local citizens and gain a more in-depth appreciation of the impacts of development and the dilemmas.

- With education, distinctions between companies can be communicated. With trust, support of disgruntled community groups may even be possible.

- Engagement reduces the risk of critics condemning DEF Corporation's operations. Reputation risk is very relevant for DEF Corporation in relation to this project.

Navigating Frontier 3: Aligning Corporate Integrity Values, Talk, and Walk in Relation to Community Participation

In order to navigate Frontier 3 in business integrity, the following questions are posed:

The external corporate stakeholder asks: What do you intend by your commitment to the community? How do you create, assess, and manage alignment between corporate commitments to the community and actual corporate practices?

The internal corporate stakeholder asks: What is our corporate commitment to the community? How do we create, manage, and assess ongoing alignment between our corporate commitments and our corporate actions?

Phase 3: Create, Manage, and Assess Alignment between Corporate Commitments to Community Participation and Actual Practices

Phase 3A: Identifying the corporation's commitments to community participation

Phase 3B: Plotting departmental/divisional commitments to community participation and corporate commitments to community participation on the Integrity Ladder

Phase 3C: Applying the Integrity Grid—plotting department/division talk and walk regarding community participation on the Integrity Grid (introduced in Chapter 4):

- *Before* multidepartment brainstorming session on feasible alternatives (reactive)
- *After* multidepartment brainstorming session on feasible alternatives (proactive)

Phase 3 involves application of the Integrity Ladder and the Integrity Grid. The Integrity Ladder is introduced and discussed in Chapter 2 and the Integrity Grid is introduced and discussed in Chapter 4.

Phase 3A: Identifying DEF Corporation's Commitments to Community Participation

The building blocks for DEF Corporation's commitments to the community are alluded to in several corporate documents, including:

- Corporate principles and value statements
- Corporate vision statement
- Codes of conduct
- Public statements in the media
- Formal reports to shareholders

DEF Corporation's commitments to community stakeholders are vague, and there are no guidelines to address community relations, engagement, investment, or participation strategies or best practices. The commitments to community at a corporate level are generally linked to the corporation's reputation and local licence to operate. The company has no commitments regarding its relationships with Aboriginal communities. The company has no commitments to human rights and local community stakeholders.

Phase 3B: Plotting Departmental/Divisional Commitments to Community Participation and Corporate Commitments to Community Participation on the Integrity Ladder

In Phase 3B, the objective is to identify alignments and gaps between the corporation's commitments to integrity, and the commitments of individual departments within DEF Corporation. Using the Integrity Ladder, applied as set out below, the corporation's integrity commitments are identified in the column "Integrity Commitment to Communities (as a Corporation)" and individual departments' commitments are plotted in the column "Integrity Commitment to Communities (by Individual Departments)."

In order to identify the corporation's integrity commitments in relation to community stakeholders, look to the outcomes of Phase 3A; in order to identify individual departments' integrity commitments, go back to the integrity commitments plotted on the Integrity Ladder for each department as set out in Phase 1B earlier in the chapter.

Integrity Ladder

RUNG	PRIMARY MOTIVATION	INTEGRITY COMMITMENT TO COMMUNITIES (BY INDIVIDUAL DEPARTMENTS)	INTEGRITY COMMITMENT TO COMMUNITIES (AS A CORPORATION)
10	Future generations		
9	Sustainable positive social impact		
8	Leverage budget to achieve positive social impact		
7	Leverage budget to do no harm	Environment, health, and safety	
6	Compliance plus proactive risk management		
5	Compliance with rules	Operations	
4	Reputation and reactive risk management	Finance/CEO	DEF Corporation
3	Minimum legal compliance	Government relations/legal/ human resources	
2	Avoid being caught with "dirty hands"	Public relations	
1	Avoid jail		
0	Self-preservation		

This exercise underscores the wide range of departmental commitments to community within DEF Corporation. The environment, health, and safety and operations departments' overstatement of the corporation's values on community participation is problematic as this will raise stakeholders' expectations, which the corporation as a whole cannot support.

DEF Corporation may be willing to clarify its express corporate commitments to community participation in relation to communities affected by North American and European investments. To the extent that DEF Corporation invests outside these geographical regions (including Indonesia), it may be nervous about clarifying commitments to community stakeholders.

Phase 3C: Applying the Integrity Grid

In order to assess the integrity alignment (and gaps) between departments within DEF Corporation, and to identify alignment (and gaps) between individual departments and the organization as a whole, Phase 3C uses the Integrity Grid tool to plot individual departmental commitments and actions.

Individual departmental commitments and actions on integrity are plotted twice in this exercise to reflect differences between proactive and reactive business integrity management practices.

The first plotting is done on the basis of departmental positions prior to the multidisciplinary brainstorming on feasible options (Phase 1 Integrity Ladder outcomes). This plotting reflects the state of DEF Corporation's departmental integrity commitments and actions in a *reactive* mode.

The second plotting is done on the basis of departmental positions after the multidisciplinary brainstorming on feasible options (Phase 2 Stakeholder and Dilemma Analysis outcomes). This second plotting reflects the state of DEF Corporation's departmental integrity commitments and actions in a *proactive* mode.

First Plotting on Integrity Grid: Department Commitments and Department Actions *before* the Stakeholder Grid and Impact Assessment Process

Corporate commitments and individual departmental commitments and actions are considered based on the discussion set out in Phase 1 of this process, and depicted on the grid as follows:

	CODE	ACTIONS	COMMITMENT	DEPARTMENT INTERNAL GAP (ACTIONS MINUS COMMITMENTS)
Corporate	C	–	4	–
Individual departments:				
Chief executive officer	CEO	2	4	–2
Environment, health, and safety	EHS	7	7	0
Public relations	PR	2	2	0
Government relations	GR	3	3	0
Operations	O	4	5	–1
Finance	F	5	4	+1
Legal	L	3	3	0
Human resources	HR	3	3	0

To achieve alignment between individual departmental commitments and actions, the preferred departmental internal gap is zero for the column "Department Internal Gap (Actions Minus Commitments)." There are five departments within DEF Corporation that have aligned their own departmental commitments and actions. The operations and finance groups have a variance where the alignment gap is not that significant. In operations, commitments exceed the departmental actions; in finance, actions exceed departmental commitments. The CEO has a significant gap between commitments and actions.

For DEF Corporation, the greatest lack of alignment is between departments. The corporation's integrity commitment level to community stakeholders is at rung 4; corporate departmental commitments range from a low of rung 2 to a high of rung 7. This lack of alignment is quite problematic for DEF Corporation's reputation, timelines, and operational effectiveness.

The data in the chart above (which is based on Phase 1 Integrity Ladder inputs) is plotted on the Integrity Grid to depict the following:

- Corporate Talk Line (DEF Corporation's commitments to integrity at rung 4 based on Phase 3B plotting)

- Equal Alignment Line (a 45-degree reference line that reflects equal alignment of departmental talk and departmental walk)

- Plot intersection of individual departmental commitments and actions

Observations from the Integrity Grid plotting exercise:

CEO: The CEO is one of the organization's weakest links. His commitments are at rung 4 in line with the company. However, his actual practices are exceedingly low at rung 2. The board of directors should seriously consider reforming or replacing the CEO before irreversible reputation damage results from his behaviors.

Environment, health and safety: This department's commitments and actions are very strong on a relative basis to the rest of the organization. Within the department, there is alignment between commitment and actions. However, there is a wide disparity between this department's

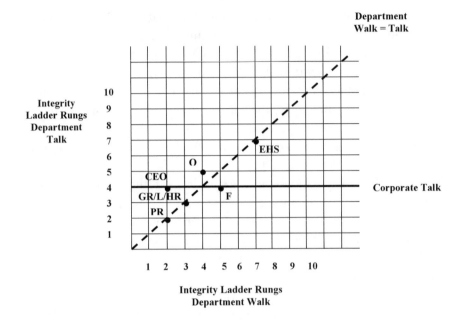

commitments and actions (rung 7) and the commitments of the organization (rung 4). Given this differential between departmental commit-
ments/actions and corporation commitments, this department should
also be identified as a priority for focus.

Public relations: This department is another very weak organizational
link, capable of causing irreparable reputation damage to the corporation
as a whole. Commitments and actions are aligned, but only at rung 2.
Community stakeholders and support groups could be galvanized to
action by the offensive behaviors of this department.

Government relations: This department is marginally higher on the
rungs of the Integrity Ladder than public relations. The department's
commitments and actions are aligned at rung 3 and the alignment is positive, but this department's talk and walk is a rung lower than the corporate level of commitment. This department's commitments and actions
need attention. Local communities could well be enraged by this department's perceived hubris.

Operations: The operations department commits to rung 5 integrity
performance in relation to community stakeholders, but performs at rung

4. This misalignment in departmental commitments and actions should be addressed, as communities will be confused. Operations groups engage frequently with communities. As well, the department's commitment is a rung higher than the corporate level of commitment.

Finance: The finance department is not quite aligned in its commitments and actions. Finance's commitment to integrity is at rung 4, consistent with the corporation's commitment level, but its actions are at rung 5. With a little focus, this department could be aligned with the organizational expectations.

Legal: The land/legal group is aligned in its commitment and practices at rung 3, a rung lower than the corporate level of commitment. This department needs to work with head office to allow some empowerment and decision making at the local project level, and latitude to be more responsive to community stakeholders' expectations. Compensation and reward structures within the company will have to be observed to ensure that empowered personnel are not penalized.

Human resources: The human resources department is aligned at rung 3 in its departmental commitments and actions. Again, the department's integrity commitments and practices are lower than the organizational level of commitment. This lower level of performance could be misleading to community stakeholders. The department has been operating in this manner for over a decade, and would benefit from refreshed thinking on community engagement best practices.

Second Plotting on Integrity Grid: Department Commitments and Department Actions *after* the Stakeholder Grid and Impact Assessment Process

The second plotting is done on the basis of departmental positions after the multidisciplinary brainstorming on feasible options (Phase 2 Stakeholder and Dilemma Analysis outcomes). This second plotting reflects the state of DEF Corporation's departmental integrity commitments and actions in a *proactive* mode.

Overall corporate and individual departmental commitments and actions are considered based on the discussion set out in Phase 2 of this process, and depicted on the grid as follows:

	CODE	ACTIONS	COMMITMENT	DEPARTMENT INTERNAL GAP (ACTIONS MINUS COMMITMENTS)
Corporate	C	5	—	—
Individual departments				
Chief executive officer	CEO	5	5	0
Environment, health, and safety	EHS	6	6	0
Public relations	PR	3	4	–1
Government relations	GR	3	3	0
Operations	O	5	5	0
Finance	F	5	5	0
Legal	L	5	4	+1
Human resources	HR	5	5	0

To achieve alignment between individual departmental commitments and actions, the preferred departmental internal gap is zero for the column "Department Internal Gap (Actions Minus Commitments)."

On the basis of processes set out in Phase B of this framework, remarkable outcomes have been fostered. The corporation as a whole has agreed that the corporate commitment to integrity in relation to community stakeholders on this gas development project must be elevated to a rung 5. The CEO has received an edict from the board of directors to commit and act on integrity at rung 5, and he is cooperating. The human resources manager on this project has retired early, and the new manager is motivated to apply best practices to this development project. Other departments are moving closer to the corporate commitment level on this project—rung 5—and the wide differential between departments is closing. Some work must be done to achieve alignment within the public relations and legal departments, but the most work needs to be done by the public relations and government relations groups to raise the level of commitments and actions.

Shifts up the Integrity Ladder by the company as a whole on this project have enabled shifts within individual departments:

- CEO has moved from rung 2 to rung 5, a substantial jump

- Environment, health, and safety has moved down only one rung to rung 6, and must continue to move down to the corporate project rung at rung 5 or the group may become a lightning rod for critics.

- Public relations has moved from rung 2 to 4 in commitments and rung 3 in integrity actions. More work is necessary to raise the level of this department's performance to the project level. Given the risks, the group is asked not to act in support of this development project until that alignment is achieved; operations is speaking on behalf of the project team.

- Government relations has remained unchanged at rung 3—this group's wait-and-see approach to change will not be tolerated by the project and, like public relations, this group has been asked to stand aside until they are aligned with the project integrity commitment and practice level.

- The operations department has aligned its commitments to be consistent with its actions at rung 5 and is aligned with the overall project commitment level. The head of operations has also moved into the local community.

- The finance department is aligned in commitment and actions at rung 5, and is aligned with the project commitments. This group is well positioned to discuss financing needs for the pipeline project with lenders.

- The legal department is not yet fully aligned with the project commitment level at rung 5. Although the local representative of this department is acting in alignment with the project's level of integrity commitment at rung 5, the head office influence is still relevant and there is a reluctance to commit beyond compliance.

- The human resources department is benefiting from the injection of new thinking in the group. The new manager is motivated to evaluate best practices and to implement them in relation to this gas development project.

When applying these business tools and processes, the first priority is to identify misalignments within individual departments between commitments and actions; the next priority is to work within the individual departments to align the departmental commitments/practices with the organizational commitments.

In this case, the organization's ability to move its integrity commitment level up a rung on the Integrity Ladder was a boost for departmental thinking and alignment. There was no extensive misalignment between individual departmental commitments and actions in DEF Corporation—the priority was narrowing the range of integrity commitments between departments. The departmental brainstorming and innovation fostered ideas that could be presented to head office.

Although head office was not willing to change the entire organization's level of commitment to community stakeholders, the project proponents and managers were able to achieve some shift in relation to this project. If the project's outcomes are successful, the corporation is likely to adopt these practices and commitments across the organization.

The data in the chart above (which is based on Phase 2 Stakeholder Impact and Dilemma Analysis outcomes) is plotted on the Integrity Grid to depict the following:

- Corporate Talk Line (DEF Corporation's commitments to integrity based on Phase 3B plotting)

- Equal Alignment Line (a 45-degree reference line that reflects equal alignment of departmental talk and walk)

- Plot intersection of individual departmental commitments and actions

The second plotting of the Integrity Grid is shown below:

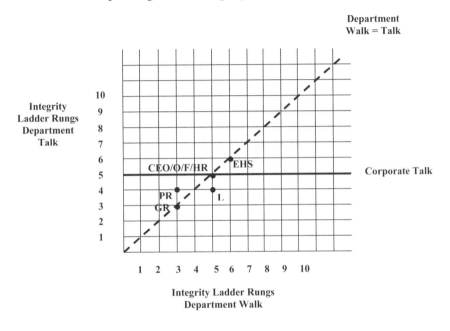

Navigating Frontier 4: Understanding Differences Between Corporations Regarding Corporate Values, Commitments, and Action on Community Participation

To navigate Frontier 4 in business integrity, the following questions are posed:

- What motivates corporate behavior to value community participation and to make commitments to the community? How are these commitments and values manifested in practice?

- What are the differences in corporate motivations in relation to community participation values, commitments, and practices? What are the outcomes of these differences in motivation?

Phase 4: Identifying, Assessing, and Implementing Best Practices for Community Participation

Phase 4A: Applying the Community Investment Strategy tool

Phase 4B: Applying the Permeation of Change model

Phase 4C: Applying the Adapted Best Practices tool

Phase 4D: Applying Benchmarking Practices

Phase 4A: Applying the Community Investment Strategy Tool

What are the models for community participation available to DEF Corporation? How will DEF Corporation and its joint venture partners decide on an effective model? How will DEF Corporation monitor and measure the impacts of community participation?

The Community Investment Strategy tool introduced in Chapter 5 enables corporations to distinguish elements of community participation practices and to clarify their corporate objectives in community participation. By using this tool, DEF Corporation identifies the options in relation to the gas development project in the following table.

Community Investment Strategy Tool

DEFINE THE NATURE OF THE COMMUNITY INVESTMENT	REGULATORY AND CONTRACTUAL COMMITMENTS TO COMMUNITIES	VOLUNTARY COMMUNITY INVESTMENT	PHILANTHROPIC INVESTMENT
Examples	Environmental measures to limit gas flaring and reduce compressor noise; safety regulations for employees	Design access routes in collaboration with local stakeholders; commit to no gas-flaring practices; give ample notice before accessing surface rights; commit to environmental standards to provide comfort to communities on water quality; commit to same safety standards for contractors and employees	Support creation of a research unit to focus on impacts of gas development on water aquifers; provide funding to build capacity of local civil society organizations; fund independent research into Colorado's governance model (Are changes in practices necessarily to give citizens comfort that laws are being enforced?)
Corporate motivation	Compliance with laws	Risk management and securing local licence to operate; can incorporate intent to do no harm and/or foster positive social impact; focus is on this project	Same motivators as voluntary community investment, but less linkage to securing local licence to operate; focus is on supporting dialogue/impact assessment for all development projects in Colorado
Short-term and/or long-term impacts	Generally short term	Both short-term and long-term impacts	Longer term

continued

DEFINE THE NATURE OF THE COMMUNITY INVESTMENT	REGULATORY AND CONTRACTUAL COMMITMENTS TO COMMUNITIES	VOLUNTARY COMMUNITY INVESTMENT	PHILANTHROPIC INVESTMENT
Stakeholder engagement strategy	Engagement with communities, regulators, commercial partners	Direct engagement with community stakeholders is a priority	Limited engagement with community stakeholders—act as a funding source
Allocate percentage of corporate community investment budget	Contracts and regulations prescribe level of commitment	Level of commitment will be set by the project's joint venture partners	Level of commitment set by DEF Corporation on a corporate-wide basis
Corporate approval process	Part of traditional project management process	Can be managed within an individual project's management process; ultimately, these strategies can operate under the umbrella of DEF Corporation's broader business integrity corporate management system	In this case, will be managed on the basis of an alliance between the project lead and head office

Phase 4B: Applying the Permeation of Change Model

Applying the Permeation of Change model introduced in Chapter 5, DEF Corporation's management team identifies its corporate Initiators, Interesteds, Wait-and-See, Followers, and Non-Compliers. Each group is assigned a distinct task in the identification and assessment of best practices:

GROUPS	EFFECTING CHANGE IN BUSINESS INTEGRITY STRATEGY
Initiators: Human resources; environment, health, and safety	• Identify emerging and innovative best practices of corporations on the leading edge of community participation, including private/public sector partnership models for multistakeholder initiatives • DEF Corporation must manage the risk of Initiators making mistakes that affect the company's reputation and/or discourage others • Encourage Initiators to identify/adopt pilot projects and define success criteria to control risks • *Sample initiative:* Create a pilot project to foster alliance between private sector and public sector in addressing and understanding environmental and social impacts of gas development on landowners in Colorado
Interesteds: Finance, operations	• Identify business integrity best practices of competitors in similar projects • Invite Interesteds to work with Non-compliers on implementation of change to shore up the weakest links • *Sample program:* Finance and operations to evaluate other similar projects and assess the need for an integrated impact assessment for this development project; may choose to work with lenders at later stages of this program
Wait-and-Sees: Legal, CEO	• Proactive monitoring of evolving community stakeholder expectations in Colorado • Wait-and-See groups prioritize opportunity management and are strongly motivated by others

continued

GROUPS	EFFECTING CHANGE IN BUSINESS INTEGRITY STRATEGY
	• *Sample monitoring objective:* Legal department (in Colorado and at head office) and CEO work collaboratively to identify key community stakeholders in this gas development project and monitor their expectations; this monitoring approach can then be adopted for use at head office and in other projects (with corresponding changes in rigidity of adherence to corporate precedents)
Followers: Public relations	• Monitor implementation of new corporation policies and strategies on community participation • Followers groups prioritize risk management • *Sample risking strategy:* Ask the public relations group to monitor impacts of community strategies on corporate reputation
Non-compliers: Government relations	• Encourage the Interesteds to support the Non-compliers in change. • Participation in program must be mandated • *Sample program:* Demand that the government relations group work with finance and operations to assess benefits of an integrated impact assessment for this project; the head of the department may also benefit from external integrity training

Phase 4C: Applying the Adapted Best Practices Tool

Stage 1: Identifying business integrity best practices in relation to community

Stage 2: Assessing best practices based on risk/impact and ease of implementation

Stage 3: Selecting practices for DEF Corporation and determining implementation tactics

Stage 1: Identifying Business Integrity Best Practices in Relation to Community

Based on its analysis of the Integrity Grid outcomes and use of the Community Investment Strategy tool, DEF Corporation has identified the following best practices for business integrity in relation to the community:

- *Pilot project:* The environment, health, and safety and human resources departments will create and launch a pilot project to foster alliance between private sector and public sector in addressing and understanding environmental and social impacts of gas development on landowners in Colorado.

- *Use of integrated impact assessments for large projects:* The finance and operations departments will evaluate other similar projects and assess the need for an integrated impact assessment for this development project; they may choose to work with lenders at later stages of this program.

- *Relocate corporate personnel into communities:* The corporation will relocate its key personnel into the communities as residents; it will empower local personnel, and will reduce dependency on third-party contractors.

- *Monitoring project:* The legal department (in Colorado and at the head office) and the CEO will work collaboratively to identify key community stakeholders in this gas development project and monitor their expectations; this monitoring approach can then be adopted for use at head office and in other projects (with corresponding changes in rigidity of adherence to corporate precedents).

- *Links to reputation:* DEF Corporation will more closely link impacts of community strategies to corporate reputation.

- *Training for personnel and joint venture partners:* Training programs will be designed and implemented to embed community participation commitments and practices across the joint venture.

Referring back to the Permeation of Change model, the management team then decides that different groups within the corporation will be assigned responsibility for distinct components of the best practices identification and assessment process:

GROUP	TASK
Initiators	• Identify emerging and innovative best practices of corporations on the leading edge of business integrity • *Method:* Evaluate models for private/public partnerships and impacts of civil society structures • *Deliverable:* Models for civil society
Interesteds	• Identify business integrity best practices of competitors • *Method:* Monitor what other oil and gas companies are doing to assess impacts of large projects • *Deliverable:* Review use of integrated impact assessments in the sector
Wait-and-Sees	• Proactive monitoring of evolving stakeholder expectations on community participation practices • *Method:* Set up process for engagement with community stakeholders in this project • *Deliverable:* Report on meeting outcomes at quarterly meetings and to board of directors
Followers	• Work with corporate risking groups on assessment of corporate reputation risks and strategies to manage • *Method:* Design project to assess corporate reputation value and risks, and identify recommendations for public relations strategies and qualifications • *Deliverable:* Corporate reputation report for the board of directors
Non-compliers	• Force to understand community impacts of development and reflect DEF Corporation's commitments to communities • *Method:* Focused training programs implemented by human resources or outside experts to reinforce understanding of impacts to communities and corporate community strategies • *Deliverable:* Mandatory attendance in training

Stage 2: Assessing Best Practices Based on Risk/Impact and Ease of Implementation

Best practices for business integrity must then be assessed and prioritized by corporate management based on the practices' potential impacts and ease of implementation for DEF Corporation.

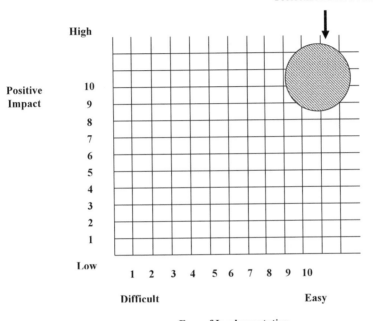

Ease of Implementation

Stage 3: Selecting Best Practices for DEF Corporation and Determining Implementation Tactics

On a project basis, DEF Corporation selects the best practices in the upper right-hand quadrant of the grid for implementation. It encourages individual departments or divisions to select best practices for implementation within their groups as pilots.

Once DEF Corporation has decided to be more responsive to the expectations of its community stakeholders, the corporation has to choose the mechanisms for this community investment. Some corporations elect to manage community investment directly, while other corporations elect to assign management of community investment initiatives to third parties. This delegation of management of community investment can be achieved through engagement with local or international foundations, charities, or through partnerships with other corporations or organizations. Co-managed programs are also feasible.

A decision to develop internal corporate capacity to design and implement community investment programs has many advantages:

- Relationships established between corporate personnel and community stakeholders are direct.

- Corporate skills in marketing, purchasing, human resources, management, and other functions can be effectively applied to community investment projects.

- Engendering cross-functional teams within corporate departments can also be rewarding.

The operations group is particularly interested in developing corporate capacity to engage directly with communities.

Corporations may also choose to implement community investment objectives by engaging with other stakeholders or third parties. DEF Corporation's voluntary community investments can be implemented through participation with other corporations in business groups, through contributions to locally developed foundations or nongovernmental organizations, through partnerships with local or international nongovernmental organizations, or through employee volunteer programs. The human resources and environment, health, and safety departments at DEF Corporation are particularly interested in working collaboratively with other organizations to test pilot community investment projects.

Phase 4D: Benchmarking Practices

At this time, DEF Corporation will not participate in benchmarking surveys conducted in relation to investment in Colorado or in industry benchmarking surveys. The company's community participation strategies in relation to the gas development project in Colorado are intended to test the corporate capacity and abilities. If the results are encouraging, the company will then apply the practices for community participation across the company, and will then elect to participate in benchmarking surveys. Internal benchmarking of corporate departments or divisional effectiveness (financial and nonfinancial) in response to community participation values may be conducted as an interim assessment tool.

Navigating Frontier 5: Accountability for Community Participation

Key challenges to be navigated in Frontier 5 are the design and implementation of dependable and strategic corporate accountability systems and processes that manifest community values and build trust with community stakeholders.

Phase 5: Accountability for Community Participation

Phase 5A: Clarifying accountabilities with the Business Integrity Accountability Cycle

Phase 5B: Implementing an accountability strategy for community participation

Phase 5C: Developing continuous improvement

Phase 5A: Clarifying Accountabilities with the Business Integrity Accountability Cycle

Corporations prioritize relationships with communities where they operate, but frequently fail to manage community participation as a strategic business integrity objective. To ensure that community participation strategies are managed and accounted for, DEF Corporation has clarified its commitments to community stakeholders and practices using the Community Investment Strategy tool.

DEF Corporation's project team must keep checking back with this management tool as a framework to ensure effective accountability and assurance of the corporation's community values through:

The Business Integrity Accountability Cycle

- Dependable management systems that support community values
- Community participation measures and monitoring
- Community participation verification processes
- Community participation reporting structures

Use of the Business Integrity Accountability Cycle will help the DEF project team clarify accountabilities for integrity commitments and actions. Much work must be done within the project group, and ultimately within the overall company, to clarify how the company measures, monitors, and verifies outcomes of community participation commitments and actions. Reporting on the outcomes will also be challenging; once the public relations team is better equipped to understand the links between corporate reputation and commitments to community stakeholders, this group can lead the reporting process. In the interim, it is best for the operations group to lead.

Phase 5B: Implementing an Accountability Strategy for Community Participation

- Implement strategies to address dilemmas/issues

- Monitor/measure outcomes as described in Part 1, Chapter 6

- Measure outcomes on Integrity Grid at defined intervals (at least quarterly)

- Verify and report on outcomes

Phase 5C: Developing Continuous Improvement

The first priority is to identify misalignments within individual departments between commitments and actions; the next priority is to work within the individual departments to achieve alignment between the departmental commitments/practices and the organizational commitments. In the case of DEF Corporation, the critical alignment issue is the extreme differentials between departments in integrity commitment to community stakeholders. The organizational commitment bar for the project has been elevated to rung 5. The next challenge is to bring DEF Corporation to that functioning level in relation to this gas development project and its other projects.

Observations for DEF Corporation: Impacts of Reactive or Proactive Management of Business Integrity

Outcomes vary when a corporation decides to adopt a proactive or reactive approach to business integrity management.

If DEF Corporation had applied a reactive approach to this gas development project in Colorado, the company would not be positioned to:

- Recognize the wide gaps between departments in commitments to community stakeholders

- Identify the public relations group and the CEO as the weakest links

- Identify the risks associated with such a wide range of commitments and practices within the company

Although the company may have been tempted to develop and implement community participation strategies on a reactive basis in response to complaints from the community, this strategy is likely to have caused great angst among community stakeholders. The public relations, government relations, and legal departments and the CEO were headed on a path of irretrievable corporate reputation damage. Recovering from allegations of hubris and arrogance would have been challenging, costly, and time-consuming for the project. Project timelines would undoubtedly have been stretched, and budgets would have to be increased to fund a defensive strategy.

The decision to move corporate personnel into the local communities and empower these individuals to make decisions, speak for the company, and take risks will be a proactive corporate culture shift that may allow the company to anticipate risks with local communities and more effectively design and implement community participation strategies. The corporate personnel need to thoroughly understand community impacts in order to anticipate the dilemmas. It is unlikely that people will ever be happy about a gas pipeline in their backyard, but the company's proactive strategies allow them to anticipate the impacts and dissent, and manage the dilemmas. The community stakeholders will be more likely to trust the corporation and the joint venture.

The joint venture's participation in the broader issues—balancing local community stakeholder impacts and the country's need for gas reserves—remains uncertain. DEF Corporation and its partners may elect to participate in dialogue on this dilemma, or they may elect not to participate because this dilemma is not within their sphere of influence.

The joint venture will also need to focus on some key stakeholder groups, including Aboriginal communities directly and indirectly affected by the project. The best practices identified and applied in other local communities may need to be tailored to be effective with Aboriginal communities. The company may choose to engage experts for advice on relationships with these communities, and must resist the tendency to apply their strategies with all communities on a cookie-cutter basis.

DEF Corporation has many more decisions to make about its corporate strategy with communities. The company's board of directors has been alerted to this process of anticipating dilemmas, and recognizes that serious reform of management practices is an imperative. The CEO has been given the opportunity to reform his integrity practices, and changes implemented in relation to the gas project suggest that transformation is feasible.

Adopting a proactive approach to community stakeholders and strategy will ultimately save money and time for DEF Corporation and its joint venture partners. But, at the outset, as personnel's time is spent designing and implementing programs with seemingly intangible results, there may be disquiet, even grumbling, about the budget and resource allocations necessary to design, discuss, and implement community participation strategies. The company must continuously reinforce the value of this work to the company and the joint venture.

There is a lot of work ahead to determine how to ensure joint venture accountability for community participation commitments and actions, which will draw employees away from the technical aspects of the project and compliance with regulations. The project team will need unequivocal support from head office on the value of this work: if community participation strategies are not supported and mandated as a business imperative, the project team will be tempted to slip back to focusing on tangible project outcomes. If the company reverts to a reactive mode, the corporation's efforts will have been in vain, and the company may in fact be worse than when it started because community stakeholders' expectations will have been raised.

PART 3

The Road Ahead for Corporate Integrity

The Horizon:
The Finish Line Is Still Moving

The finish line in business integrity has moved, and it is predictable that the expectations of stakeholders and responsive best practices will continue to evolve.

In the 1970s and 1980s, many corporations resisted but ultimately responded to internal and external corporate stakeholder demands to design and implement comprehensive safety and environmental policies and practices. In the 1990s and into the twenty-first century, corporations are challenged to design and implement comprehensive business integrity systems that respond to the evolving priorities of traditional stakeholders and those of emerging stakeholders.

To keep abreast of these changes in business operating environments, corporate managers are encouraged to stay focused on identifying and closing the integrity gaps in their organizations. Also, corporate leaders are encouraged to assess when their organizational commitments to integrity need to be moved up a rung on the Integrity Ladder.

The Incentive: Carrots or Sticks?

Some corporate managers, motivated by strict legal compliance, will capitulate to stakeholders' demands for changes to corporate management systems and business integrity practices only when regulated to do so by governmental or quasi-governmental authorities. In defense of this reactive strategy, these corporate managers point to the risks of corporations being exposed to incremental liability if commitments made to social accountabilities are not sufficiently clear or are misinterpreted by stakeholders.

Other corporate managers will link business integrity policy and strategy to their organization's overall risk management and corporate reputation strategies. These corporate managers will be motivated by a combination of sticks and carrots.

Finally, there will be a contingent of corporate leaders who proactively choose to address business integrity as a critical and integrated strategy to facilitate corporate contribution to the social fabric of their investment environments. Carrots motivate these leaders.

Motivation Continuum: Options to Stimulate Corporate Integrity

LEGISLATE CORPORATE INTEGRITY	CORPORATE WATCHDOG CULTURE	EXTERNAL STAKEHOLDER CRITICISM	REWARD CORPORATE INTEGRITY	REWARD INDIVIDUAL INTEGRITY	VOLUNTARY INITIATIVES/ ALLIANCES
Stick	Stick	Stick	Carrot	Carrot	Carrot

From the external stakeholder's perspective, which is the more effective and sustainable motivator—carrots or sticks? Perspectives are wide-ranging.

Some would argue that sticks should not replace strategy: the majority of companies have tended to be reasonable in defining their social accountabilities without government bullying, and companies are most effective as social volunteers by responding to their stakeholders' unique interests. For example, cosmetics manufacturers and other companies that sell products targeted to women support breast cancer research; extractive sector companies operating in Africa support HIV/AIDS research. Imposition of one-size-fits-all regulations can undermine enthusiasm for volunteerism and detracts from individual companies' ability to focus on their distinctive strengths.

Conversely, in some operating environments, legislated social mandates (coupled with transparent and enforceable consequences for noncompliance), arguably, have material impact. For example, in 2003, South Africa released a list of nineteen conditions that mining companies were to comply with to have licences renewed. The conditions included teaching workers to read and write, developing communities near mines, building infrastructure such as houses and roads, bringing more women into mining operations, not discriminating against foreign migrant labor, and purchasing goods from companies owned by blacks.

In order to motivate all categories of corporate leaders, a blend of carrots and sticks is evolving in practice.

The Stick as Motivator

Motivating corporate behavior with a stick encompasses a broad range of actions, including:

- *Corporate management:* can adopt a "watchdog" corporate culture to monitor compliance by corporate personnel with laws, regulations, and the organization's own rules

- *Governing authorities:* can use legal and regulatory systems to impose, regulate, and monitor organizational and individual behaviors.

- *External stakeholders:* can publicly criticize or exclude corporations and individuals who misbehave.

Corporate Watchdog Culture

Corporate managers may tighten their oversight of corporate personnel to ensure that integrity is not breached. Corporate employees' unauthorized access to sensitive information, such as bids on tenders or the release of financial information, can seriously compromise a corporation. In-house security precautions can be increased and whistle-blowing may be adopted as best practices to ensure that corporate behaviors are monitored.

Corporate watchdog practices can be effective. For example, accounting software makers are developing computer programs that flag unusual bookkeeping practices, and can even launch investigations with little human intervention. Software manufacturers point to WorldCom to demonstrate the merits of this watchdog practice—the company's capital spending was markedly higher than its competitors'. Tailored watchdog software may have identified the anomalies for corporate auditors and executives.

Taken to excess, these watchdog measures do, however, risk fostering a culture of distrust within corporations. The inadvertent or intentional behavior of corporate employees is an acknowledged threat to corporations. The risks range from theft, misuse of data, or cyber-vandalism to more unintentional behaviors that leave corporations vulnerable.

While these risks require management, some corporate teams are cautious in imposing watchdog or whistle-blowing practices given their potential impacts on corporate culture. Considerable clarification of the pressing need for watchdog practices is required to foster employee support. Employee participation in designing these practices can be helpful in mitigating negative implications to organizational culture.

Regulating Corporate Behaviors

Advocates for more onerous legislative and regulatory controls on corporate behaviors have been successful in lobbying for stronger laws to govern corporate behaviors, and governmental and regulatory bodies are listening. The Sarbanes-Oxley Act, supported by the United States Securities and Exchange Commission, is the heavyweight in this evolving legislative regime. The United Kingdom is evaluating the merits of a corporate social responsibility bill and many European Union countries are considering regulatory motivators for corporations, particularly in the wake of the Parmalat scandal.

There are two critical outstanding questions in the debate about the effectiveness of regulatory compliance as a stick to motivate corporate integrity behaviors. Firstly, to what extent does more legislation positively influence corporate behaviors and, secondly, how do governmental and regulatory bodies monitor and ensure compliance with the burgeoning layers of legislated behaviors?

Looking at the first question, to what extent does legislated behavior result in more ethical corporate behavior? This is a question that requires further understanding and analysis. For companies with embedded integrity practices, additional regulation may not alter corporate integrity outcomes. For companies with integrity gaps or companies primarily motivated by compliance, additional regulation may stimulate enhanced integrity practices.

In order to respond to citizens' appeals for corporate accountability, regulators are being mandated to craft legislation with teeth. The public demands that corporations and individuals who fail to comply with legislative mandates be publicly censured and financially accountable. Consequences of noncompliance are increasingly sufficient to deter potential violators: fines are reaching record levels; a corporation's right to operate may be compromised; and jail terms are imposed when the potential consequence of misbehavior is significant or deterrence is a priority.

For example, in 2003, the media heralded the announcement that an Atlanta-based pipeline corporation, Colonial Pipeline Corporation, would pay $34 million in fines under the United States' Clean Water Act as a consequence of oil spills, "the largest civil penalty ever paid by a corporation in the 32-year history of the Environmental Protection Agency."

Beyond the imposition of fines and penalties, the risk of public censure for violating laws can detrimentally affect a corporation's reputation, exacting an even greater and long-lasting financial and nonfinancial toll.

But questions still remain about the regulation of corporate behaviors: does more regulation generate more corporate integrity? A recent study by a World Bank team observed the correlation between regulation of business and national income in 130 countries. The World Bank team's report reflected that the poorest countries have the most rules. As the report suggests, the rules were no doubt drawn up with the best of intentions, but rules themselves do not alleviate poverty, and may even become a barrier to investment if they dampen entrepreneurial risk taking and provide an avenue for corruption.

Beyond the impact of rule promulgation, we must also assess a regulatory or legislative body's motivation and ability to monitor and assure corporate compliance with laws and rules. If enforcement of rules becomes arbitrary, the level playing field required to stimulate corporate investment and impact is compromised. If corporate compliance with rules can only be haphazardly monitored—for example, because regulatory bodies cannot afford to deploy more enforcement officers or inspectors—public enthusiasm for rules will wane.

Stakeholder Wrath

Stakeholder groups—consumers, advocacy organizations, investment fund managers, and communities—can influence corporate behavior by publicly criticizing business integrity practices or by excluding corporations from participation in certain activities or organizations.

Consumer boycotts of a corporation's products can be organized to channel the wrath of stakeholder groups. Particularly successful boycotts have been organized by advocacy groups to target name-brand companies within larger consumer markets—for example, gas station chains such as Exxon and Shell; popular sporting and apparel companies such as Nike and Adidas; and producers of hygiene products such as Unilever and Proctor & Gamble.

Nestlé's experiences with consumer boycotts, and even threats of boycotts, are extraordinary. In 2002, Nestlé relented to international pressure following bad publicity about its attempt to recover a £6 million debt from the government of Ethiopia. Just a threat of consumer activism made the Swiss corporation backtrack. For Nestlé, the wrath of stakeholders has seemed unrelenting. Nestlé's attempts to partner with a leading breast cancer charity in the United Kingdom were rejected in part at least due to ethical concerns over the corporation's promotion of infant baby formula milk in the developing world.

Corporate management's vulnerability to advocacy by nongovernmental organizations, citizens groups, and consumers is criticized by some. Reebok's response to sweatshop allegations in Asia was to withdraw business from a subcontracted factory in Thailand as proof of its corporate responsibility. Although workers at the Bangkok factory were paid above minimum wage and had access to health and safety rights that few local manufacturers could offer, the corporation elected to pull out of this link in its supply chain in response to advocacy. Some corporate stakeholders questioned the merits of this decision; what was more responsible: to provide employment to peasants in Thailand, or to withdraw from Thailand because of the reputation risks?

Community stakeholders are often positioned to reward or condemn corporate behaviors. Members of local communities are frequently motivated to band together to ask probing questions about corporate development projects, for example, the relaxation of zoning regulations that allow the construction of a new plant or office building in a quasi-residential neighborhood. Private sector projects in the developing world frequently encounter community-championed advocacy, some of which can be quite constructive. In Nigeria, protests led by local women have proven to be an effective means for host communities in the Delta region. Peaceful protests by local women have raised awareness of the environmental impact of oil production and unfair allocations of the benefits of oil operations; these protests have been beneficial in guiding corporate response.

Advocacy by fund managers can also be very influential. Pension fund managers and ethical fund managers have significant motivation and ability to withhold benefits from corporations assessed as lacking integrity. The California Public Employees Retirement System (Calpers), with an estimated U.S. $150 billion in assets, is a strong advocate for socially responsible investing. In 2003, Calpers stunned Asian markets when it suggested that it might sell off roughly U.S. $1 billion in assets in the Philippines, Thailand, Indonesia, and Malaysia because these operating environments did not meet new standards ranging from trading liquidity to human rights. Socially responsible investing is clearly no longer just a left-wing political agenda and is becoming more and more mainstream.

In view of deeply rooted philosophical differences of opinion regarding the role of corporations, it is likely that the future will see a continuation of stakeholder groups wielding sticks to motivate corporate behaviors. It is also appropriate to note the limitations of this advocacy: nonpublic companies are predictably less intimidated by advocacy that threatens corporate reputation on a short-term basis, and consumer boycotts are not a practical means to express dissatisfaction with the vast majority of corporations that do not market to the public.

Finally, these advocates will also have to innovate ways to constructively influence the integrity behaviors of corporations from non-Western cultures. Non-Western companies are increasing their investment thresholds in Western operating environments, and are more likely to partner with Western companies. Traditional sticks wielded by advocates have not as yet proven as effective in influencing the integrity commitments of non-Western companies.

The Carrot as Motivator

Motivating corporate behavior with carrots also encompasses a broad range of actions:

- *Corporate management:* can adopt a reward system that recognizes and compensates individuals' alignment to integrity commitments.

- *Governing authorities:* can use legal and regulatory systems to reward corporate and individual behaviors that are responsive to business integrity.

- *External stakeholders:* can publicly applaud or encourage corporations that demonstrate responsiveness to business integrity commitments

Corporate Recognition and Reward Strategies

In earlier chapters, the crucial links between corporate commitments to integrity and personnel compensation and reward strategies were examined. In order to encourage corporate walk on integrity, employees must be rewarded for behaviors that are aligned to the corporate talk on integrity.

A corporation's clarity in defining business integrity expectations and measuring outcomes of strategy influences its organizational ability to assess individual, departmental, and overall organizational business integrity performance. If there is a lot of talk about the importance of business integrity—but without corresponding recognition and rewards for positive employee and departmental alignment with corporate business integrity expectations in corporate compensation schemes—the commitments quickly become nothing more than rhetoric. If individuals and departments are not reprimanded for failure to adhere to corporate business integrity commitments, what is the incentive for individuals or departments to support the organization's business integrity vision?

Regulatory Incentives

When the rule of law is contemplated as a motivational tool, stakeholders generally think of laws and regulations as sticks to be wielded to punish poor corporate behavior.

Laws and regulations can also be used to reward good corporate performance on business integrity. At this time, there are only a few precedents for regulatory incentives to reward corporate integrity. Access to some government funding (for example, capital and insurance accessible through export credit agencies) may be conditional on business integrity track records. As well, certain taxation incentives and governmental or regulatory recognition awards are available only to companies that demonstrate integrity. Social fund managers are able to recognize certain companies in their funds on the basis of a corporation's integrity track record. FTSE4Good in the U.K. and The Jantzi Social Index in Canada are good examples.

As corporations and their key stakeholders enhance their ability to measure and report on business integrity indicators, the scope for regulatory incentives to corporations operating with integrity can be expanded.

Stakeholder Engagement and Voluntary Action Models

Most emerging practice in business integrity is evolving in the field of stakeholder engagement and volunteer action. In an effort to achieve impact and sustainability in integrity practices, alliances and partnerships among multiple stakeholder groups are increasing.

Corporations are hiring former advocacy campaigners, funding think tanks, and supporting alliances with advocacy groups modeled on the campaigns launched against them. Companies are routinely hiring former heads of nongovernmental organizations to manage stakeholder relations.

Partnerships among corporations, academic institutions, advocacy groups, and nonadvocacy nongovernmental organizations are on the rise. Some of these alliances are strategic, and some alliances flounder. Corporate stakeholders are encouraged to carefully evaluate partnership synergies before embarking on a course of engagement that is intended to be sustainable.

Models of emerging alliances include the following:

Alliances among corporations within industry groups and among corporations

- The International Petroleum Industry Environmental Conservation Association joined the International Association of Oil and Gas Producers to conduct joint studies of social impacts of oil and gas projects.

- The Mining Association of Canada's stewardship initiative "Toward Sustainable Mining" endorses environmental and stakeholder inclusion practices for member companies to help the industry sector earn its social licence to operate on an individual and collective basis.

Alliances between institutions and corporations

- Santa Clara University, Markkula Center for Applied Ethics, hosts corporations and other stakeholders at conferences to address business ethics issues.

Alliances between advocacy nongovernmental organizations and corporations

- Oxfam has engaged with major investors in GlaxoSmithKline over developing countries' access to AIDS drugs.

- The Swiss branch of Clean Clothes Campaign launched a pilot project in 2000 seeking garment retailers to adopt a model code of conduct and to ensure implementation of the code through its supply chain. Heeding this call, three Swiss garment retailers adopted the code and agreed to test the feasibility of establishing an independent mechanism to monitor implementation of the code in India and China. The Swiss garment retailers were Migros, Switcher, and Veillon.

- An evaluation of human rights and business was conducted by Amnesty International and the Prince of Wales Business Leaders Forum. A joint report was issued, entitled *Human Rights: Is It Any of Your Business?*

Alliances between nonadvocacy nongovernmental organizations and corporations

- Microsoft Corporation partners with not-for-profits—Mercy Corps and Save the Children—to link technology and society.

Alliances among corporations and governments

- The Extractive Industries Transparency Initiative was announced by U.K. Prime Minister Tony Blair in 2002 at the World Summit on Sustainable Development in Johannesburg.

- The Extractive Industries Review consultation was organized by the World Bank Group.

Alliances among corporations and multilateral organizations

- The UN's Global Compact encourages corporations to commit to social accountability practices and report on the outcomes. The Global Compact has facilitated policy dialogue on many subjects, including the private sector role in conflict zones.

- The World Bank's Business Partners for Development encourages and supports partnerships among corporations invested in targeted countries and alignment in approach in addressing social accountabilities.

- *Investing in People: Sustaining Communities through Improved Business Practice* is a guide published by the International Finance Corporation in 2003.

Alliances among multiple stakeholder groups and corporations

- George Soros's "publish what you pay" campaign brought together multiple advocacy and nonadvocacy nongovernmental organizations. This campaign was directed to corporations invested in countries where the host governments do not disclose revenues from foreign investment. The campaigners advocated for corporations to disclose to the public what they paid in taxes and royalties to host government coffers.

- The Marine Stewardship Council, an independent, global, nonprofit organization, is working to reverse the continued decline of the world's fisheries. First established by Unilever and WWR in 1997, the program works through a multistakeholder partnership approach.

- A Canadian partnership among Mount Royal College, Petro-Canada, and the Centre for Affordable Water and Sanitation Technology was declared in April 2003. This innovative partnership was formed to develop the training materials and curricula for extension courses in low-cost water and sanitation technologies and practices.

Evaluating the Benefits of Alliances

Many of the stakeholder engagement and voluntary actions profiled in this chapter have been effective vehicles for advancing corporate responses to business integrity mandates. However, some public/private sector partnerships have not borne fruit. The lessons learned can be important for corporate leaders and their stakeholders.

Some critics publicly question how nongovernmental organizations can be both adversarial and collaborative. It is readily accepted that corporations can gain market intelligence and credibility through closer ties with the not-for-profit world. However, benefits of partnership for the not-for-profit partner are sometimes questioned and, in the case of advocacy groups where reputations depend on their independence, alliances can even be detrimental.

When Greenpeace joined forces with energy corporations BP and Royal Dutch Shell to urge governments to tackle climate change at the Johannesburg summit on sustainable development, the public/private partnership was viewed skeptically, the alliance being openly referred to an "unholy" alliance. Likewise when World Wildlife Foundation, the world's largest conservation group, partnered with a French company seeking to build a massive quarry on the island of Harris, Friends of the Earth International, another major environmental group, claimed that WWF International was being cynically used by the company.

To some, public/private partnerships will remain contentious and suspicious. Accusations that corporations are hijacking earth summits and pushing their own agenda of free trade in developing countries are abating, but suspicions continue.

In their 2004 report entitled *Behind the Mask: The Real Face of Corporate Social Responsibility*, Christian Aid went so far as to assert that business is using corporate social responsibility as a shield behind which to campaign *against* environmental and human rights regulations. Even the self-interest of multinational corporations in delivering aid is questioned. Some charities and stakeholder groups accuse corporations of entering into water, sanitation, and electricity partnerships only to foster privatization of these infrastructure environments for the benefit of big business. The cycle of recrimination can be challenging to break.

Integrity Frontiers

It would be impossible to predict all emerging integrity dilemmas, but there are a few noteworthy trends that corporations may choose to monitor. If corporate systems and practices are sound, emerging dilemmas can be anticipated and managed on a proactive basis. Emerging integrity dilemmas include the following issues:

Revenue Allocation: Local Benefit Issues

Stakeholders at local, national, and international levels are increasingly adept at evaluating the overall economic benefit of private sector investments and monitoring allocations of the revenue pie among key stakeholder groups. In cases where local communities do not derive significant benefit from corporate investment, questions are being asked. Corporate investors may find themselves at the crossroads of this discussion.

This issue can manifest in many forms:

- *Impacts of tax havens, harmful tax avoidance, and evasion:* Some nongovernmental organizations advocate establishing standards discouraging corporations from the use of tax havens, harmful tax avoidance, and tax evasion as part of the corporate social responsibility agenda. Advocates, including Oxfam, demand that standards be established to require corporations to make information available, and to refrain from aggressive tax planning, the use of transfer pricing, thin capitalization, and the use of conduit and base corporations for the purpose of modifying tax bases. The tax-planning industry is encouraged to establish codes of conduct to provide a socially responsible, rather than merely legal, dimension to the tax advice that is offered to transnational corporations. Fund managers are beginning to assess corporations on these criteria, downgrading corporations that are evasive. Henderson Global Investors recently decided to contact all the companies in the FTSE 350 index to ask about their tax affairs.

- *Push for transparency:* To enhance the transparency of government benefits of foreign investment, George Soros's financial transparency campaign "publish what you pay" encourages corporations to disclose taxes and royalties paid to host governments.

- *Benefits of development:* There is heightened stakeholder sensitivity to the social, environmental, and economic impacts of sudden increases in foreign direct investment and revenues, particularly in developing countries with authoritarian leadership. For example, the possibility of substantial oil development in the tiny African state of São Tomé e Principe or in Mauritania raises questions about the impacts of oil revenues on local economies.

- *Imposition of controls on government revenue sources:* Multistakeholder governance structures were imposed to support the private sector development of the Chad-Cameroon pipeline. The World Bank's support of the pipeline's construction was endorsed by local and international stakeholder groups on the condition that a significant portion of oil proceeds paid to the government of Chad be managed by a group of trustees representing multilateral organizations, not-for-profit organizations and local government representatives. This governance and oversight structure was imposed in anticipation of the risk of the Chad government not applying the newfound oil revenues to social development priorities in the country.

- *Sharing benefits with future generations:* There is advocacy in support of the creation of future generation funds to ensure that host governments apply proceeds of investment for future stakeholders. These funds have been created during boom periods in Alberta, Canada.

Debt Forgiveness by Corporations

Campaigners have in recent years successfully persuaded the International Monetary Fund and the World Bank to forgive some of the hefty debts owed by poor countries. These same campaigners and others are now turning their attention to foreign debts that corporations owe as a result of their successful compensation claims for corporate assets expropriated by the governments of poor countries.

In 2003, two substantial corporations—Nestlé and Big Food—capitulated to public relations campaigns launched by advocacy groups. Jubilee Debt Campaign launched a campaign against Big Food, the parent of Iceland, a British supermarket chain, and persuaded the corporation to drop its claim against the government of Guyana for U.S. $19 million in compensation for sugar mills seized in the 1970s (and now worth a reported U.S. $1 billion). Nestlé, under pressure from Oxfam, chose to give up a long-standing claim against Ethiopia for assets seized by the country's 1970s Marxist dictatorship.

Allegations of Corporate Complicity in Human Rights Violations

Multinational corporations risk allegations of being complicit with human rights violations. Allegations of corporate complicity with human rights offenses of host governments, local partners, and other corporate stakeholders can encompass a wide range of human rights charges, including torture, forced child labor, and denial of freedom of expression.

Unocal Corporation was alleged to be complicit in human rights abuses during the construction of a U.S. $1.3 billion pipeline in Myanmar. Critics alleged that Unocal entered into a business relationship with the brutal military regime in Myanmar, knowing that the military would violate many human rights to further the project. The accusations resulted in a lengthy judicial battle which was settled out of court in late 2004.

Amnesty International and the Prince of Wales International Business Leaders Forum published a research report in 2002 on this mounting risk. The study, entitled *Business and Human Rights: A Geography of Corporate Risk*, points to problems associated with corporations' supply chains and misuse of goods after production. Corporations and their stakeholders are already familiar with the allegations of corporate complicity made against extractive corporations operating in countries where the host governments sanction the use of torture. This Amnesty International/Prince of Wales report suggests that the scope for allegations of corporate complicity in human rights violations may extend to include supply chains and misuse of goods after production. For example, information technology corporations may come under attack if their products are used by repressive regimes to violate privacy or curtail freedom of expression. Likewise, chemical corporations can face complicity accusations if their products are misused.

Corporate Liability for Business Integrity Commitments

The consumer activist lawsuit recently lodged against Nike, alleging that the sportswear manufacturer violated California's false-advertising code by making false statements in a variety of communications to the public, represents a new type of threat to corporations that make business integrity statements.

In the lawsuit, allegations were made that Nike's public relations campaign falsely guaranteed that it had complied with health, safety, and environmental regulations in factories where its shoes are made and falsely represented the conditions for 450,000 workers who make Nike shoes.

California courts determined that the purpose of the Nike public relations campaign was to "maintain its sales and profits" and, as a result, was a form of commercial speech not entitled to full First Amendment free speech protection if it contained false statements. The unfortunate consequence of limiting the reach of freedom of speech protections for corporations may be to discourage corporations from publicly reinforcing their business integrity commitments.

The Long Arm of Corporate Liability

Multinational parent corporations are increasingly being held to account in Western courts for damages they cause in the developing world. Applying the legal principle of the corporate veil between subsidiaries and a parent corporation, multinationals have contended that a parent corporation is a mere shareholder of a subsidiary corporation and should not be held legally liable for subsidiaries' actions. However, parent corporations are being held to account for their global operations.

In the OK Tedi case, thousands of Papua New Guinea landowners successfully sued BHP, the multinational mining company, in Australian courts for contaminating their land. In the United Kingdom, the parent companies of Rio Tinto, Cape PLC, and Thor Chemicals have been the subject of several rulings by the Court of Appeal and the House of Lords. In the United States, multinational corporations Unocal and Talisman have been subject to the jurisdiction of United States courts for alleged damages inflicted outside the United States under the Alien Tort Claims Act.

As well, there is a rise in class action litigation against corporations. Zealous lawyers are motivated to test new corporate liability frontiers, for example, by launching lawsuits against McDonald's on the basis of obesity impacts. As advocates and the media raise awareness of emerging stakeholder expectations of corporations, litigation is a predictable corollary.

Accountability of Not-for-Profit Organizations

Nongovernmental organizations are pressuring corporations to demonstrate business integrity and transparency, and the tables are turning. Corporations are now pressuring nongovernmental organizations to demonstrate integrity and transparency. Increasingly, corporations are asking activist groups to demonstrate the same level of transparency that is being asked of corporations—specifically, asking advocacy groups to disclose their supporters and clarify their decision-making processes.

Shareholder Activism

Shareholder activism is gaining momentum, and the impacts of shareholder-championed initiatives are a progressively more powerful influence on corporate behaviors. Annual general meetings are becoming a more common venue for debate of integrity issues. Behind the scenes, institutional investors often wield significant clout.

Shareholder resolutions may be focused objections to the corporation's investments in certain projects or geographical locations, or changes in compensation arrangements for corporate directors and executives may be questioned.

Increasingly, shareholder challenges are including more wide-sweeping, ideologically based recommendations on business integrity management within corporations. For example, 2003 proposals lodged by shareholders of Manulife Financial Corporation included recommendations that the board of directors create an ethics committee to ensure that the corporation uses all necessary means to foster a corporate culture founded on the highest ethical standards.

Similarly, at the 2003 annual meeting for shareholders of Imperial Oil Ltd. in Toronto, the corporation faced a shareholders' resolution calling for the corporation to disclose its financial risks associated with reducing greenhouse gas emissions to meet the Kyoto Accord. Kairos, a church organization, brought the resolution forward on behalf of three Imperial shareholders—the Presbyterian Church, the Sisters of Saint Anne, and Les Soeurs de Saint-Joseph de Saint-Hyacinthe.

Industry Self-Regulation

Part 1 identified the phenomena of the weakest links within corporations. Within industry sectors, competitors or other corporations in a supply chain can compromise the reputation and opportunity of their peer group, thus becoming the weakest link in the sector.

Although slightly contradictory to traditional notions of competition, it is increasingly more important for corporations to be aware of and concerned about their ethical practices within their industry sector. Industry associations are recognizing that their reputation with some stakeholder groups is frequently a shared reputation. It is challenging, but industry associations are extending their mandates to incorporate collective response to the weakest links in their sector. Working collaboratively, industry associations are raising the floor on business integrity within their sectors. In doing so, these associations are reducing liability exposure of the sector and managing collective reputation.

Attempts to Integrate Social Impacts into Project Assessments

To anticipate social impacts of private sector projects and to manage anticipated risks, corporations are attempting to incorporate social impacts into environmental impact assessments. The results of these efforts are patchy.

As a general observation, private sector project proponents are relatively aware of environmental metrics for projects, and understand the financial and operational consequences of associated environmental risk management practices. Corporations are frequently less comfortable with social impact assessments and the corresponding mitigation practices. Social impact assessments are routinely included in environmental impact assessment frameworks with limited precision as to exactly what is to be evaluated, and there is even less clarity about what to do to eliminate or mitigate anticipated negative social impacts in a project.

Financiers of large-scale projects have collaborated to adopt the Equator Principles, a voluntary set of guidelines developed by private lenders to assess and manage the social and environmental impacts of development projects. One year after its inception, twenty-five lenders—twenty-three banks and two public financial institutions—have endorsed the Equator Principles.

The voluntary principles for lending to development projects were established based upon the policies of the World Bank and the International Finance Corporation. Proponents of the Equator Principles envision an investment environment where, regardless of the funding sources, development projects will be subject to comparable environmental and social screening processes.

Cultural and Regional Context

Corporate integrity rationales have the optics of originating in North America and Europe, with multinational enterprises applying practices to operations on a global basis. At the risk of appearing to have dual standards (which would be repugnant to some corporate stakeholders), corporations are alert to the dangers of applying cultural relativism theories to business integrity. It is generally agreed that companies' social accountabilities should apply universally regardless of a project's physical location. For example, bribery is not acceptable in any country, regardless of local norms; gas flaring harms the environment whether or not the host country constrains flaring; and sexual harassment is offensive across the globe.

However, cultural context can be quite relevant. In many Islamic countries, for example, corporate social accountabilities are motivated by religious belief systems that encourage companies to contribute roughly 10 percent of their profits to charity. This same belief system discourages companies from publicly reporting these charitable contributions. Hence, local companies in Islamic cultures are sometimes reluctant to report on business integrity outcomes.

Cultural influences in corporate integrity need to be better understood. In particular, we need a better understanding of how to make business integrity practices, accountabilities, and reporting more relevant in non-Western investment environments.

Stakeholder advocacy groups have wielded their sticks to motivate the behaviors of Western investors operating in the developed and the developing world. These advocacy groups require a more thorough understanding of what motivates non-Western corporations if their advocacy is to be effective in motivating business integrity expectations more universally.

Managing Integrity Frontiers Beyond Compliance

Carrots and sticks will continue to be used as social and political tools to motivate corporate integrity practices. Corporate social responsibility gained widespread support in the last decade as a voluntary measure that allowed business to fill gaps in regulatory frameworks. The pendulum is now swinging back in favor of legislating corporate behavior. The pendulum, which swings back and forth from carrots to sticks, will no doubt continue to shift. Corporate managers must be aware of these shifts, but leaders must also remain strategically focused on the objective of *managing* integrity.

Corporations are under enormous pressure to comply with evolving governance laws and legislated accountabilities. The consequences of noncompliance with regulatory mandates has a financial and a reputational wallop. The public is not yet entirely convinced of corporate motivation to pursue voluntary practices under the corporate social responsibility mantra and continues to be skeptical.

As discussed in Part 1, corporations need to understand what motivates their commitments to business integrity. The credibility and outcomes of integrity practices depend on underlying corporate motivators. If an organization's integrity drivers are situated at rungs 3, 4, or 5 of the Integrity Ladder, then compliance is a predictable stimulus.

However, some corporations are motivated to manage business integrity frontiers beyond compliance and through proactive risk management. These corporations avoid causing harm to others or focus on social return on corporate investment as a desired and intended by-product of a financial investment. Compliance with regulations will not be enough to embed the corporate integrity aspirations of these companies.

If a corporation's response to emergent legislative and regulatory strength is a renewed focus on compliance, it may be essential to reevaluate corporate motivators. Do leaders within a company intend to engender support for a rules-based approach to integrity with compliance as a key motivator? Or are corporate leaders motivated to inspire a principles-based approach to integrity with strategic management of integrity frontiers as a key motivator?

Inspiring a corporate response to business integrity beyond compliance is not easy. Legislative volleys, intended to prescribe corporate behaviors and negative media attention, may throw corporations and their leaders off their strategic course. If a corporation is motivated to manage business integrity beyond compliance, corporate leadership must be committed to stay the course. Leaders must also be able to inspire others to join in strategically managing integrity frontiers. Managing integrity frontiers beyond compliance will be a test of leadership for corporate managers in the twenty-first century.

APPENDIX:
Business Tools

Integrity Ladder
Stakeholder Grid and Impact Assessment Tool
Integrity Grid
Permeation of Change Model
Adapted Best Practices Tool
Benchmarking Practices
Community Investment Strategy Tool
Business Integrity Accountability Cycle
Evaluation and Decision-Making Process for Business Integrity
  Management

Integrity Ladder

RUNG	QUESTIONS TO ASK TO REVEAL MOTIVATION (COMMITMENT)	PRIMARY MOTIVATION	EXAMPLE	CONTINGENCY PLAN (ACTION)
10	Will my children and grandchildren appreciate my decisions to help others?	Future generations	George Soros's personal commitment to transparency Bill Gates's personal commitment to fight HIV/AIDS	Individuals create trusts and foundations to support philanthropy Altruism
9	Are there ways to leverage my corporate budget to achieve a positive social impact that has long-term sustainability?	Both social return on corporate investment and financial return on corporate investment are intentionally of substantial importance	Corporate alliances with other stakeholders to respond to host community health care needs	Consider impact of investment beyond the operating timetable Capacity building in host jurisdiction
8	Are there ways to leverage my corporate budget to achieve a positive social impact?	Social return on corporate investment is a desired and intended by-product of financial investment	Corporate responses to host community health care needs	Consider commercial and social benefit of community investment, respect for environment, and relations with host government

7	How do we leverage our corporate budget to ensure that we do no harm?	Avoid causing harm to others	Corporate decision to ensure operating budget includes environmental and social impact assessment and response	Consider universal health, safety, and environmental practices if cost effective
6	How do we comply with both the letter and spirit of applicable laws and company policy?	Compliance motivation supplemented with proactive risk management.	Investments are subject to proactive decision-making process	Create multidisciplinary teams to properly evaluate and manage risks
5	What do we need to do to comply with the letter of the law and company policy?	Compliance with rules	Strict compliance with host government environmental practices, even if inferior to international standards	Hire many lawyers to draft and interpret rules
4	Will this action or inaction detract from my public reputation or private relationships?	Reputation protection; reactive risk management	Apply different practices to less visible investments	Hire a public relations firm to engage with stakeholders
3	How do I comply with the minimum legal requirements and stay in business?	Minimum compliance	Allegations against Nike and its supply chain in Asia	Challenge legal interpretations/ jurisdiction Accept double standards No sense of social accountabilities

continued

RUNG	QUESTIONS TO ASK TO REVEAL MOTIVATION (COMMITMENT)	PRIMARY MOTIVATION	EXAMPLE	CONTINGENCY PLAN (ACTION)
2	How can I avoid being caught with "dirty hands"?	Personal safety/self-preservation	Allegations against Elf in Africa	Outsource the "dirty work" Minimize the paper trail
1	Will I go to jail?	Personal safety/self-preservation	Enron management	Plea-bargain Turn in someone else
0	How do I cover up?	Personal safety/self-preservation	Richard Nixon in Watergate scandal	Hire high-priced lawyer Obfuscate

Stakeholder Grid and Impact Assessment Tool

STAKEHOLDER CATEGORIES	TYPES OF IMPACT				
	REPUTATION	PHYSICAL ASSETS (HARM OR LOSS)	PERSONNEL (HARM OR LOSS)	TIMELINES	SHARE VALUE
Corporation (parent)					
Employees working on project					
Media					
Regulators					
Investors					
Insurers/ lenders					
Customers					
Suppliers					
Advocacy NGOs					
Nonadvocacy NGOs					
Partners					
Agents					
Host communities					
Host government					
Other relevant governments					

Impact Assessment: –5 = most negative impact potential
                     0 = no impact
                    +5 = most positive impact potential

Impact assessment must evaluate both the stakeholders' motivation and ability to cause the impact.

Further detail can be incorporated into the matrix to clarify the magnitude of the harmful action. For example, harm or loss to personnel could include a range of impacts from personal injury, detention, kidnapping, homicide; impacts to physical assets could include theft, sabotage, destruction of assets, or other types of infrastructure impacts that are unique to a business operation or operating environment. Reputation impacts can be further refined to identify a variety of triggers, for example: lack of transparency, corruption, unfair sharing of benefits, environmental degradation, social/cultural impacts, discrimination, human rights abuses, or Aboriginal interests. Share value impacts can be assessed over various timelines: immediate, monthly, financial quarter, annual, life of the project, three to five years, longer term. Impacts to timelines can be charted against the project timeline.

Integrity Grid

Using the Integrity Ladder, overall corporate commitments to integrity, and individual departmental commitments and actions on integrity, are considered and depicted on the chart on the opposite page.

To achieve alignment between individual departmental commitments and actions, the preferred departmental internal gap is zero (depicted in the column "Department Internal Gap"). As well, to achieve alignment between the departments and the overall corporate commitments to integrity, the preferred corporate/department gap is zero (depicted in the column "Corporate/Department Gap").

The data in the chart on page 297 (which is based on Integrity Ladder inputs) is plotted on the Integrity Grid as shown on page 298.

	CODE	COMMITMENT	ACTIONS	DEPARTMENT INTERNAL GAP (DEPARTMENT ACTIONS MINUS DEPARTMENT COMMITMENT)	CORPORATE DEPARTMENT GAP (DEPARTMENT COMMITMENT MINUS CORPORATE COMMITMENT)
Overall corporate	C	7	—	n/a	—
Individual departments:					
Security	S	2	2	0	-5
Environment, health, and safety	EHS	3	3	0	-4
Investor relations	IR	4	4	0	-3
Government relations	GR	4	4	0	-3
Operations	O	4	5	+1	-3
Finance	F	6	6	0	-1
Legal	L	6	7	+1	-1
Human resources	HR	8	8	0	+1

- Corporate Talk Line (corporation's overall commitment to integrity)
- Equal Alignment Line (a 45-degree reference line that reflects equal alignment of department commitments = department actions)
- Plot intersection of individual departmental integrity commitments and actions

Integrity Grid plotting:

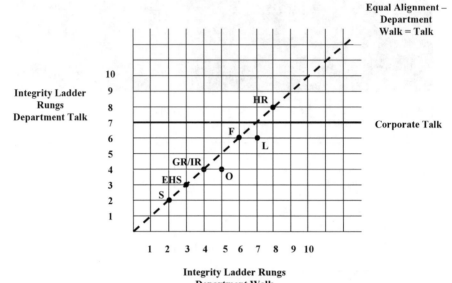

S =   Security Department
EHS = Environmental, Health and Safety Department
IR =   Investor Relations Department
GR =   Government Relations Department
O =   Operations Department
F =   Finance Department
L =   Legal Department
HR =   Human Resources Department

Permeation of Change Model

GROUPS WITHIN ORGANIZATIONS	CHARACTERISTICS IN INNOVATION DIFFUSION
Initiators	• Manage the risk of Initiators making mistakes that affect the company's reputation and/or discourage others • Encourage Initiators to adopt pilot projects and define success criteria to control risks
Interesteds	• Invite Interesteds to work with Non-compliers on implementing change to shore up the weakest links
Wait-and-Sees/ Followers	• Wait-and-See and Follower groups prioritize risk management and are strongly motivated by others • Recommend that Wait-and-See and Follower groups proactively monitor evolving stakeholder expectations
Non-compliers	• Business integrity Non-compliers can become the weakest links in an organization and must be prioritized for change • Encourage the Interesteds to support the Non-compliers in change. Initiators are not likely to be effective in supporting change within the Non-compliers group

Adapted Best Practices Tool

Stage 1: Identifying corporate integrity best practices

Stage 2: Assessing best practices based on risk/impact and ease of implementation

Stage 3: Selecting and implementing best practices

Stage 1: Identifying Business Integrity Best Practices

GROUP	TASK
Initiators	• Identify emerging and innovative best practices of companies on the leading edge of business integrity
Interesteds	• Identify business integrity best practices of competitors
Wait-and-Sees/ Followers	• Proactive monitoring of evolving stakeholder expectations of corporate best practices on business integrity
Non-compliers	• Force to examine and implement best practices within their own company

Stage 2: Assessing Best Practices

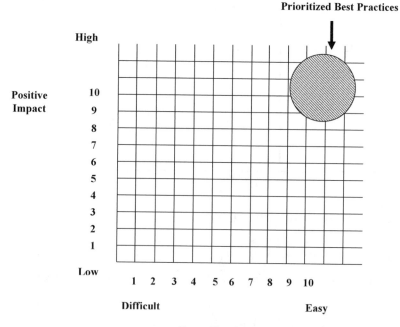

Prioritized Best Practices

High

Positive Impact   10 9 8 7 6 5 4 3 2 1

Low

1 2 3 4 5 6 7 8 9 10

Difficult   Easy

Ease of Implementation

Stage 3: Selecting and Implementing Best Practices

It is recommended that a few best practices be selected for implementation on a corporate-wide basis. Also, individual departments or divisions may select best practices for implementation within their groups as pilots.

Initiators and Interesteds within an organization may also be encouraged to consider best practices that fall outside the high impact/ease of implementation quadrant of the grid.

Are there best practices with high impact that rank low on implementation? Can the company modify implementation approaches to enhance the ease of implementation scoring?

Are there best practices with ease of implementation that rank low on impact? Can potential impacts to the company be reduced through practice innovation?

Benchmarking Practices

In order to maximize the value of benchmarking, companies can participate in benchmarking surveys conducted by independent organizations. Internal benchmarking between of corporate departments or divisions can also be constructive.

Community Investment Strategy Tool

DEFINE THE NATURE OF THE COMMUNITY INVESTMENT	REGULATORY AND CONTRACTUAL COMMITMENTS TO COMMUNITIES	VOLUNTARY COMMUNITY INVESTMENT	PHILANTHROPIC INVESTMENT
Examples	Technical training commitments; environmental compliance	Capacity-building initiative for community benefit; upgrades to local infrastructure	Donation to support cancer or AIDS research; donation to wildlife protection fund
Corporate motivation	Compliance with laws	Risk management and securing local licence to operate; can incorporate intent to do no harm and/or foster positive social impact; focus is on individual project	Same motivators as voluntary community investment, but less linkage to securing local licence to operate; more corporate focus and less project focus
Short-term and/or long-term impacts	Generally short term, some long term	Can be either or both	Generally longer term
Stakeholder engagement strategy	Engagement with communities, regulators, commercial partners	Direct engagement with community stakeholders is a priority	May have limited engagement with community stakeholders

Allocated percentage of corporate community investment budget	Contracts and regulations prescribe level of commitment	Level of commitment can be set by a company generally on a project basis	Level of commitment generally set by company on a corporate-wide basis
Corporate approval process	Part of traditional project management process	Can be managed within an individual project's management process or within a broader business integrity corporate management system	Routinely managed within a broader business integrity corporate management system rather than on a local project basis

The Business Integrity Accountability Cycle

Business Integrity
Values/Principles

Reporting

Business Integrity
Best Practices

Verification
Processes

Corporate
Management
Systems

Performance Measures
Monitoring

Evaluation and Decision-Making Framework for Managing Business Integrity

Phase 1: Establish the Business Integrity Baseline

Phase 1A: Assessing integrity commitments and action (historical) of individual departments within the corporation

Phase 1B: Applying the Integrity Ladder (introduced in Chapter 2) analysis to the corporation

Phase 2: Identify Stakeholders, Assess Stakeholder Impacts, Anticipate Stakeholder Expectations of a Corporation, Identify Potential Dilemmas

Phase 2A: Applying the Stakeholder Grid and Impact Assessment tool (introduced in Chapter 3) to identify key stakeholders in a project and assess potential stakeholder impacts

Phase 2B: Anticipating stakeholders' expectations of the corporation and identifying potential dilemmas arising from project impacts and these expectations

Phase 2C: Creating opportunity for innovation with multidisciplinary brainstorming to identify feasible options to manage dilemmas

Phase 3: Create, Manage, and Assess Alignment between Corporate Commitments to Business Integrity and Actual Practices

Phase 3A: Identifying corporate commitments to business integrity

Phase 3B: Plotting departmental integrity commitments and corporate integrity commitments on the Integrity Ladder

Phase 3C: Applying the Integrity Grid—plotting departmental integrity talk and departmental integrity walk on the Integrity Grid (introduced in Chapter 4):

- *Before* multidisciplinary brainstorming of feasible strategies (reactive)
- *After* multidisciplinary brainstorming of feasible strategies (proactive)

Phase 4: Identify, Assess, and Implement Best Practices in Business Integrity

Using the Community Investment Strategy Tool, Permeation of Change model, the Adapted Better Practices tool, and Benchmarking Practices (tools introduced in Chapter 5) to identify, assess, and implement best practices that will enhance strategic management of business integrity frontiers

Phase 5: Respond to Business Integrity Accountabilities

Phase 5A: Clarifying accountabilities with the Business Integrity Accountability Cycle (introduced in Chapter 6)

Phase 5B: Implementing tactics

Phase 5C: Implementing continuous improvement

Index